Studia Fennica
Ethnologica 14

The Finnish Literature Society was founded in 1831 and has from the very beginning engaged in publishing. It nowadays publishes literature in the fields of ethnology and folkloristics, linguistics, literary research and cultural history.

The first volume of Studia Fennica series appeared in 1933.

Since 1992 the series has been divided into three thematic subseries: Ethnologica, Folkloristica and Linguistica. Two additional subseries were formed in 2002, Historica and Litteraria. Subseries Anthropologica was formed in 2007.

In addition to its publishing activities the Finnish Literature Society maintains a folklore archive, a literature archive and a library.

Where is the Field?

The Experience of Migration Viewed through the Prism of Ethnographic Fieldwork

Edited by Laura Hirvi & Hanna Snellman

Finnish Literature Society • Helsinki

Studia Fennica Ethnologica 14

The publication has undergone a peer review.

VERTAISARVIOITU
KOLLEGIALT GRANSKAD
PEER-REVIEWED
www.tsv.fi/tunnus

The open access publication of this volume has received part funding via
Helsinki University Library.

A digital edition of a printed book first published in 2012 by the Finnish Literature Society.
Cover Design: Timo Numminen
EPUB Conversion: Tero Salmén

ISBN 978-952-222-388-3 (Print)
ISBN 978-952-222-762-1(PDF)
ISBN 978-952-222-761-4 (EPUB)

ISSN 0085-6835 (Studia Fennica)
ISSN 1235-1954 (Studia Fennica Ethnologica)

DOI: http://dx.doi.org/10.21435/sfe.14

Contents

THE TOLD AND THE UNTOLD

LAURA HIRVI AND HANNA SNELLMAN

Introduction: Nine Tales of the Field

E thnographers seek to achieve a better understanding of the human
experience through the exploration of different kinds of life worlds by
conducting fieldwork. This method is often understood to include interviews,
participant observation, informal conversations and the recording of field
notes along the way. Thanks to its ability to assist in highlighting the interplay
between global processes and (trans-)locally lived lives, ethnographic
fieldwork methods have also been found valuable in research on human
migration. However, when setting out to gather their data, researchers who
are eager to explore the experiences of migrants and their descendants
often come across stumbling blocks for which their academic training as
ethnographers has not adequately prepared them. This edited volume does
not seek to provide a comprehensive answer to the question of how to deal
with such challenges that not only apprentice ethnographers but also more
experienced scholars encounter in the course of carrying out their fieldwork;
instead, it offers the reader nine 'tales of the field'.[1] These tales, which have
been written by both junior and more experienced scholars working in
different parts of the globe, bring to the fore the various moments of online
and offline encounters that take place between fieldworkers and the people
they encounter. In addition, the contributions to this volume contain the
authors' reflections on how they have dealt with the obstacles, challenges
and also the opportunities that they have encountered in the course of their
fieldwork endeavours. This book seeks to offer a close-up view of the various
coping strategies developed and applied by scholars who are conducting
fieldwork and in this vein hopes to serve as a useful resource for future
ethnographers who are setting out to study the mysteries, both hidden and
overt, of the cultural and social worlds.

---

1   The work of editing this book has been part of an NOS-HS funded project
    entitled *Sikh Identity Formation: Generational Transfer of Traditions in the Nordic
    Countries* (project number 212061). Kristina Myrvold (Lund University, Sweden)
    is the principal investigator of this project, which began in 2009. The Finnish
    co-investigator is Hanna Snellman (University of Helsinki), while Laura Hirvi
    (University of Jyväskylä) has been writing her doctoral dissertation under the
    auspices of this project.

Recording how individual ethnographers deal with the challenges that they face with regard to their fieldwork is, we believe, an enlightening and relevant venture as it contributes to a process that fosters the development and transmission of ethnographic research skills. As Allaine Cerwonka points out in the first chapter of a volume which she co-authored with her former supervisor, Liisa Malkki, apprentices who are in the process of acquiring skills for conducting fieldwork are often left to figure out certain aspects of the method that 'go without saying' by carefully listening to the tales told by senior fieldworkers.[2] In a similar vein, Billy Ehn and Orvar Löfgren note how in Sweden it seems that students learn how to become ethnologists by following an unwritten syllabus.[3] Often, this 'informal socialization'[4] of the novice into the art of doing fieldwork takes place outside university classrooms. Information about what ethnographers actually do when they conduct ethnographic fieldwork is commonly disseminated in the form of informal talk after class, sometimes in passing, behind closed doors or over coffee in a department's staff room. In order to be able to catch at least a fragment of this valuable 'corridor talk',[5] students as well as colleagues who are eager to learn from the experiences of others have to depend in many instances on serendipity and can only hope that they manage to join such random discussions at the right moment in time.

In order to reduce the role of serendipity and to contribute to a growing body of fieldwork methods for 'research in arenas in which Malinowskian conditions of fieldwork are most challenged',[6] the chapters presented in this volume set out to document in a formal manner some examples of this kind of 'corridor talk' on ethnographic methods. In this way, we hope to facilitate the transmission of fieldwork skills, which would otherwise run the risk of remaining on an oral level or passing unnoticed if they are only published as mandatory parts of doctoral dissertations, which often fail to reach a wider readership. Producing a collection of accounts in which the authors reflect on their use of ethnographic research methods is particularly relevant in the field of migration studies, where, as several contributions to this volume indicate, research is often carried out in contexts that challenge the traditional canon of fieldwork methods. The reason for this is that researchers conducting research on mobile people, who in some of the cases that are discussed in this book have settled in urban environments, often seem to struggle with the task of delimiting their research site in spatial terms. Considering the increasing popularity that the use of fieldwork enjoys in migration studies, we would suggest that there is a need for a book that focuses not only on research methods as applied generally in the study of human migration[7] but also on ethnographic fieldwork methods in particular.

2   Cerwonka 2007, 3.
3   Ehn & Löfgren 1996.
4   Cerwonka 2007, 3.
5   Marcus 2006, 113.
6   Marcus 2009, 19.
7   See for example Vargas-Silva 2012.

By documenting and highlighting the various ways in which ethnographers who are studying immigrants in different parts of the world not only deal with moments of despair and respond to possible difficulties but also take the opportunities that are presented to them in the course of their fieldwork, this book offers some innovative, creative and concrete examples of how to be flexible and improvise in the field.[8] Thus, similar to the aim of *Ethnologia Europea*'s recent special issue entitled *Irregular Ethnographies* edited by the Swedish ethnologists Tom O'Dell and Robert Willim, one goal of this volume is to enlarge our understanding of some of the 'diverse forms of ethnographic practice' carried out by ethnographers in the 21st century.[9] The overall intention of this book is to offer insights into the art of conducting field research that will be equally useful both for students and for more senior researchers working in the field of migration studies and beyond. On a more general level, this book may also be of value for policy-makers and others who are interested in learning more about the experience of migration and how it affects people's everyday lives. The intimate character of many of the accounts included in this book serves to promote this objective.

Furthermore, agreeing with George E. Marcus, who is currently the Director of the *Center for Ethnography* at UC Irvine (USA), we consider 'telling about fieldwork experiences' to be an essential exercise that provides the necessary background to stimulate discussions about ethnographic methods.[10] Ethnographers can only learn how others have coped with similar challenges when their experiences are shared in writing. The possession of such information is maybe beneficial in trying to navigate through one's own fieldwork project. It can be also useful when one writes research proposals since being aware of what may happen in carrying out fieldwork makes 'the dreamer' who writes a research proposal better informed and permits her/him to visualise what a planned fieldwork project might look like. Participation in the process of updating fieldwork methods is important because, as Akhil Gupta and James Ferguson remind us, the art of fieldwork can only ensure its continuity if it adapts to the changing environment, and 'for that to happen, as Malinowski himself pointed out, such tradition must be aggressively and imaginatively reinterpreted to meet the needs of the present'.[11]

The present, as understood in this volume, manifests itself in the form of globalization, which is characterised by an increase in mobility. This has been furthered by ever cheaper and faster modes of transportation and a higher degree of interconnectedness in the world. Eager to explore what impact globalization has on the everyday lives of ordinary people, scholars from various disciplines have become increasingly interested in investigating the experiences of migrants. This interest has given rise to the emergence of

---

8   See Malkki 2007 for a thought-provoking discussion of the role that improvisation plays in ethnographic fieldwork.

9   O'Dell & Willim 2011, 12.

10   Marcus 2006, 114.

11   Gupta & Ferguson 1997, 39–40.

an interdisciplinary field that is known today as 'migration studies', and it has resulted in the establishment of centres around the world that focus on research related to the topic of human migration. It has also spurred the foundation of multidisciplinary associations[12] and journals[13] that promote research carried out in the field of migration studies and help to disseminate its findings.

The fact that researchers around the world who are working in different disciplines are contributing to the field of migration studies also becomes evident when one takes a closer look at the backgrounds of the contributors to this volume. We selected the authors' contributions from approximately twenty abstracts which were received in response to an international 'Call for papers' circulated through various mailing lists in autumn 2009. Based on our own research projects, we saw a need for a work in which contributors would examine the experience of labour, migration and labour migration while critically reflecting on their ethnographic fieldwork experiences. Owing to the small number of proposals on the subject of labour, we eventually decided to concentrate on producing a book that on the one hand would examine the life worlds of immigrants in different parts of the globe, and on the other hand critically scrutinize the methods used in carrying out fieldwork in such settings. In other words, this volume arose of our joint interest in producing a work that could function as a handbook of fieldwork methods and at the same time would provide insights into the experiences of migrants. As it stands, this book also represents our modest desire to connect scholars from abroad with the Finnish academic world in general and Finnish ethnology in particular. It also reflects our endeavour to create an academic dialogue that would reach not only across disciplinary boundaries but also across national borders and thereby acknowledge the interconnected (academic) world in which we live.

The field of migration studies accommodates, among others, scholars of history, ethnology, geography, sociology, anthropology, psychology and religious studies. Many of the scholars from these academic backgrounds share an interest in shedding more light on the causes of human migration and the impact it has on people's lives in order to reach a better understanding of the world we live in. In order to do so, migration scholars are increasingly turning to the method of fieldwork, as it provides an appropriate tool for producing studies that are capable of capturing the perspective of migrants and for describing the complexity of the social and cultural worlds in which they operate. Furthermore, as the contributions to this volume show, using fieldwork as a method in the field of migration studies can produce research that gives a human face to the ways in which the experience of migration affects people's lives.[14] In the context of Finland, for example, the application

---

12 See e.g. *The Society for the Study of Ethnic Relations and International Migration (ETMU)* (http://www.etmu.fi/index_eng.html) in Finland.

13 See e.g. the open access *Nordic Journal of Migration Research* (http://versita.com/njmr/).

14 See in particular Mapril; Roseman; Vogt, in this volume.

of ethnographic fieldwork methods to the study of human migration has resulted in a number of insightful studies that explore emigration from,[15] and immigration to, Finland[16].

However, as we emphasise, the present conditions in which researchers carry out their fieldwork have significantly changed from the time when Bronislaw Malinowski and his contemporaries carried out their empirical studies, as no longer is the fieldwork site that many of today's researchers encounter one that can be easily explored on foot.[17] As a consequence of these changed conditions, ethnographers are often left with an uncertain feeling when it comes to the question of what research practices to apply in the name of ethnographic fieldwork methods. Is, for example, talking on the phone to an interviewee who is physically located in another country participant observation in the Malinowskian sense, asks Ulf Hannerz.[18] Or, one might ask, with reference to Saara Koikkalainen's contribution to this volume, whether data collection via Skype constitutes 'real' fieldwork? The question that is at stake here is whether the dominating image that we attach to the idea of 'real fieldwork' is still characterized by an idea of spending a year alone in some faraway 'exotic' place cut off from 'home'?[19] In addition to the problems related to the question of how to carry out fieldwork in today's world, contemporary ethnographers often 'do not seem to know what the field is, or where it should be, if it is real or perhaps virtual, and even if there has to be one at all'.[20] As a consequence, many who are beginning or are in the middle of conducting fieldwork see themselves confronted like Deborah d'Amico-Samuels with the simple but at the same time complex and tricky question: 'Where is the field?'[21]

Multi-sited fieldwork

In this context, there arises the question of what sites researchers should turn to in order to make sense of the experiences of people who lead lives and conduct practices that 'cut across national borders'[22] and take place in the online as well as the offline world? How should one go about studying people whose lives are marked by mobility, transnationalism or the consciousness of belonging to a diaspora; who are both here and there, and who feel at times that they are nowhere but everywhere or in between? The acknowledgment that people may maintain their cultural

---

15 See e.g. Lähteenmäki & Snellman 2006; Snellman 2005; Tuomi-Nikula 1989; Lindström-Best 1988.
16 See e.g. Martikainen 2004; Tiilikainen 2003; Wahlbeck 1999.
17 Falzon 2009, 6.
18 Hannerz 2006b, 28.
19 See Clifford 1997, 55.
20 Hannerz, U. 2006a, 23.
21 D'Amico-Samuels 1991, 69, quoted in Ferguson & Gupta 1997, 35.
22 Glick Schiller et al. 1992, 1.

practices and social relationships over great geographic distances has given scholars reason to reflect more closely on the form of research designs and fieldwork practices. One of the most notable proposals to emerge out of such contemplations on how to conduct ethnographic research in present times has been formulated by George Marcus in an article that outlines his ideas concerning multi-sited ethnography.[23] As a method, it aims to enable the study of the 'circulation of cultural meanings, objects, and identities in diffuse time-space'.[24] This form of ethnography is marked by mobility, and rests on the idea of 'follow[ing] people, connections, associations and relationships across space', as Marc-Anthony Falzon puts it with reference to Marcus[25] in an introduction to a recent volume in which the contributors reflect on multi-sited ethnography.[26]

In the present work, many of the contributors have applied this approach in a similar way to other scholars who have conducted research on migrants.[27] This can be seen as a reflection of the prominence that the method of multi-sited fieldwork enjoys in the field of migration studies. José Mapril's chapter, for example, is based on fieldwork that he carried out on the one hand in the environment where the immigrants he studied had settled (Portugal), and on the other hand in the place from where they originally departed on their journey of migration, which in this case was Bangladesh. Shifting the emphasis to an investigation of how the lives of immigrants originating from one country unfold in two different settlement sites, Laura Hirvi's contribution describes the challenges she encountered during her trans-Atlantic fieldwork carried out among Sikhs from northern India who are now living in California and in Finland. Saara Koikkalainen, in turn, explores in her work the experiences of educated Finns living and working in different countries of the European Union by using the Internet to track them, thus illustrating the ways in which researchers can follow people by taking a virtual path. In other words, her work seems to suggest that the act of following does not necessarily imply the need for physical movement and that researchers may follow people to different sites using the Internet as a 'vehicle of transportation'.

Wendy Vogt explains at the beginning of her contribution how she initially set out to literally follow Central American refugees and migrants on their passages to the United States. But as she soon realized, instead of following people who were on the move, it seemed more feasible to become momentarily immobile herself in order to be able to grasp the experiences of people in transit. A similar insight seems to emerge from Lisa Wiklund's chapter, which is based on fieldwork that she carried out among young Japanese persons living and working in New York; she argues that it is

---

23 Marcus 1995.
24 Marcus 1995, 96.
25 Marcus1995.
26 Falzon 2009, 1–2.
27 See e.g. Huttunen 2010; Leonard 2009; Paerregaard 2008.

perhaps preferable 'to study cosmopolitanism without moving too much'.[28] Hence, both Vogt and Wiklund seem to suggest that in order to study people whose lives are marked by a high degree of mobility fieldworkers should seriously consider the option of remaining in place.

In the study of immigrants, one may choose – at least in the initial phase of fieldwork – to remain stationary in a few selected sites. The sites chosen for this purpose should be venues which by their functions attract people who are on the move in their daily lives. In the case of immigrants, as the chapters in this volume suggest, such sites could be shelters,[29] religious places of worship[30] or institutions connected with the bureaucracy involved in the process of migration.[31] Other sites that lend themselves to the study of immigrants are festivals, parades or social gatherings like weddings and birthday parties that have been arranged by immigrants, although such occasions tend to be more fleeting in character.

The framework of this book

'Where is the field?' is a thought-provoking question, as this volume hopefully demonstrates, because it invites ethnographers to reflect, among other things, on their own role in shaping and finding the field that they end up studying.[32] The contemplation of this question is a characteristic common to all the contributions in this book. Furthermore, all the authors discuss and reflect on their fieldwork experiences in connection with projects that focus on migrants. Thus, despite the heterogeneity of the contributors' disciplinary backgrounds, they are all migration scholars who have based their data-gathering process on ethnographic fieldwork methods. In short, what unites the chapters in this book is the authors' interest in studying the experiences of migrants who are in the process of moving or have moved from one country to another together with the overlap in the methods they have chosen to gather their data.

In order to provide the readers with some possible threads that they can follow when going through this volume, we decided to arrange the chapters under three broad sub-themes that reflect some of the similarities and overlaps between the various chapters. Thus, the first half of the book contains four chapters in which ethnographers reflect on the question of how to 'reach the hard-to-reach'. For Laura Hirvi, who in the first chapter discusses her research on Sikhs immigrants and their descendants living in two different countries, the initial challenge was to gain access to people who are hard to reach in Finland because of their 'invisibility' in the public

---

28 Wiklund, this volume, 124.
29 Vogt, this volume.
30 Mapril; Meintel & Mossière; both this volume.
31 Hasselberg and Meissner; this volume.
32 See in particular Meissner & Hasselberg and Wiklund, both in this volume.

landscape stemming from the relatively small size of the group. 'Being there' in the field was thus impeded by the problem of 'getting there', and only by resorting to online methods was she able to gain access to the previously 'invisible' public and private offline world of Sikhs in Finland. Ethnographic research that is conducted online raises a number of ethical concerns, and these are highlighted in her reflections on applying the social networking service Facebook as a research tool. The definition of privacy, for example, becomes less clear when situated in the online world. Hirvi also takes up the discussion of exit in the context of fieldwork and suggests an alternative reading of what ethnographers might mean when speaking about departure from the field, namely the mental journey that researchers need to make in order to leave their work behind.

Saara Koikkalainen likewise elaborates in her contribution in Chapter Two on the usefulness of the Internet and the various tools it offers for conducting fieldwork. Her case study examines the labour market experience of educated Finns working in the European Union and scattered all over the European continent. In order to gain access to their life worlds, one option for Koikkalainen would have been to apply the method of multi-sited ethnography by literally following her informants on their journeys abroad. But gathering data in such a manner is a slow and expensive task, for which it might be hard to receive the necessary funding. Therefore, Koikkalainen decided to transfer her initial stage of data-gathering to the online world by conducting fieldwork from her office using Skype and other Internet programs. In her reflections, she concludes that the Internet is useful for ethnographers as it can be used to locate relatively small migrant groups scattered in different countries and localities.[33]

Perhaps, one of the book's most intriguing studies is that of Wendy Vogt. Focusing on the journey undertaken by migrants, instead of studying them in their sending or receiving countries, Vogt succeeds in witnessing migrants in transit from very close range. Vogt is interested in examining the social world of Central American refugees and migrants in Mexico on their way to the United States, and initially she planned to follow them on their journey northwards. However, she soon realized that studying people in transit did not mean that she herself had to be in transit as well. Instead, she decided to stay in one of the established migrant shelters, which was used by vulnerable migrants, such as women and children, on their passage towards North America. This strategy had the advantage of enabling her to gain access to undocumented and vulnerable migrants, who come under the category of people who are hard-to-reach. Towards the end of her contribution, Vogt also critically reflects on her own position in the field and her struggle to maintain the 'intimate distance that is required in ethnographic research'.[34]

The last chapter included under the sub-theme 'Reaching the Hard-to-reach' is co-authored by Fran Meissner and Inês Hasselberg. Hasselberg's

33 Koikkalainen, 62, this volume; see also Hirvi, this volume.
34 Vogt, this volume, 82.

project focuses on examining the experiences of long-term migrants who face deportation from the UK. The other project discussed in this chapter was conducted by Meissner and explores how migrants who originate from a particular geographic area and who constitute numerically small groups establish social contacts in urban areas of London and Toronto marked by super-diversity. Based on their individual fieldwork projects, both authors point out how methods, defined *a priori*, often 'have to be adjusted and creatively re-imagined'[35] in the light of the actual fieldwork, especially in studies that try to access a hidden population. In their chapter, Meissner and Hasselberg also offer their experience-based reflections on how access to informants and research locations can transform the notion of the field from that which a researcher sets out to study – an illustration of the fact that the malleability innate to the field is 'part and parcel of the research process'.[36]

Chapter Five, written by Lisa Wiklund, provides a smooth transition from the first section of this book to the second, which is entitled 'Creating Communities'. In her fieldwork conducted among young Japanese adults who have moved to New York City to work in creative jobs, Wiklund wrestles, like the authors of the studies presented in the preceding four chapters, with the question of how to gain access to the group of people she would like to study. In her case, however, an even more significant challenge is posed by the question of how to keep up with people whose daily lives are marked by a high degree of mobility. Her methodological strategy for coping with these questions is to imitate the field she is studying, for example by hunting down her informants just as they as freelancers hunt for jobs; Wiklund calls this technique 'mirroring'. In addition, and with reference to the book's second sub-theme, Wiklund reflects on how far the process by means of which she constructed her field led to the creation of 'a community where there is none'.[37]

Deirdre Meintel's and Géraldine Mossière's contribution to this book is also concerned with the issue of creating communities. In their chapter, however, it is not so much the fieldworkers who are responsible for creating communities, but rather religious affiliation is considered to be the driving force behind the process through which communities are created. As part of a larger collaborative study that seeks to document religious diversity and the significance of religion in people's everyday lives in Quebec, this chapter focuses particularly on data that have been collected by means of fieldwork conducted among religious groups that mainly attract immigrants in Montreal. The study suggests that religious groups often provide their members with an experience of fellowship and thus help to 'replace community ties fractured by migration'.[38] Further, religious groups provide moral communities that form an important point of reference in immigrants' post-migration lives. The challenge Meintel and Mossière see in conducting

---

35 Meissner & Hasselberg, this volume, 92.
36 Meissner & Hasselberg, this volume, 102.
37 Wiklund, this volume, 122.
38 Meintel & Mossière, this volume, 134.

fieldwork in religious groups is that researchers may experience a stronger need to position themselves in the field that they have entered.

Chapter Seven takes the reader closer to the lives of Bangladeshis living in Lisbon. José Mapril was initially primarily interested in exploring the ritualisation of transnational space, and gathered his data conducting multi-sited fieldwork in several different regions of Portugal as well as in Bangladesh. A second reading of his material, however, revealed to him that his informants' foodscapes were another area worth exploring in more detail. On the basis of ethnographic data, Mapril shows in his case study how food and its daily consumption can reveal a great deal about the manner in which immigrants' experience and position themselves in the life worlds they are part of. His study further demonstrates that food, and in particular the sharing of it, assists in the creation of new relationships among immigrants and helps to produce a feeling of community in religious groups.

In the first chapter located under the section title 'The Told and the Untold', Clara Sacchetti critically examines 'how one goes about gathering ethnographic data in the field'.[39] With reference to other researchers who have reflected on this matter from a perspective of poststructual feminist ethnography, she argues for an acknowledgement of the central role of ethnographic unknowability (or the unexplained, or fieldwork failures) for reaching a better understanding of the research object. The moment of ethnographic unknowability is illustrated in one of the chapter's vignettes, in which Sacchetti describes how in a formal interview situation an Italian woman is unable to tell about her experience of migration to Canada. But instead of looking at such moments of unknowability as failures in fieldwork that need to be overcome, Sacchetti pleads that they should be accepted in their own right as part of the field because also the untold, the unsaid and the unexplained tell the researcher something about the studied field.

If we think of this book as imitating and following an immigrant's possible life path, then it could be argued that the last contribution, authored by Sharon R. Roseman, appositely fits such an imagined time line. Her focus is on an elderly couple, of whom the husband had previously worked for years as a seasonal worker in Switzerland. Now, about ten years later and after finally settling down back in his home country, Spain, he and his wife reflect on this experience in the conversations they have with the author. On the basis of an analysis of her ethnographic data, Roseman demonstrates how 'studying migration through storytelling practices' allows her to examine the wife's and husband's 'intersubjective connections with other people as they emerge from the past, and merge into the future'.[40] In her case, the field is a told one that the practice of narrating stories helps to create.

---

39 Sacchetti, this volume, 190.
40 Roseman, this volume, 197.

What next?

So what can students and others who are eager to carry out fieldwork in today's world learn from the reflections presented in this volume? A central concern in many of the accounts seems to be the question of how to get in touch with the people one is eager to learn more about through ethnographic fieldwork. What becomes clear in several of the case studies discussed in this book is that the gatekeeper still plays an important role in enabling or denying the researcher access to the field. It is interesting to note that in their reflections on access and the challenges of fieldwork, none of the contributors to this volume explicitly addresses the question of language. Traditionally, as Hannerz points out, an anthropologist like Evan-Pritchard was expected to communicate with informants solely 'through their own language'.[41] The prerequisite for successfully accomplishing fieldwork was to learn the language of the group the ethnographer set out to study. But working among people who, owing to their backgrounds as migrants, often live and grow up in multi-lingual environments has perhaps made the task of learning the informants' language less urgent, as often the informants have adopted the ethnographer's mother tongue and transformed it into one of their 'own languages' in the process of settling down. Or in some cases the informant and the ethnographer share a lingua franca, such as English, and use this as their medium of communication. Certainly, the picture is more complex and suggests the need for future research on the ethnographic methods practised at the beginning of the 21st century in order to investigate in more detail the role that language plays in contemporary fieldwork projects.

Another topic that needs to be addressed in more detail in future studies is the question of what researchers actually do with the material that they have collected by means of ethnographic fieldwork. And here we do not mean the 'writing-up' of the ethnography, but rather the stage between the collection of the data and the writing: the act of analysing the material. As Richard Wilk points out, in teaching ethnographic research methods in class or in writing monographs, there is rarely any discussion of what happens when ethnographers 'sat down to write, and how they made a narrative out of their mess of notes, charts, photographs and sound recordings'.[42] He uses the metaphor of cooking to describe how ethnographers usually portray what ingredients they have collected and used to cook a ready meal, i.e. the ethnography. However, only rarely do ethnographers make clear the efforts that went into processing the ingredients that eventually lead to the production of the meal (ethnography).[43] Hence, the question that should be addressed in more detail is: What exactly do researchers mean when they state in their writings that their studies are based on 'ethnographic analysis'? What are the steps by which this process takes place?[44]

41 Hannerz 2003, 202.
42 Wilk 2011: 23–24.
43 Wilk 2011.
44 What we have in mind here is the kind of reflections presented by Laura Huttunen (2010), for example.

Another issue that needs to be discussed in more detail with reference to recent discussions concerning research ethics is related to the question of data management. What do researchers do with the gathered data after a project has come to an end? Should they delete interviews, fieldnotes and photographs in order to protect the people who have participated in the research, or should they store them in archives in order to make them available for future research?

In summary, it can be said that the contributions to this book offer an insight into the making of ethnographies in a present that is marked by a high degree of mobility and interconnectedness. The chapters in this work also illustrate how this mobility and interconnectedness is experienced by different groups of migrants, such as those who are currently in the process of migrating,[45] those who intend to stay only temporarily abroad,[46] those who face deportation,[47] those who have permanently settled in the countries they or their ancestors have migrated to,[48] and those who have returned for good to their native lands after a period of seasonal migration.[49] This work communicates an idea of the identities of the people who move and the great variety of places from and to which they migrate. It also draws a colourful picture of the complex fieldwork sites in which ethnographers currently carry out their research. The clear-cut distinction between home and the field gets lost along the way and is replaced with a more fluid definition that acknowledges the overlap between the two. Finally, the reader of this volume might justifiably demand an answer to the question raised in the title of the book: 'Where is the field?' On the basis of our reading of the chapters, we would suggest that the field appears to emerge in the encounter between the informant and the ethnographer. Without this encounter, there would be no field.

45 Vogt, this volume.
46 Koikkalainen, this volume.
47 Hasselberg, this volume.
48 See in this volume Hirvi; Sacchetti.
49 Roseman, this volume.

Bibliography

Cerwonka, A. 2007: Nervous Conditions. The Stakes in Interdisciplinary Research. In: A. Cerwonka & L. H. Malkki: *Improvising theory: Process and temporality in ethnographic fieldwork*. Chicago: University of Chicago Press.

Clifford, J., 1997, *Routes. Travel and Translation in the Late Twentieth Century*. Cambridge: Harvard University Press.

D'Amico-Samuels, D. 1991: Undoing Fieldwork: Personal, Political, Theoretical and Methodological Implications. In: F.V. Harrison (ed.), *Decolonizing Anthropology: Moving Further toward an Anthropology for Liberation*. Washington: Association of Black Anthropologists, American Anthropological Association, 69; quoted in A. Gupta & J. Ferguson, 1997: Discipline and practice: 'The field' as site, method, and location in anthropology. In: A. Gupta & J. Ferguson (eds), *Anthropological locations. Boundaries and grounds of a field science*. Berkeley, Los Angeles, London: University of California Press, 35.

Ehn, Billy & Orvar Löfgren, 1996: *Vardagslivets etnologi. Reflektioner kring en kultur-vetenskap*. Natur och kultur. Stockholm.

Falzon, M. 2009: Introduction. Multi-sited Ethnography: Theory, Praxis and Locality in Contemporary Research. In M. Falzon (ed.) *Multi-Sited Ethnography. Theory, Praxis and Locality in Contemporary Research*. Aldershot: Ashgate.

Glick Schiller, N., L. Basch & C. Blanc-Szanton, 1992. Transnationalism: A New Analytical Framework for Understanding Migration. In: N. Glick Schiller, L. Basch & C. Blanc-Szanton (eds), *Towards a Transnational Perspective on Migration: Race, Class, Ethnicity and Nationalism Reconsidered*. New York: New York Academy of Science.

Gupta, A. & J. Ferguson1997: Discipline and Practice: "The Field" as Site, Method, and Location in Anthropology. In: A. Gupta & J. Ferguson (eds), *Anthropological Locations. Boundaries and Grounds of a Field Science*. Berkeley, Los Angeles, London: University of California Press.

Hannerz, U. 2003: Being there...and there...and there!: Reflections on Multi-Sited Ethnography. *Ethnography* 4: 2, 2001–2016.

Hannerz, U. 2006a: Studying Down, Up, Sideways, Thorough, Backwards, Forwards, Away and at Home: Reflections On A Field Worries Of An Expansive Discipline. In: S. M. Coleman & P. Collins (eds), *Locating the Field: Space, Place and Context in Anthropology*. Oxford: Berg Publishers.

Hannerz, U. 2006b: Introduktion: När fältet blir translokalt. In: U. Hannerz (ed), *Flera fält i ett: Socialantropologer om translokala fältsstudier*. Stockholm: Carlssons.

Huttunen, L. 2010: Sedentary Policies and Transnational Relations: A 'Non-sustainable' Case of Return to Bosnia. *Journal of Refugee Studies*, 23: 1, 41–61.

Huttunen, L. Tiheä Kontekstointi: Haastattelu Osana Etnografista Tutkimusta. In: J. Ruusuvuori, P. Nikander, & M. Hyvärinen (eds), *Haastattelun Analyysi*. Tampere: Vastapaino, 39–63.

Leonard, K. I. 2009: Changing Place: The Advantages of Multi-sited Ethnography. In: M-A. Falzon (ed.) *Multi-sited Ethnogrpahy. Theory, Praxis and Locality in Contemporary Research*. Farnham, Burlington: Ashgate, 165–180.

Lindström, V. 1988: *Defiant Sisters: A Social History of Finnish Immigrant Women in Canada*. Toronto: Multicultural History Society of Ontario.

Lähteenmäki, M. & H. Snellman, (eds) 2006: *Passages Westward*. Studia Fennica Ethnologica 9. Helsinki: SKS.

Malkki, L. H. 2007: Tradition and Improvisation in Ethnographic Field Research. In: A. Cerwonka & L. H. Malkki: *Improvising Theory: Process and Temporality in Ethnographic Fieldwork*. Chicago: University of Chicago Press.

Marcus, G. E. 2009: Introduction: Notes towards an Ethnographic Memoir of Supervising Graduate Research through Anthropology's Decades of Transformation. In: J. D. Faubion & G. E. Marcus (eds), *Fieldwork Is Not What It Used to Be. Learning Anthropology's Method in a Time of Transition.* Ithaca and London: Cornell University.

Marcus, G. E. 2006: Where Have All the Tales of Fieldwork Gone? *Ethnos* 71: 1, 113–122.

Marcus, G. E., 1995: Ethnography in/of the World System: The Emergence of Multi-Sited Ethnography. *Annual Review of Anthropology,* 24, 95–117.

Martikainen, T. 2004: Immigrant Religions in Local Society: Historical and Contemporary Perspectives in the City of Turku. Dissertation. Åbo: Åbo Akademi.

O'Dell, T. & R. Willim, 2011: Irregular Ethnographies. An Introduction. *Ethnologia Europaea,* 41: 1, 5–15.

Paerregaard, K. 2008: *Peruvians Dispersed. A Global Ethnography of Migration.* Plymouth, UK: Lexington Books.

Snellman, H. 2005: *The Road Taken. Narratives from Lapland.* Inari: Kustannus Puntsi.

Tuomi-Nikula, O. 1989, *Saksansuomalaiset: tutkimus syntyperäisten suomalaisten akkulturaatiosta Saksan Liittotasavallassa ja Länsi-Berliinissä.* Helsinki: SKS.

Tiilikainen, M. 2003: *Arjen islam. Somalinaisten elämää Suomessa.* Tampere: Vastapaino.

Vargas-Silva, C. (ed.) 2012: *Handbook of Research Methods in Migration.* Cheltenham, Northampton: Edward Elgar.

Vertovec, S. 2009: *Transnationalism.* London and New York: Routledge.

Wahlbeck, Ö. 1999: *Kurdish Diasporas: A Comparative Study of Kurdish Refugee Communities.* London: Macmillan

Wilk, R. 2011: Reflections on Orderly and Disorderly Ethnography. *Ethnologia Europaea,* 41: 1, 15–25.

REACHING
THE HARD-TO-REACH

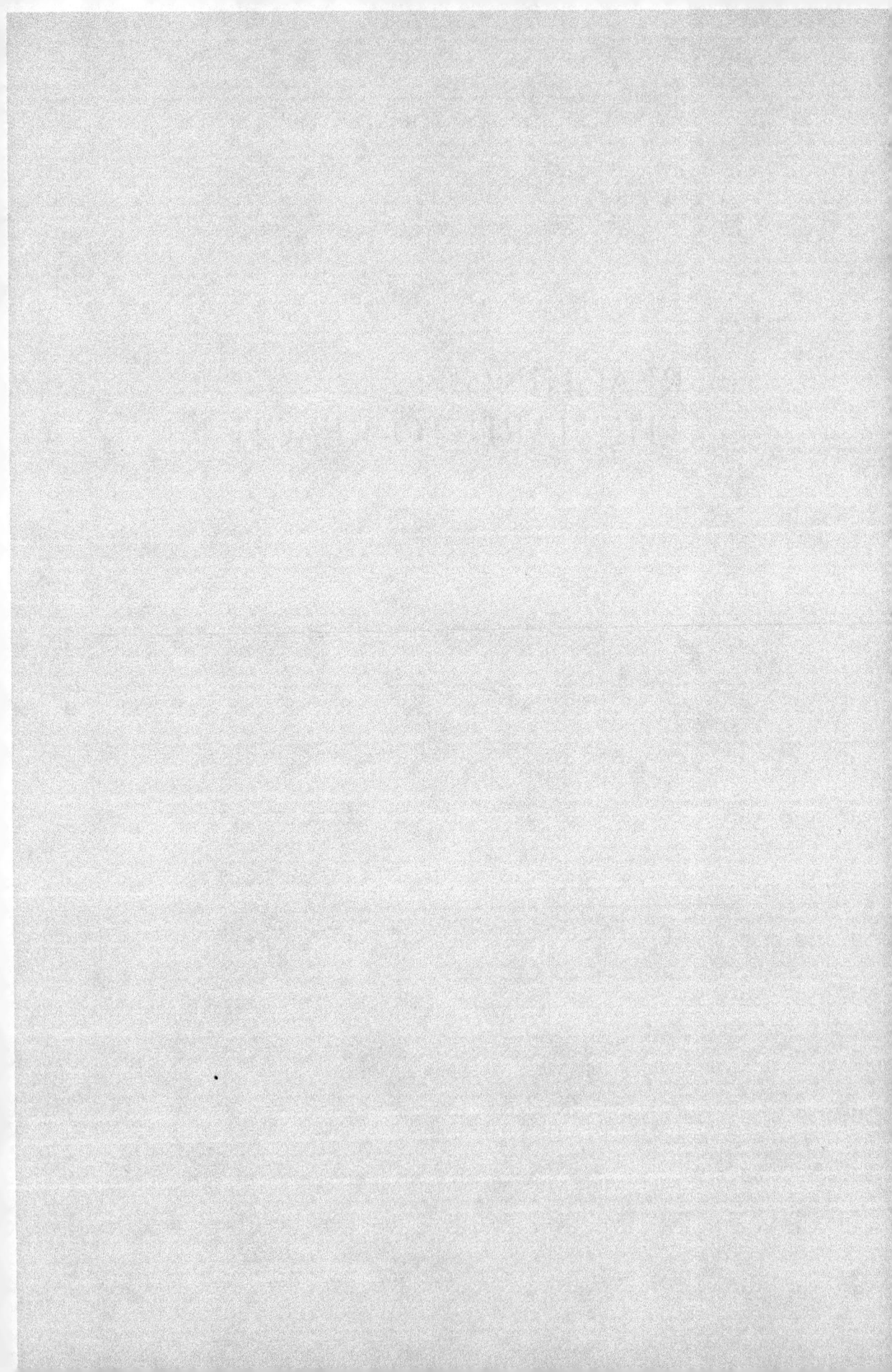

Laura Hirvi

Multi-sited Fieldwork amongst Sikhs in Finland and California

Reaching the Offline via the Online

S itting in a train from Jyväskylä to Helsinki, the capital of Finland, on my way to the birthday party of one of my Sikh informants, I receive a phone call from an Indian *giani* (learned man, priest). He calls me from Copenhagen, Denmark, to inform me of his intention to visit the *gurdwara* (Sikh temple) in Finland the next day. Nine months earlier, I had conducted fieldwork in the rural town of Yuba City in California, for a research project. During the almost three months I spent there, carrying out research amongst local Sikhs, I followed online the political campaign of one of my Sikh informants in Finland.

These persons, events and locations are all in some way linked to my fieldwork experience amongst Sikhs with a migration background, on the basis of which I seek to explore the complex processes through which identities are negotiated. In this study, I focus on Sikhs who have identified themselves as such and who migrated from northern India to two different cities; one Helsinki, the capital of Finland, and the other Yuba City, a rural town in California. Throughout the chapter, I use the word 'Sikh' to refer both to those Sikhs who actually migrated from India to Helsinki or Yuba City and to their descendants who were raised in their respective new home countries.

Sikhs started migrating to Finland in the late 1970s. Their faith, Sikhism, is a monotheistic religion that has its origins in the Punjab in Northern India, and Sikhs gather for congregational worship in a Sikh temple called a *gurdwara*. In Finland, there is only one *gurdwara*, which is located in Helsinki. Most Sikhs have settled down in the area around Helsinki, working either as employees or as entrepreneurs in the restaurant business.[1] Today, there are approximately 600 Sikhs living in the country. In contrast to Helsinki, the first Sikh settlers already arrived in Yuba City at the beginning of the twentieth century, and since then their number has increased to an estimated 8% of the city's total population. Initially, the Sikh pioneers

1   Hirvi 2011.

View from train in Finland, 2009, Laura Hirvi.

worked on farms, but today they can be found in all kinds of occupations. From November 2009 to November 2010, for example, Yuba City had its first Sikh mayor. Sikhs have a long and successful history in this town, which makes a trans-Atlantic comparison with the still small and rather young Sikh community in Finland especially interesting.

This chapter is based on data that I gathered for my doctoral dissertation research by means of multi-sited fieldwork. I spent the period October to December 2008 in Yuba City interviewing 38 male and female Sikhs belonging to different age groups and also carrying out participant observation. In addition, I returned in November 2009 to observe and take part in the local Sikh parade for a second time. In Finland, I conducted fieldwork amongst Sikhs in a 'yo-yo' manner during the period February 2008 to December 2011. The term 'yo-yo fieldwork' has been coined by Helena Wulff, and is used to describe fieldwork that consists of various field stints instead of a continuous presence in the field.[2] During my fieldwork in Finland, I conducted 27 interviews and took part in numerous cultural, religious and social events. In an effort to share my research results with my informants, I sent copies of my publications to Sikhs who were interested in reading them.

The opening narrative of this chapter already indicates that my fieldwork experience was marked by a high degree of mobility and a struggle to reach people who were spatially often quite dispersed. The aim of this chapter is to reflect on the role that the Internet played in the course of this type of

2   Wulff 2002.

fieldwork. In this vein, I wish with this chapter to add to a growing body of literature that seeks to update the corpus of conventional fieldwork methods. In particular, I am eager to explore how the use of the Internet, including the social networking site Facebook, can expand the body of traditional fieldwork methods in cases where 'being there'[3] is hindered by problems related to the question of 'getting there'. In addition, this contribution outlines some thoughts concerning the manner in which the advent of modern technologies has altered the researcher's relationship to the field and vice versa. The last section of the chapter addresses some ethical considerations related to online fieldwork methods, particularly in connection with Facebook. However, before shifting the focus to a more detailed discussion of the role of the Internet in the study of mobile people, I begin with a brief elaboration of how the 'field' is conceptualized in this study.

Conceptualizing the field as a bounded network

The thoughts put forward in this chapter are based on the idea that the field cannot simply be understood as a spatially bounded location.[4] Rather, I conceptualize the field as being made up of people and their practices, material objects and social sites. At the same time, it has to be kept in mind that the researcher constructs the field through a constant process of decision-making.[5] The procedure of selecting, choosing and deciding can therefore be seen as an important activity through which ethnographers bound their fields and transform the 'initial indeterminacy of field experience into a meaningful account'.[6] Implicit here is the idea that the field site cannot be defined *a priori* by the actual fieldwork project but rather emerges out of the ongoing data-gathering process.[7]

It is only during the actual fieldwork that a researcher decides who to talk to, what places to visit and what photographs to take. During one of my first visits to the *gurdwara* in Finland, for example, I was actively looking for people whom I could interview. Once, after I had finished eating the *langar*, the free food that is served to all at a Sikh temple, I walked to the congregational hall where I saw groups of women sitting on the floor. There I stood, wondering which group I should join and who to talk to in order to find people who would be willing to participate in my study. Confronted with such situations, 'fieldworkers find themselves at a metaphorical crossroads at which they have to make a choice in order to proceed. Eventually, these choices are going to have an impact on the shape of the evolving ethnography. In the following, I highlight the kind of choices that informed the process through which the field that I ended up studying came into being.

3   See Geertz 1988.
4   Gupta & Ferguson 1997.
5   Amit 2000, 6.
6   Candea, 2009, 27.
7   Burrell 2009, 184.

Choices are motivated by different, sometimes overlapping factors. During my fieldwork, I primarily aimed to make strategic choices. This means that whenever possible I preferred the option that seemed more significant and interesting for the ongoing research. However, when the alternatives appeared to be of equal importance, I let pragmatic considerations consciously influence my decisions. In Yuba City, for instance, I often had to rely on my bike in order to get from place A to B. On those Sundays when I had no one to pick me up by car, I therefore preferred to go to the *gurdwara* at Tierra Buena Road, since it was considerably closer to me than the other big temple in town. Some of the decisions that I made in the course of my fieldwork were partly also guided by 'intuition', such as in situations where I had to select a person out of a larger group of people to ask for an interview. In the context of this discussion it is important to point out that the task of making meaningful choices is not only limited to the time one spends gathering data through ethnographic fieldwork but continues at the stage of analysis and writing. When a researcher decides what to include and what to exclude in her/his work, s/he determines the boundaries of the field *post hoc*.[8] Further, one has to keep in mind that the process of constructing a field is not only restricted to the decisions the researcher makes but also the fact that the research participants are actively involved in shaping the field that a researcher ends up studying. Hence, like other scholars, I consider the construction of the field to be based on 'collaboration between researcher and the researched groups'.[9] Applied to the concrete fieldwork experience, this meant that I was only able to visit the homes and birthday parties of those people who were willing to invite me. And naturally I could only interview and talk to those Sikhs who agreed to it. Thus it can be argued that social relationships play an important role in shaping an ethnography as they enable the researcher to access realms that otherwise would have remained unseen, unnoticed or inapproachable. Or, as Vered Amit has put it: 'The scope of activities which an ethnographer can observe, in which s/he can participate, his/ her vantage point and premise of involvement are contingent on the nature of the relationships s/he is able to form with those engaged in these situations'.[10]

Sometimes being engaged in certain relationships can also close the doors to possible other contacts.[11] I realized this when talking to a Sikh couple in Yuba City. I had started a conversation with them at their work place, and we were just talking about the Sikh Parade that is annually organized in Yuba City. In this context, I mentioned the name of a male Sikh who is a quite public and controversial figure in town. Soon after mentioning his name, I noticed how the husband's attitude towards me and my inquiries changed. He exchanged a few words in Punjabi with his wife, who turned to

---

8   Coleman & Collins 2006, 6.
9   Burrell, 2009, 196; see also Coleman & Collins 2006, 12.
10   Amit 2000, 1–2.
11   Davies, 1999, 78.

Sikh gurdwara in Yuba City, California, 2008, Laura Hirvi.

me and said, 'Ok, thank you, and bye bye.' And before I realized it, the fragile moment of trust was gone and they walked away.[12]

Then again, relationships can also function as door-openers. This became most evident in my use of the snowball method, in which one initial contact leads to an ever increasing number of new ones. As I came to realize in the course of my fieldwork, the first contact does not necessarily need to belong to the group of people a researcher wants to study. During my research, I experienced several occasions on which I was put in contact with a future informant with the help of a person who was not a Sikh her-/himself. In one case, for example, I met an informant through a non-Sikh in Yuba City. This Sikh then eventually helped me to find six other people whom I interviewed for my study. And in Helsinki, a non-Sikh mailing list subscriber put me in contact with a Sikh woman who enabled me to recruit five other Sikhs living in Finland.

Getting there: the role of the Internet

As scholars have pointed out, cultures are not rooted in 'soil'.[13] This becomes particularly evident in the study of immigrants, when people travel carrying across their cultural maps in order to navigate through life. One of my informants in Yuba City explains it thus: 'I was born in India; I came to

12 Fieldnotes Laura Hirvi, December, 2008.
13 Inda & Rosaldo 2002, 13.

Khanda sign hanging from a car's rear-view mirror in Yuba City, California, 2009, Laura Hirvi.

this country [the USA]; my culture came with me.'[14] Although they often considerably alter and adjust their cultural maps to changing contexts, many Sikh migrants are eager to maintain certain cultural and religious traditions and strive to transmit them to the following generations of Sikhs who grow up outside the ancestral homeland. Religious places of worship, such as the Sikh *gurdwara* in Helsinki, can play a significant role in this enterprise.[15]

Sikhs in Yuba City already have four *gurdwaras*. In my fieldwork, I focused mainly on Yuba City's first *gurdwara*, which was built on the outskirts of the town in 1970. The temple annually arranges a *Nagar Kirtan*, also known as the Sikh Parade, which I had the chance to attend twice, once in 2008 and again in 2009. The parade, together with the activities that are carried out in connection with it, has in recent years attracted more than 70,000 visitors over the weekend when it is held. The intention of this religious procession is to bring God's message through the singing of divine hymns (*kirtan*) to the city (*nagar*). The procession consists of a leading float that carries the *Guru Granth Sahib*, the holy book of the Sikh faith. It is followed by numerous floats representing different Sikh congregations or organizations, such as the Punjabi clubs of high schools or universities. It was easy for me 'to be there', to attend this particular event, as it was open to the public.

Sikh immigrants have been arriving in Yuba City since the beginning of the twentieth century, and today their presence has created a significant and visible landscape. In Yuba City, the people, events and material objects

14 Interview with Suraj, December 17, 2008.
15 See Hirvi 2010.

Sign indicating in English as well as in Punjabi to the visitors of the Sikh parade that parking is not allowed here, Yuba City, California, 2009, Laura Hirvi.

that constitute a field were located right in front of my modern version of the Malinowskian tent – in other words, the flat in town that I had rented for the period of my fieldwork. When going to the supermarket or dropping off my daughter at her pre-school around the corner, I often encountered something that I considered relevant for my fieldwork experience. I saw men with turbans riding their bikes towards the temple at Tierra Buena Road, and when shopping for groceries I saw women wearing the traditional Indian dress called *Salwar kameez*. Often I would notice cars that displayed the *Khanda*, which is an important symbol in Sikhism. The *Khanda* was either hanging from the car's rear-view mirror or displayed in the form of a sticker pasted on the back window. Thus, in the case of Yuba City, most of the time I could feel sure that everything I did could be justified as being part of my fieldwork.[16]

In Helsinki, on the other hand, getting to 'be there' was not as simple as in Yuba City. The local Sikh community is only a small minority of the total population of Helsinki, and the chances of running into a Sikh by accident are few. From my initial perspective, the community I set out to study seemed invisible. Since I did not know the location of the *gurdwara* – as a matter of fact I was not even sure that there was one – and without having any pre-existing contacts with Sikhs living in Finland, inventiveness was needed. This initial period resembled the fieldwork experience of the anthropologist Cordula Weissköppel, which she describes as follows: 'My task at making first contacts was more like looking for a needle in a haystack

16 See Kurotani 2005, 204.

than fieldwork in the conventional sense, where the anthropologist is surrounded by the society to be studied.'[17] Soon I realized that, like many other ethnographers in the contemporary world, I was trying to conduct fieldwork in a setting in which 'the Malinowskian conditions of fieldwork' were seriously challenged.[18] How to start fieldwork under such circumstances became a question that urgently needed to be addressed.[19]

As it turned out, the Internet was for several reasons the solution to undoing the Gordian knot that I felt myself confronted with. To start with, the Internet turned out to be an extremely valuable recruitment tool that helped me find the first participants for this study.[20] I posted an email to the mailing list of the Finnish Society for the Study of Ethnic Relations and International Migration (ETMU), and in response I received from one of the list's subscribers an offer to put me in contact with a Sikh family, whose daughter and mother both eventually turned out to be my first informants. Another subscriber to the list put me in touch with a Sikh woman, whom I ended up interviewing together with her husband, and who since then has been inviting me to her children's birthday parties. Thus online methods have enabled me to enter the 'offline lives'[21] of the people whom I was interested in studying.

In addition, I used Facebook, the social networking website, to look for possible informants, by searching the social network of Finland for people with the last name 'Singh' or 'Kaur', as these are common last names for Sikhs who are close to the heritage of Sikhism. Keen to convey my identity as a researcher and to apologise for disturbing their privacy, I drafted the following letter and sent it to altogether 18 people on two separate occasions:

> Hello!
> My name is Laura, and I am doing research about the Sikh community in Helsinki. Mostly I am interested in the everyday life of Sikhs living in Finland, which would include leisure time activities, religious practices and the relationship to India and Finland.
> At the moment I am looking for Sikhs to interview, and I was wondering, whether you, due to your surname (SINGH/ KAUR), belong

---

17 Weisskö ppel 2009, 254; See also Powdermaker (1966, 213), who reports on a similar problem in her study of Hollywood.

18 See Marcus 2009, 19.

19 See also Meissner and Hasselberg (this volume) for similar experiences during their fieldwork.

20 Sanders 2005; see also Meissner and Hasselberg (this volume) for a similar approach.

21 Sanders (2005, 79) argues: "The Internet is an appropriate and useful tool where the virtual can be used to access 'real life'". Her use of 'real life', even though written in inverted commas, is problematic as it seems to suggest that online worlds are not part of the real world. Thus I prefer the use of "offline lives", which I consider to be more accurate in terms of its connotations. See also Boellstorff (2008, 21), who prefers the term "actual world" when referring "to places of human culture not realized by computer programs through the Internet".

to the Finnish Sikh community? In case you do, it would be great if we can arrange an interview. You can contact me by sending me an email: lajoschw@cc.jyu.fi. / or via Facebook. In case you do not belong to the Sikh community, I apologize for having bothered you!

Best regards,
Laura Hirvi
University of Jyväskylä

As Table 1 indicates, out of the 18 messages I sent via Facebook, eleven received responses, three of them from females and eight from males. One of the men offered help in locating the *gurdwara*, and two others agreed to meet me for a face-to-face interview. Two of the respondents, one female and one male, initially agreed to participate in my study, but suddenly withdrew this offer without any further explanation. Other studies which have applied Internet-based methods have reported similar problems connected with the sudden withdrawal of informants.[22] When no further explanation is given, one can only speculate on the reasons behind such a sudden interruption of communication. Perhaps they disliked the idea of meeting a person they had only met online in the offline world. Or maybe they were just too busy or not interested enough in the research project and hence decided to end the computer-mediated conversation. In a face-to-face meeting, hardly anyone would leave in the middle of a conversation without bidding farewell, but cyberspace seemed to make this an easier option, possibly owing to the impersonal character of our exchange at that early stage of communication. And, of course, this choice on the part of a potential informant side has to be respected.

The other Facebook respondents did not take part in this research because they either belonged to another religion, or were atheist, or did not identify themselves as Sikhs despite having Sikh parents. The number of messages sent out is not enough to permit generalisation, but it seems that, at least in this case study, gender played a role in my success in recruiting informants via an online social network site. Out of the nine women I tried to contact, only three responded, and the one who did agree to an interview withdrew at the last minute. By contrast, of the nine men who had been contacted all but one replied. Eventually, I ended up interviewing two male respondents, who identified themselves as Sikhs, as well as one respondent's friend, who turned out to be one of my most valuable contacts, keeping me up to date with the cultural events he organized for the community. Further, it can be noted that none of the participants found through Facebook was older than 35.[23] While the number of interviews obtained by means of this Facebook method may seem meagre, it is important to note that the answers given by

---

22 See e.g. Kivits 2005, 45.
23 Here it has to be noted that at the time when I adopted this online research method, Facebook had just arrived in Finland and thus the number of people using it was probably lower than it is today.

Total 18	Responded	No response	Agreed to interview/ help	Withdraw from interview/ help	Interviewed/ helped	Parents Sikh but respondent not	Other religion/ atheist
Female (9)	3	6	1	1	0	1	1
Male (9)	8	1	4	1	3	3	3

Table 1. Response to letter sent via Facebook.

respondents who had Sikh parents but did not identify themselves as Sikhs also provided significant insights for this research project, and I could have explored these insights further if I had recognized this potential earlier.

James Clifford argued about a decade ago: 'When one speaks of working *in* the field, or *going* into the field, one draws on mental images of a distinct place with an inside and outside, reached by practices of physical movement'.[24] But like Saara Koikkalainen's contribution in this volume, I have shown in this paragraph that at the beginning of the 21st century the Internet and its various forms of communication have helped to decrease to some extent the need for physical movement by offering the researcher the option of online movement instead.[25]

Gathering data through the Internet

Besides providing assistance in the search for informants, the Internet offers a chance to conduct part of the actual data-gathering online. One option is to go online in order to observe. This alternative seems to be especially attractive in cases where the information is not available anywhere else or where physical movement is restricted owing to limited funds and/or to the impossibility of being physically in two different places at the same time. It was for the second reason that I was not able to attend Yuba City's 15th Annual Punjabi American Festival. But thanks to the option made available by the Internet, I still had the opportunity to observe the event a couple of months later from my office at the University of California in Santa Barbara. Going online, I was able to read newspaper articles that reported and commented on the event, look at numerous photographs displayed on the organizers' homepage and watch a video produced by the local newspaper which included interviews with the organizers and members of the audience. Travelling with the help of the Internet in this way enabled me to observe

24 Clifford 1997, 54, original emphasis.
25 See Koikkalainen, this volume.

Entrance to the gurdwara in Helsinki, Finland, 2010, Laura Hirvi.

the Punjabi American Festival without having to physically leave my office. In applying this method, however, it has to be kept in mind at the stage of analysis that others, in this case journalists, photographers and website administrators, have predefined the perspective from which one is able to observe.

Besides offering an alternative site for making observations, the Internet, and in particular computer-mediated communication (CMC), can serve as a practical tool for conducting interviews. It has been argued that the advantage of gathering data by means of CMC is that it offers statements that are already in written form.[26] Further, it obviates the need for physical travel by both researchers and informants, and thus it is a method that is low in costs.[27] In addition, it is a tool that enables both researcher and respondent to engage in the conversation at their best convenience thanks to its asynchronous and place-independent character.[28]

During my fieldwork, I used CMC in the case of Chintan[29], whom I had met at the *gurdwara* in Finland. When I met him for the first time, Chintan was about to move back to India for good, and so we agreed to conduct the interview via emails. Meeting him face-to-face at the *gurdwara* had helped to establish a rapport. Even so, I was eager to create an atmosphere of trust

26 However, "the ease of obtaining data in virtual worlds can also be a curse" (Boellstorff 2008, 75) because handling such a large amount of data poses a particular challenge for the ethnographer at the phase of analysis.
27 See Kivits 2005, 35.
28 Hine 2000, 45.
29 I use pseudonyms in order to protect the identity of my informants.

by including my own ideas and experiences in the email conversation in order to 'create a comfortable and friendly context for interviewing'.[30] Chintan was a very patient respondent, who was committed to the research project and willing to share his thoughts concerning his stay in Finland. But after six emails, which already had produced a valuable set of data, I felt that the natural flow of communication had ebbed away. Mail by mail his responses had got shorter, and I could not blame him because writing long answers demands a lot of time and energy. Eager not to exploit his kindness, I therefore decided to bring our email exchange to an end. Eight months later, I came across his emails while going through my data. Spontaneously, I decided to send him an email to see how he was doing. At that time, I was spending a year as a Fulbright student at UCSB, and Chintan – to my great surprise – had returned together with his newly wed wife to Finland to work in a local company. Thus, after my return to Finland, I eventually ended up interviewing Chintan and his wife offline. Compared with the email-based conversation, the face-to-face interview conducted in their Finnish home contained a wealth of information which would have been difficult to gather via an exchange of emails.

Nevertheless, emails are a useful research tool in situations where it is hard to arrange an offline meeting. In other words, if Chintan had not returned to Finland, the email-based interview would have provided the only, albeit valuable as such, source of information. Further, as this case demonstrates, the e-mail exchange enabled me to follow an informant's life over a longer time span. Thanks to our computer-mediated correspondence I found out that Chintan had moved back to Finland together with his wife, and in order to get this information I did not have to rely on serendipity; in other words, the chance of meeting him at the *gurdwara* or of hearing about his return from someone else, for example.

Emails are not only helpful for conducting interviews, but together with other technological media such as cell phones they also constitute an effective tool in enabling researcher to stay in touch with the people they have met during the time spent physically in the field, as Wendy Vogt's and Lisa Wiklund's contributions to this volume clearly show.[31] My informants and I were able to stay connected whether we were in Jyväskylä, Helsinki, Yuba City, Santa Barbara, India or somewhere else in the world.[32] Certain informants in Finland kept me informed about upcoming events via emails and sometimes also text messages – happenings that I otherwise would not have noticed owing to the somewhat invisible and non-public character of the events organized by the Sikh community in Helsinki. Therefore, it can be claimed that modern technology enables researchers to access realms that would perhaps otherwise have remained unseen or unnoticed. Further, repeated communication via emails and text messages ensured that I never really had the feeling of having left the field for good. In contemporary

---

30 Kivits 2005, 40.
31 Vogt, this volume; Wiklund, this volume.
32 See, for example, the vignette at the beginning of this chapter.

ethnographic fieldwork, it seems to be a more and more common feature for researchers to stay in touch with the people they have met in the course of fieldwork after physically departing from the field.[33] This calls into question once again the relationship between 'home' and 'the field'.

The question of exit

The Internet made access to the research target group, and in particular to the Sikhs living in Finland, significantly easier. But at the same time, as I argue in the following, together with other modern technologies it made 'exiting' the field much more challenging. Once the fieldwork got going, research-relevant experiences and events seemed to pop up everywhere. Thus it seems that, like the fieldwork experience of the anthropologist Joanne Passaro amongst homeless people in New York, these experiences were all part of the texture that constituted my field.[34] However, experiencing and conceptualizing the field in such a manner makes a distinction between home and the field difficult, as for example the sociologist Marja Tiilikainen's reflections on her fieldwork with Somali immigrant women in Finland demonstrate when she asserts that, whenever she was in the field, she was not entirely there, and, when at home, it was difficult for her to leave the field completely behind.[35]

James Clifford argues that modern technology, with its ability to 'compress space', makes exiting the field a more difficult task.[36] The Internet and mobile phones have the power to tear down the walls of various constructed spheres, such as 'the field' and 'home'. This happened to me, for example, on one Friday evening when a young Sikh man, whom I had interviewed earlier that day, kept on sending me text messages late into the night. Or on a Saturday afternoon, when I was spending time with friends, I received a phone call from an informant I was supposed to meet the next morning in Helsinki. What if I had not answered their calls and messages? Would this have risked losing them as informants? Karin Norman concludes in her reflections on fieldwork conducted 'at home' that, when the field 'spills over in one's everyday life', it can be 'both emotionally and intellectually rewarding or quite difficult to manage, emotionally, and also practically'.[37] Such potential negative consequences arising from the merging of the field and researchers' constructed notion of their 'home' suggest that a deeper reflection on the process of exiting fieldwork might be in order.

So far scholars have not paid as much attention to the question of exits as they have to the question of access.[38] Stories of entry are prominent in ethnographic accounts as they function as a proof that the researchers

---

33 See e.g. Norman 2000; Wulff 2002; Wilk 2011.
34 Passaro 1997, 153.
35 Tiilikainen 2002, 275; see also Tiilikainen 2003, 94.
36 Clifford 1997, 68.
37 Norman 1999, 122.
38 Iversen, 2009, 10.

have actually been there, in the field, and are thus qualified to produce an ethnographic account of the cultural communities they have studied. However, detailed and reflective accounts of exit are rarer, and often departure is only mentioned when leaving the field is referred to as a means though which the researcher gains the necessary distance to engage in the writing of the ethnography.[39] James Fergusson condemns these 'tropes of entry to and exit from' the field in ethnographic texts since, according to him, they disregard the reality in which the researcher and the informants are positioned, that is 'within a common, shared world'.[40]

But perhaps rather than require a complete removal of these stylistic devices in the writing of ethnographies, it might be suggested that they be used with greater reflexivity. Especially with reference to 'exits', the question of what fieldworkers actually refer to when they write about exiting, departing, getting out and leaving the field could be explored in more detail. Do these metaphors refer only to physical departure? Or are such tropes of withdrawal also relevant in referring to the process of the 'intellectual distancing' needed to analyze the gathered data?[41] Or is there perhaps another meaning implied in the phrase 'exit from the field' when it functions as a rhetorical device by which fieldworkers address the problem of how to leave their work behind? Because after all, field*work*ers, who receive a grant or a university salary to conduct their research, perform (field)*work* in the sense of paid labour.[42] And even if for many this may involve a unique chance to follow a calling, ethnographers do actually work when they collect data for their research projects. However, fieldwork conducted nearby and characterized by the use of new technologies seems at times to be a job that is 24/7 in nature. The Internet and mobile phones have created the possibility that leaving informants is only a physical departure with no final impact on the researcher's connections with the field and the people in it.

Experiencing fieldwork as a job that demands permanent commitment does not run contrary to the practice of conducting traditional fieldwork projects. But unlike the latter, which are carried out in a geographic location distant from home for a pre-determined period of time, fieldwork conducted 'nearby' has no pre-determined beginning or end that is materialized in the form of a flight ticket, for instance. This gives fieldwork conducted at home a more ongoing character that makes the idea of exit much harder for the researcher to grasp and realize. Ongoing connectivity with the field and with the people in it can have certain advantages, but for the practice of fieldwork carried out nearby, this constant closeness can also pose certain emotional challenges, as it competes with a researcher's own private social life. This private social life and its concomitant obligations are often left behind in fieldwork conducted away from home, and this seems to allow fieldworkers to immerse themselves more fully in the life worlds that they

39 Clifford 1997, 90; Burrell 2009, 182.
40 Ferguson 1997, 138.
41 Davies 1999, 193.
42 See also Hastrup 1992, 118.

seek to study as they have more time to focus on the relationships with the people whom they meet in the course of doing fieldwork. But irrespective of whether researchers carry out fieldwork nearby or far from home, they need moments of retreat from fieldwork in order to reflect on their ongoing fieldwork. On the basis of these considerations, it could be argued that the question of exit becomes meaningful in so far as it is tied to the question of how to leave the work behind. How to get a break from the field when living in it? Deliberately switching off technologies is, of course, one option available to both the researcher and the researched group.

The question of ethics

Online ethnographies or studies that have integrated online methods into their fieldwork design seem to have an almost imperative need to address the question of ethics in considerable detail. In principle, it can be said that the ethical guidelines that apply to the offline world should also guide a researcher's behaviour in the online world. These guidelines often stress the researcher's responsibility to protect the informants' anonymity, to inform the researched group or people about the purpose of the study, to ask them for their consent to participate in the research and/ or to be observed, and to protect them from any possible harm that could arise as a consequence of taking part in the research project. However, transferring research ethics from the offline to the online world has turned out to be a challenging task. Among other things, as Riikka Turtiainen and Sari Östman point out, researchers seem to struggle with the question of whom and in what circumstances they need to ask for permission when gathering data on the Internet.[43] This is a tricky question owing to the fact that the Internet and the various forms it provides for communication have blurred the distinction between what is considered public and what is classified as private.[44] The fact that the Internet may have different meanings for different people complicates this discussion further.[45]

As a consequence of the difficulties of pinning down a clear and visible distinction between the private and the public on the Internet, the question of ethical conduct seems to receive special attention in studies that apply online methods as part of their ethnographic fieldwork. In discussions concerning research ethics, it is important to keep in mind that the regulations for researchers' ethical conduct may differ from country to country.[46] In the USA, for example, researchers who are affiliated to a university and plan a research project involving human beings have to get their research plan approved by an institutional review board prior to its realization. In Finland, on the other hand, no such mandatory procedures exist. Organizations that

---

43 Turtiainen & Östman 2009.
44 Bromseth 2002, 35.
45 Hine 2005, 9.
46 Sveningsson 2004, 47.

produce academic knowledge are obligated to provide sufficient instructions regarding proper research ethics, but the final responsibility for conducting ethically correct research lies with the researchers themselves.[47] With reference to research conducted through the Internet, Arja Kuula points out that it is impossible to formulate general ethical guidelines that would be applicable to all situations. Rather, ethical considerations have to be negotiated against the background of the specific research context.[48]

In this case study, as mentioned earlier, I conducted part of my observation online, for example by browsing the websites of a Yuba City Punjabi cultural organization or by visiting the homepage of a Sikh politician in Finland. Since both sites were easily accessible and designed to reach the public, studying these homepages can be regarded as unproblematic in terms of research ethics. Likewise, my email communication with certain individuals was ethically correct, I would argue, since the correspondence partners had been informed in advance about the research project and had been asked for their explicit consent to take part in this research. Similarly unproblematic was my use of mailing lists as subscribers had the option to choose whether or not to reply to my call for assistance.

A much more challenging case concerning research ethics was raised by the use of the social networking site Facebook. The site was founded in February 2004 and, according to the company's press release, has currently almost 400 million active users.[49] For this research, Facebook was used in the initial stage of the fieldwork project as a tool to recruit informants by sending a number of selected members the letter quoted above in this chapter. However, soon after sending out the first message I began to wonder whether it was ethically correct to contact these people via a social networking site.

In order to answer this question, it is helpful to start by taking a closer look at the policies and intentions of Facebook itself, since people who have subscribed to the site's services should be familiar with the terms and conditions as they have accepted them when signing up.[50] On its homepage, Facebook states that it 'is a social utility that helps people communicate more efficiently with their friends, family and co-workers. The company develops technologies that facilitate the sharing of information through the "social graph", the digital mapping of people's real-world social connections.'[51] This statement seems to suggest that Facebook is meant as an online tool to be used for keeping up with already existing connections in the offline world. However, under *Info* the company states that its mission is 'to give people the power to share and make the world more open and connected.'[52] And

---

47   Kuula 2006, 34ff.
48   Kuula 2004, 195.
49   http://www.facebook.com/press/info.php?factsheet./ Accessed 16 May 2010.
50   Providing they have really read them.
51   http://www.facebook.com/press/info.php?factsheet. Accessed 16 May 2010.
52   http://www.facebook.com/facebook?v=app_7146470109&ref=pf#!/facebook?v
     =info&ref=pf. Accessed 16 May 2010.

under *privacy policies* one can find statements such as 'Facebook is designed to make it easy for you to find and connect with others' and 'Facebook enables you to connect with virtually anyone or anything you want, from your friends and family to the city you live in to the restaurants you like to visit to the bands and movies you love'.[53] Do these statements thus legitimate the use of Facebook for finding people to take part in a study?

If they agree that they do, researchers who want to approach people via Facebook should take into account paragraph 5.7 of the company's *Rights and Responsibilities*, which states: 'If you collect information from users, you will: obtain their consent, make it clear [that] you (and not Facebook) are the one collecting their information, and post a privacy policy explaining what information you collect and how you will use it.'[54] With these considerations in mind, I sent out the letter in the sincere conviction that it would not harm or offend the receivers or put them at risk, and that the recipients had the possibility to choose whether or not to engage in this form of social networking. At that time I believed that people who had set up a Facebook profile were aware of its public, because accessible, character. But what if they were not? Because I sent out too many messages with the same content over a short period of time, the Facebook system reacted, and I was warned about possibly spamming other people. Spamming other people was far from my intention. But now I asked myself the question: Was I disturbing their right to privacy? Initially I did not think so, based on the fact that I understood this to be a site whose subscribers accepted it for its ability to support and broaden the options for social networking. And at least the eleven people who answered the message did not show any signs of anger, offence or surprise over the letter. But what about the seven other recipients who did not answer the message? Did they construe it as spam that was disturbing their privacy? Did they have different expectations concerning the purpose of Facebook?

By later improving the options for adjusting a user's privacy settings, Facebook seems to have realized that the people who use its services may do so for different purposes. While some subscribers strictly use it for keeping up with already existing contacts, others use it for social networking with colleagues, and some groups and celebrities may use it as a channel for recruiting supporters and for communicating with them. In the context of discussing this case study, I would argue that a better, and without doubt ethically less questionable, option for recruiting informants with the help of this particular social network site would have been to post a request to join this research project on the Facebook page of the *gurdwara* in Helsinki after asking the administrator of this page for permission. However, at the time this research project started, Sikhs in Finland did not yet have any collective Facebook pages, or any general Internet presence.

53 http://www.facebook.com/settings/?tab=privacy&ref=mb#!/policy.php. Accessed 17 May 2010.
54 http://www.facebook.com/terms.php. Accessed 16 May 2010.

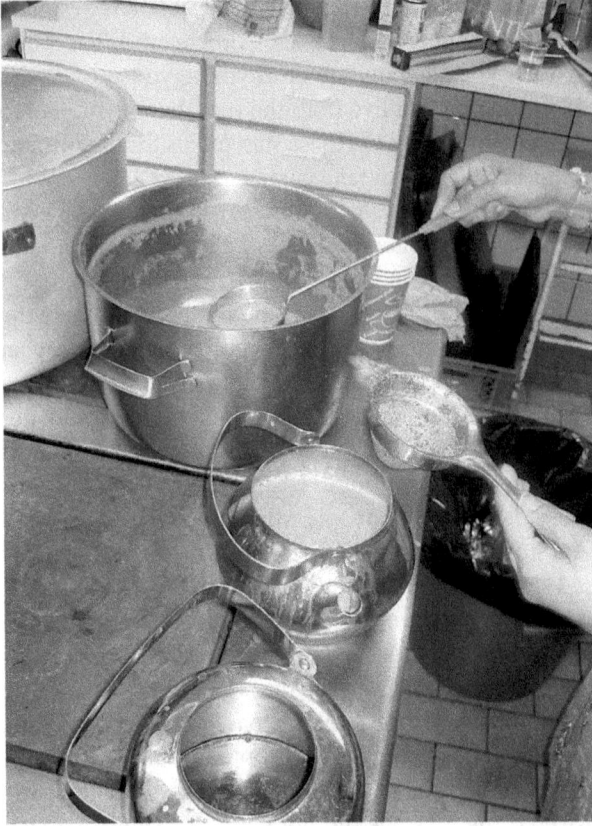

*Preparation of
Indian tea at
a Sikh birthday
party in Helsinki,
Finland, 2008,
Laura Hirvi.*

Concluding Remarks

This paper has highlighted the crucial role that the Internet – with its unique ability to establish connections between people and places in multiple ways – played in the success of this fieldwork endeavour. In a recent publication of articles reflecting on the methods of ethnographic fieldwork, George Marcus calls for a reform of the fieldwork craft. As he points out, there is 'the need to shape a discourse that escapes the restrictive constructions of fieldwork while preserving its valued characteristics'.[55] Such efforts do not aim to downplay the importance and relevance of the research practices related to what Marcus describes as the 'Malinowskian tradition of fieldwork'.[56] Rather, the intention is to encourage acceptance of alternative approaches towards fieldwork methods and to openly incorporate them into the existing canon of practices as applied in contemporary fieldwork endeavours.

Such a reform in fieldwork methods would support thinking outside the box, which eventually could lead to an enlargement of what the box of

55 Marcus 2009, 5.
56 Marcus 2009, 7.

fieldwork methods is perceived to contain. Ten years earlier, Marcus together with his colleague Michael Fischer acknowledged in their introduction to the second edition of *Anthropology as Cultural Critique* that the advent of CMC and visual technologies demands 'different norms of fieldwork and writing'.[57] This seems to support the argument that discussions surrounding a rethinking of fieldwork methods have to take the Internet into account more seriously because it may play a crucial role in enabling, improving and sometimes easing the fieldwork enterprise, as this chapter has hopefully demonstrated.

However, the Internet is not only opening up alternative options for the conduct of fieldwork, but it can also affect other realms related to the production of ethnographies and the dissemination of research findings. Concerning the latter, homepages are particularly useful as they allow scholars to easily share information about their ongoing research projects and their findings with a larger audience. Further, more and more ethnographers working at the beginning of the 21st century have discovered the activity of blogging as a means to document their fieldwork experiences and the writing process. It can be assumed that the practice of posting blog entries of this kind has a positive impact on increasing the transparency of the research process. In the future, it would be interesting to see how ethnographers could in their ethnographic writings make more extensive use of the tools provided for them by the Internet, including the ability to provide informants with an avenue to continuously comment on the research in progress.

Summarizing the thoughts presented in this chapter, it can be said that in this case study the Internet served as an effective tool that provided the fieldworker with the beginning of a thread that would eventually lead to an informant to interview or a place to visit in person.[58] Further, it helped in gaining supplementary data that enabled a deeper understanding of the context. However, unlike studies such as the one conducted by Tom Boellstorff, which seeks to explore online worlds in their own right,[59] this research project had as its main focus people's lives and cultures as lived and practised in an offline context. Therefore, my presence in the offline world, where I was able to see, listen, taste, smell and touch, was crucial to fully experiencing, in the sense of *erleben*,[60] what I was trying to understand. Without the bodily and sensory experiences of dancing the *bhangra* (a Punjabi dance) with the women and children at birthday parties and weddings, smelling Indian food or tasting sweet *prashad* (blessed food) at the *gurdwara*, touching the floor with my forehead when bowing in front of the *Guru Granth*, or hearing the life stories told by my informants shared

---

57 Marcus & Fischer 1999, xxv.

58 See Koikkalainen in this volume for a similar conclusion.

59 Boellstorff 2008.

60 The German word "Erlebnis" has been translated as "lived experience" (see e.g. Frykman & Gilje 2003, 15); "erleben" is the verb from which this noun is derived.

with me over a cup of *chai* (tea) or Starbucks' *caffè latte*[61], I would not have been able to fully grasp the richness of the various elements that form the socio-cultural worlds in relation to which identities are negotiated.

Thus, on the basis of the fieldwork experience discussed in this chapter, I agree with Judith Okely, who asserts that fieldworkers do learn 'through all the senses, through movement, through their bodies and whole being in a total practice'.[62] It is the experience of fieldwork with its sensual richness and gripping intensity that supports the complex learning process through which ethnographers eventually seek to understand what they study. Therefore, I would argue that 'being there' physically was mandatory for this particular research project but without the help of the Internet the act of getting there might have been a lot harder and slower and prevented me from seeing the online dimension that is part of my informants' lives.

Bibliography

Allen, C. 1996: What's Wrong With the 'Golden Rule'? Conundrums of Conducting Ethical Research in Cyberspace. The Information Society: *An International Journal* 12: 2, 175–187.

Amit, V. 2000: Introduction: Constructing the Field. In: V. Amit (ed.), *Constructing the Field: Ethnographic Fieldwork in the Contemporary World*. London: Routledge.

Boellstorff, T. 2008: *Coming of Age in Second Life. An Anthropologist Explores the Virtual Human*. Princeton and Oxford: Princeton University Press.

Bromseth, J. C. H. 2002: Public Places - Public Activities? Methodological approaches and ethical dilemmas in research on computer-mediated communication contexts. In: A. Morrison (ed.), *Researching ICT's in Contexts*. InterMedia Report 3/2002, Oslo: University of Oslo.

Burrell, J. 2009: The Field Site as a Network: A Strategy for Locating Ethnographic Research. *Field Methods* 21: 2, 181–199.

Candea, M. 2009: Arbitrary Locations: In defence of the bounded field-site. In: M. Falzon (ed.), *Multi-sited Ethnography. Theory, Praxis and Locality in Contemporary Research*. Aldershot: Ashgate.

Clifford, J. 1997: *Routes. Travel and Translation in the Late Twentieth Century*, Cambridge, London: Harvard University Press.

Coleman, S. M. & P. Collins 2006: Introduction: 'Being ... Where?' Performing Fields on Shifting Grounds. In: Coleman, S. M. & P. Collins (eds.), *Locating the Field: Space, Place and Context in Anthropology*. Oxford, New York: Berg Publishers.

Davies, C. A. 1999: *Reflexive Ethnography: A Guide to Researching Selves and Others*. London: Routledge.

Faubion, J. D. & G. E. Marcus (eds.) 2009: *Fieldwork Is Not What It Used to Be. Learning Anthropology's Method in a Time of Transition*, Ithaca and London: Cornell University.

61 My intention in making this point is not to advertise a certain popular American company but to emphasize the diverse conditions under which modern fieldwork can and does take place. Publishing such accounts supports the idea of what Clifford (1997, 90; see also Passaro 1997) has termed 'Subway ethnographies' and aims at including them in the paradigm of accepted modes of fieldwork practices.

62 Okely 1992, 16.

Ferguson, J. 1997: Paradoxes of Sovereignity and Independence. 'Real' and 'pseudo' nation-states and the depoliticization of poverty. In: K. F. Olwig & K. Hastrup (eds.), *Siting cultures. The shifting anthropological object*. New York: Routledge.

Frykman, J. & N. Gilje 2003: Being There. In: J. Frykman & N. Gilje (eds.) *Being There. New Perspectives on Phenomology and the Analysis of Culture*. Lund: Nordic Academic Press.

Geertz, C. 1988: *Works and Lives. The Anthropologist as Author*. Stanford: Stanford University Press.

Gupta, A. & J. Ferguson 1997: Discipline and Practice: 'The Field' As Site, Method, and Location in Anthropology. In: A. Gupta & J. Ferguson (eds.), *Anthropological Locations. Boundaries and Grounds of a Field Science*. Berkeley, Los Angeles, London: University of California Press.

Hastrup, K. 1992: Writing Ethnnography. State of the Art. In: J. Okely & H. Callaway (eds.), *Anthropology & Autobiography*. London, New York: Routledge.

Hine, C. 2000: *Virtual Ethnography*. London, Thousand Oaks, New Delhi: SAGE Publications.

Hirvi, L. 2010: The Sikh Gurdwara in Finland: Negotiating, Maintaining and Transmitting Immigrants' Identities. *South Asian Diaspora* 2: 2, 219–232.

Hirvi, L. 2011: Sikhs in Finland: migration histories and work in the restaurant sector. In: K. A. Jacobsen and K. Myrvold (eds.) *Sikhs in Europe: Migration, Identities, and Representation*. Aldershot: Ashgate. 95–114.

Inda, J. X. & R. Rosaldo 2002: Introduction. A World in Motion. In: J. X. Inda & R. Rosaldo (eds.), *The Anthropology of Globalization*. Malden, Oxford, Victoria: Blackwell Publishing.

Iversen, R. R. 2009: 'Getting out' in Ethnography: A Seldom-told Story. *Qualitative Social* Work 8: 1, 9–26.

Kivits, J. 2005: Online Interviewing and the Research Relationship. In: C. Hine (ed.), *Virtual Methods: Issues in Social Research on the Internet*. Oxford: Berg Publishers.

Kurotani, S. 2005: Multi-sited Transnational Ethnography and the Shifting Construction of Fieldwork. In: L. Hume & J. Mulcock (eds.), *Anthropologists in the Field: Cases in Participant Observation*. New York: Columbia University Press.

Kuula, Arja 2006: *Tutkimusetiikka. Aineistojen hankinta, käyttö ja säilytys*. Tampere: Vastapaino.

Marcus, G. E. & M. J. Fischer 1999: *Anthropology as Cultural Critique. An Experimental Moment in the Human Sciences. Second edition*. Chicago and London: University of Chicago Press.

Marcus, G.E. 2009: Introduction. Notes Towards an Ethnographic Memoir of Supervising Graduate Research through Anthropology's Decades of Transformation. In: J. D. Faubion & G. E. Marcus (eds.), *Fieldwork is not what it used to be. Learning Anthropology's Method in a Time of Transition*, Ithaca and London: Cornell University.

Norman, K. 2000: Phoning the Field. Meanings of Place and Involvement in Fieldwork 'at Home'. In: V. Amit, (ed.), *Constructing the Field: Ethnographic Fieldwork in the Contemporary World*. London: Routledge.

Okely, J. 1992: Anthropology and Autobiography: Participatory Experience and Embodied Knowledge. In: J. Okely & H. Callaway (eds.), *Anthropology & Autobiography*. London, New York: Routledge.

Passaro, J. 1997: 'You Can't Take the Subway to the Field!'. 'Village' Epistemologies in the Global Village. In: A. Gupta & J. Ferguson (eds.), *Anthropological Locations. Boundaries and Grounds of a Field Science*. Berkely, Los Angeles, London: University of California Press.

Powdermaker, H. 1966: *Stranger and Friend. The Way of an Anthropologist*. New York, London: W.W. Norton & Company.

Sanders, T. 2005: Researching the Online Sex Work Community. In: C. Hine (ed.), *Virtual Methods: Issues in Social Research on the Internet*. Oxford: Berg Publishers.

Sveningsson, M. 2004: Ethics in Internet Ethnography. In: E. A. Buchanan (ed.), *Readings in Virtual Research Ethics. Issues and Controversies*. Hershey, London, Melbourne, Singapore: Information Science Publishing.

Tiilikainen, M. 2002: Homes and fields, friends and informants. Fieldwork among Somali refugee women. In: T. Sakaranaho, T. Sjöblom, T. Utriainen & H. Pesonen *Styles and Positions. Ethnographic perspectives in comparative religion*. University of Helsinki, Department of Comparative Religion.

Turtiainen, R. & S. Östman 2009: Tavistaidetta ja verkkoviihdettä – omaehtoisten verkkosisältöjen tutkimusetiikkaa. In: M. Grahn & M. Häyrynen, (eds.), *Kulttuurituotanto – Kehykset, käytäntö ja prosessit*. Tietolipas 230. Helsinki: SKS.

Weissköppel, C. 2009: Traversing Cultural Sites: Doing Ethnography Among Sudanese Migrants in Germany. In: M. Falzon (ed.), *Multi-sited Ethnography. Theory, Praxis and Locality in Contemporary Research*. Aldershot: Ashgate.

Wilk, R. 2011: Reflections on Orderly and Disorderly Ethnography. *Ethnologia Europaea. Journal of European Ethnology*. Special Issue: Irregular Ethnographies. 41:1, 15–25.

Wulff, H. 2002: Yo-yo Fieldwork: Mobility and Time in a Multi-Local Study of Dance in Ireland. *Anthropological Journal on European Cultures* 11: 117–136.

Online

http://www.Facebook.com/press/info.php?factsheet./ Accessed 16 May 2010.
http://www.Facebook.com/press/info.php?factsheet/ Accessed 16 May 16 2010.
http://www.Facebook.com/Facebook?v=app_7146470109&ref=pf#!/
    Facebook?v=info&ref=pf./ Accessed 16 May 2010.
http://www.Facebook.com/settings/?tab=privacy&ref=mb#!/policy.php./ Accessed 17 May 2010.
http://www.Facebook.com/terms.php./ Accessed 16 May 2010.

Saara Koikkalainen

Virtual Fields: How to Study a Scattered Migrant Population Online

The Case of Highly Skilled Finns in the European Union

Like the objects of ethnographic inquiry – people – ethnography itself is on the move. It is moving away from 'fields' as spatially defined localities towards sociopolitical locations, networks, and multi-sited approaches. And it is moving from physical spaces to digital spaces.

Andreas Wittel: Ethnography on the Move: From Field to Net to Internet (2000).

Introduction

In the last decade transnational migration has reached unprecedented levels. The United Nations estimated that in 2010 the number of international migrants exceeded 200 million.[1] The number consists of labour migrants, refugees, students, families, retirees, highly skilled migrants and irregular migrants who cross national borders in clandestine ways in search of a better life. The increasing importance of transnational mobility and migration calls for new and innovative ways of studying this phenomenon, of bringing a human face[2] to the study of global mobility.

Ethnographic fieldwork provides excellent tools for studying the migrant experience as well as for looking at the on-the-ground influences of these transnational population movements on both the sending and the receiving localities. Some small (national) migrant groups are scattered in different places, even though their reasons for mobility and their individual characteristics are fairly similar. This article asks how the labour market experiences of such migrant groups can be studied. Are there alternatives to traditional ethnographic fieldwork, which focuses on one location, or should one conduct fieldwork in several different locations? Or is it possible to be in the field virtually and study the experiences of such groups via the Internet?

---

1 United Nations 2009.
2 Favell et al. 2006.

The development of the Internet with its online communities like Facebook, and tools such as web surveys, blogs and Skype, a free software application for making online telephone calls,[3] have offered ethnographers a new, virtual field to explore. This chapter discusses the methodological choices made in a case study of educated Finns who have moved abroad to look for work or accepted job offers in other European Union countries. The research focuses especially on the ways in which cultural capital[4] can be transferred across borders. The paths leading abroad from Finland are much more diverse today than in the 1960s and 1970s, when it was common that whole families from certain Finnish towns and villages moved to work in the industrial towns of Sweden. Many of those leaving today have higher education degrees and are free to choose their workplaces from a variety of destinations.[5] The participants of the study in question had tertiary degrees, were aged 25–44 years and had moved to different European Union countries. The key research question was to try to understand how they find work abroad and what it is like to be a highly skilled Finnish migrant in today's Europe.

The chapter discusses the possibilities of studying the experiences of such small migrant groups online against the background of some historical developments in the ethnographic method. Can collecting data from a geographically scattered migrant group online create a sample of respondents that would resemble a community – even though the people in question have never met each other? The chapter traces a narrative from armchair ethnology to what could be called 'armchair netnography'.[6] Along the way it asks if researchers who want to be in the field virtually can share the experience of the group of migrants that they study, as with traditional 'physical' ethnography.

From armchair ethnology to 'writing culture'

The anthropologists of the nineteenth-century era of 'armchair ethnology' sought to establish a general science of Man by looking at the origins of modern institutions, rituals and customs and mapping their evolution toward ever higher standards of rationality.[7] At the time, physical travel to these far away places was not necessary, as interpretations could be made on the basis of cultural artefacts gathered and travel accounts written by missionaries and traders, for example. In the early twentieth century, anthropology was established as an academic discipline unique in its capacity to produce new information based on professional fieldwork. Early fieldwork-based ethnographies belonged to the genre of ethnographic realism: the attempt

---

3   Skype can be downloaded free from www.skype.com.
4   E.g. Bourdieu 1986.
5   See e.g. Koikkalainen 2011b; Kiriakos 2011.
6   I am not the first to use this analogy; see for example Roff 2005; Haverinen 2009.
7   Marcus & Fisher 1986, 17–18.

to present a culture as it 'really was'. In many early texts, the delicate balance between the objective and the subjective was maintained by producing polished ethnographies as the end product of the fieldwork, stripped of the failures, feelings and frustrations of the anthropologist.[8] These genre conventions were contested in the 1980s, when the art of writing an account of a different culture was acknowledged to be a separate skill, along with experimenting with different kinds of ethnographic writing.[9]

One of the key contributions to the textual turn in anthropology, which dealt with the problems of ethnographic texts, was *Writing Culture: the Poetics and Politics of Ethnography* by James Clifford and George E. Marcus (1986). The discussions that preceded and followed the publication of *Writing Culture* suggested that anthropology had to either look critically at its own conventions or be reduced to producing texts that are merely subjective accounts of foreign cultures. This period has been described as a 'representational crisis' in ethnography, and some scholars later criticised it for being too self-reflective and lacking scientific value.[10] Even so, the textual turn significantly influenced our understanding of what ethnographies are. Ethnographies are not true representations of the essence of a particular culture but culturally constructed texts, since culture itself and our views of it are 'historically produced and actively contested'.[11] They are inherently partial, as the writer always chooses what to include, whose side of the story to tell and how to translate the reality of others.[12]

Today, ethnography can be seen as a 'cocktail of methodologies'[13] used in a variety of disciplines, encompassing many forms of data-gathering and suitable for a wide range of research topics. Ethnography has been extensively used in the field of interdisciplinary migration studies, and the lives of Finnish migrants have also been studied with this method. Examples of studies loosely falling into this category have, among other subjects, focused on Finnish women married to Greek men,[14] Finns working in Silicon Valley,[15] Finnish retirees moving to the south coast of Spain[16] and Finns who have moved to work in Sweden.[17]

It would be quite possible to study the experiences of educated Finns in the European labour markets using the traditional ethnographic approach. To the extent that immersion in the culture of the migrants in question is expected, the research would have to be limited to one geographical location. Of European cities, the most natural choice would be London,

8   Clifford 1986, 13.
9   Marcus & Cushman 1982, 29–30.
10 Denzin 1997, ix, 4–5.
11 Clifford 1986, 18.
12 Clifford 1986, 4–7.
13 Hobbs 2006, 102.
14 Järvinen-Tassopoulos 2007.
15 Kiriakos 2011.
16 Karisto 2008.
17 Snellman 2003; Piippola 2007.

which is a magnet for highly skilled workers from around the globe.[18] However, even in this location, the field would be dispersed and fragmented, since the Finns living in London do not form an ethnic enclave or inhabit the same neighbourhoods, nor do all of them work in the same types of jobs. It is also worth noting that concentrating on just one location, like Europe's major global city London, would inevitably alter the scope of the research. Focusing on the subjects' experiences in one location would make it difficult to answer the research question posed in the introduction to this chapter: How do educated Finns find work abroad? And further, how have they benefited from the opportunities offered by the European free mobility regime? Do they face discrimination, or does their cultural capital transfer abroad easily?

Multi-sited ethnography and ethnography as an art of the possible

There are nearly as many definitions of ethnography as there are major works written by renowned anthropologists and research methodology guides for social science students. The fact that ethnography has developed and endured many paradigm shifts and been adapted to research fields ranging from human geography to consumer behaviour and from psychology to economics testifies to the adaptability of this research approach. Many definitions of ethnography stress the personal engagement of the researcher in the life of the subjects of her/his study.[19] Ethnography is more than mere participant observation of the culture and everyday practices of a particular group in naturally occurring situations. It entails the utilisation of different types of data, such as life histories, films and photography, in-depth interviews and 'engaged listening'.[20] Other interpretations of what it means to be in the field have been suggested in addition to the traditional protracted period of fieldwork. If we wish to study phenomena that are no longer bound to certain localities then the field has to be understood more widely.[21]

One interesting departure from the traditional model is the introduction of multi-sited ethnography, most notably by George Marcus (1995), who argued that postmodern ethnographic work, which moves out from single sites, should 'examine the circulation of cultural meanings, objects, and identities in diffuse time-space'.[22] In this case, the object of study would be cultural formations produced in several different locales. Multi-sited ethnography is not just a controlled comparison of field sites but a more complex process since the objects of study are also 'mobile and multiply

18 See e.g. Favell 2008.
19 E.g. Hobbs 2006, 102.
20 Forsey 2010.
21 Hannerz 2003, 209–210.
22 Marcus 1995, 96.

situated'.[23] Marcus concludes that multi-sited research can be designed around six different themes. The first possibility is to *follow the people*. This type of approach has been used in migration, diaspora and transnational studies, where the journeys of migrants are followed from the place of origin to the country of destination.[24] The other possibilities suggested are to *follow the thing, the metaphor, the story, the life of a particular individual,* or to *follow the conflict*.[25]

If I were to follow the lead of George Marcus in formulating my study design, I should identify potential intra-European migrants while they are still living in Finland and follow their journeys to other European countries. I should sit with them in the waiting rooms of potential employers and observe how they succeed in finding a job, either starting a career abroad, moving on to a new country or returning home. There are many interesting examples of researchers tracking the lives of mobile groups that cross national borders.[26] In Europe, Adrian Favell's (2008) study of young professional 'Eurostars' used such a multi-sited approach when he interviewed transnationally mobile Europeans living in three cities: London, Brussels and Amsterdam. In the case of highly skilled Finns moving to Europe, too, this would be one possible course of action, albeit rather slow since gathering enough field data on the individual journeys of those choosing to go to cities like Paris, Rome, Brussels or Dublin would take years.

The traditional ethnographer conducted fieldwork to record, understand and explain cultural processes such as farming practices, religious acts, initiation rites or other mystical rituals. Observing transnationally mobile highly skilled individuals trying to find work in different European locations would not create the same kind of data. The migrants of interest to me are homogeneous in many respects, for example in having a tertiary degree and being within a specific age bracket. But there are differences as well: they have diverse educational backgrounds and work histories, and they encounter an equally diverse set of employers in their countries of destination. As Ulf Hannerz has argued, some of the changes affecting the ethnographic method are caused by modernity and the changing nature of work itself: participant observation makes little sense if the people you are studying spend hours alone at a desk staring at a computer screen.[27]

As also becomes clear from looking at the other contributions in this volume, there are numerous ways of conducting ethnographic research in the field of migration studies and in the contemporary world in general: the fieldwork may be deeply rooted in one local community which is a key node in a migrant network, or it may span multiple localities or include the

---

23 Marcus 1995, 102.
24 See Vogt in this volume for a description of such an approach.
25 Marcus 1995, 106–110. See also O'Reilly 2008, 145–146.
26 See e.g. Greenhalgh 2007; Hannerz 2003; Sinatti 2008; Smith 2007; Smith & Bakker 2008.
27 Hannerz 2003, 211.

act of following mobile populations commuting from one place to another.[28] As Karen O'Reilly concludes: '…the sense of a group and a locality has not gone, but there is an argument that people can no longer be understood simply in their local context, that the regional or global context must be addressed as well as political, economic, social and cultural relations.'[29] In this sense, focusing on one small and dispersed national group located in several countries can reveal something about the nature of European mobility in general and about the kinds of barriers that still exist for transnational mobility within this seemingly border-free area.

But if a long-term immersion in the culture of the mobile population in question is not feasible, one has to make do with the next-best option for gathering information and be content with what Ulf Hannerz calls 'ethnography as an art of the possible'.[30] The tools provided by the Internet are helpful in such an endeavour and can help in answering questions of a more general nature: How does intra-European mobility work in practice? How can these migrants make the best use of their education and previous work experience in a new country? Is there a European labour market that they become part of when they leave Finland?

In the world wide field of the web

In the past twenty years, information technology and new communication methods have challenged the ways in which we study culture and society. The development of different online networking tools, virtual communities and discussion platforms has created a multitude of new and exciting forums for interaction. People across the globe play interactive online games, meet in chat-rooms, share their photos on Facebook, write microblogs, create content for wikis and publish music and videos for anyone to see. The Internet was therefore the ethnographic field that I chose to enter in order to find informants who could help in answering the key questions of my study.

In her influential book *Virtual Ethnography* (2000), Christine Hine developed a methodology for an empirical investigation of the Internet and its current uses. She divided previous research into two categories. The first strand of research sees the 'Internet as culture' and has explored the rich ethnographic field-sites provided by new forms of computer-aided communication. These include the study of newsgroups, virtual communities and trying to understand online identity play. The second type of research has looked at the 'Internet as a cultural artefact' that is shaped by the social context and the technological applications used. In this approach the design of the Internet today is seen as the result of the actions of various interest

---

28 For one example of how the lives of migrants originating from one country can be studied in multiple locations, see the article by Hirvi in this volume.

29 O'Reilly 2008, 101.

30 Hannerz 2003, 213.

groups and social forces that have allowed certain types of technology to flourish, while other possible forms of communication and interaction have been sidelined. The content of the media produced and consumed can be examined through ethnography utilising categories such as producer, user and audience to understand the capabilities of technology in situated contexts.[31]

The main practical problems with these two types of virtual ethnography lie in the location of the field itself. If doing ethnographic fieldwork is understood as a prolonged engagement with a specific location and culture, then how is this engagement to be achieved online? And if one wishes to study the Internet as a cultural artefact (or a form of text), then how can one observe the everyday actions of individual web content producers when they largely engage in these actions in the solitude of their homes?[32] For Hine, the development of multi-sited ethnography, 'the interactive and engaged exploration of connectivity'[33] provides an interesting avenue to follow. Her solution to the problem of locating the field is to choose a specific topic as the object of virtual ethnography, not a bounded spatial location.[34]

Ethnographic methods have been used online in a variety of disciplines and with diverse research topics ranging from the study of sexual expression to food culture and from online fashion to cross-cultural weddings.[35] Several researchers have argued for a disciplined approach to studying the virtual world. These include Arturo Escobar (1994) with his anthropology of cyberculture, Anjali Puri (2007) with webnography, Dhiraj Murthy (2008) with digital ethnography, and Robert V. Kozinets (2010) with netnography. Yet another attempt to formulate a coherent agenda for online research is offered by Jennifer Brinkerhoff (2009), who has studied 'digital diasporas' in the field of international relations, and who sees the Internet as being 'ideally suited for connecting diasporans who are geographically scattered and removed from their homeland.'[36]

The Internet and especially social networking sites such as MySpace and Facebook provide inexpensive ways of keeping contact with those who stay at home as well as tools for building networks in their new home areas or countries. They can increase one's social capital as contact with old friends and acquaintances can be maintained across geographical distance.[37] Brinkerhoff defines diasporas as migrant groups who are dispersed, whether by choice or by force, across at least one national border; who share a collective myth or memory of their homeland and are committed to keeping that alive; who ponder on the issue of possible return one day; and who share a diasporic consciousness and hybrid identity.[38]

31 Hine 2000, 2, 14, 19, 30–33, 38–39.
32 Hine 2000, 21, 38.
33 Hine 2000, 61.
34 Hine 2000, 65.
35 Kozinets 2010, 174–175.
36 Brinkerhoff 2009, 12.
37 See e.g. Ellison et al. 2007.
38 Brinkerhoff 2009, 31.

Finns, too, have websites and discussion groups that serve expatriates living in different locations. These include commercial and non-commercial websites like www.expatrium.fi and www.ulkosuomalainen.com and discussion forums, mailing lists and Facebook groups for Finns living in London, Florence or Berlin, for example. Thus, even though their numbers are small in comparison with the global migration networks of larger groups, at least online Finns exist as a distinct migrant group. Many expatriate Finns are also active in local Finnish associations, the Finland Society or Finnish-language schools for expatriate children. These organizations are active both locally and transnationally, so expatriate Finns do engage in some forms of diaspora politics and take part in transnational advocacy networks.[39]

But whether Finns discussing matters online can be regarded as taking part in a digital diaspora[40] is debatable. Finns as intra-European migrants are privileged in having the right of free movement and being able to freely engage in circular migration or take up short-term work, language training or traineeships abroad. Their relationship with their homeland is not complicated in the same sense as that of those who have been forced to leave, nor do they generally send remittances home or plan to invest in developing their country of origin. Teaching the Finnish language to their children and applying for dual nationality are ways of keeping the Finnish heritage alive, but this does not add up to a shared myth of the homeland that is 'created and recreated across distances and generations',[41] as Brinkerhoff describes one of the key elements that define a diaspora.

It would be possible to study Finns in Europe either by openly taking part in the discussions that they have on the expatriate websites or by reading what they write about work and looking for employment as a passive observer.[42] The problem with this approach for a study like mine is that the websites that I found do not focus on discussions about finding work *per se*. More commonly they exchange information on how to find housing or affordable day-care, open a bank account or beat the local administrative bureaucracy. They provide a form of on-the-ground tacit knowledge that is shared with more recent movers, together with tips on where to find a sauna or get the cheapest flights home. If the ethnography is limited to a certain online discussion group, for example, it might be difficult to produce the kind of diversity of voices that my study is looking for.

Finding Finns in Europe: the online approach

During the development of the European Union's free movement regime over the past sixty years, crossing intra-European borders has been made so simple that it has been said to resemble regional mobility more than

---

39 Vierimaa 2011.
40 Brinkerhoff 2009.
41 Brinkerhoff 2009, 31.
42 See Beaulieu 2004, 146–147.

international migration.[43] European citizens wishing to look for work in other member states can cross national borders and do so legally without necessarily showing up on migration statistics. Researchers studying intra-European mobility have faced a difficult problem: how to reach this population that is almost invisible in the new host country, at least compared with other migrant groups such as asylum seekers or refugees who are under rigorous control?[44] Even the statistics on how many intra-European migrants there are in each member state at any given time are not fully reliable as, owing to the unique national histories of each state, the methods of collecting population data and the systems of measuring incoming and outgoing migrants are different across Europe.[45] This difficulty applies also to Finns: there is no up-dated address register of Finns living abroad, so it is impossible to draw a representative sample of this population.

The 'new map of European migration' consists of different forms of mobility and migration: students, workers, professionals, retirees and long-term tourists.[46] It has been noted that, as the standard of living rises, the reasons for international mobility also become more diverse and change from being mainly economic to being governed by other factors, such as choices concerning family, love or lifestyle.[47] This has also been observed with Finns who move abroad, whose reasons for mobility vary.[48] If at least some of the diversity of current Finnish outward migration is to be highlighted, the ethnographic focus cannot be on a single destination or route but should aim at a broader reach, despite the difficulties in obtaining the relevant data.

My study used the Internet as a tool to reach expatriate Finns scattered across the continent.[49] An online survey *Working in Europe* [Työntekijänä Euroopassa],[50] was designed with SurveyMonkey,[50] a popular online survey tool. It was publicised with the aim of reaching as many individuals as possible, from different countries and from both cities and the countryside. A combination of techniques was used in generating a sample for the survey. Three methods were combined for maximum coverage: sampling through an organisation, targeting flow populations and snowballing.[51] The organisation whose help I sought was SEFE, *The Finnish Association of Business School Graduates*, which agreed to forward my message to all its

43 Recchi & Favell 2009. For the development of the free movement regime, see Koikkalainen 2009b or Koikkalainen 2011a.
44 A method called respondent-driven sampling offers one possibility for reaching such 'hidden populations'. It was not chosen for this study owing to its emphasis on quantitative methods. See Wejnert & Heckathorn 2011.
45 Fassman et al. 2009.
46 King 2002.
47 Santacreu et al. 2009; O'Reilly & Benson 2009.
48 See e.g. Koikkalainen 2011b.
49 See also Meissner & Hasselberg in this volume for how Internet surveys have been used as a tool for reaching the 'hard to reach'.
50 For more information, see www.surveymonkey.com.
51 Richie et al. 2006, 93–94.

expatriate members.[52] I sought to draw the attention of flow populations from various discussion forums and websites that serve Finns living abroad and sent a request to discussion forums of Finns in Britain, Belgium, Germany, the Netherlands, France, Ireland, Spain, and to Finnish schools in Italy and Austria asking members to take part in the survey and to encourage their friends to do the same.

In addition, the snowballing method was used in asking friends and acquaintances as well as 30 Finns who write blogs on their life abroad to respond to the survey and to forward the message to others in similar situations. I also set up a Facebook group for the project in order to publicise it in a social medium. The respondents were advised to click directly on a link to the survey on the e-mail/web-page or to take a closer look at the research questions, objectives and research ethics from a web page that presented the study.[53] During the period from March to July 2008, 545 individuals joined the survey, and 471 (86%) of them finished the whole questionnaire. The survey consisted of 27 questions on the personal and educational backgrounds of the respondents, their international experiences and reasons for moving abroad and their labour market experiences both in Finland and abroad. Most of the questions were multiple-choice, but there were also open-ended questions about the work life experiences and future plans of the respondents.

The respondents were also asked for their e-mail addresses, should they be interested in participating in a more thorough interview later. Submitting the e-mail address was voluntary. Gathering the experiences of Finns abroad by openly requesting them to take part in the survey eliminated one of the most problematic features of online research, that of getting the consent of those being 'observed'. Engaging in participant observation by lurking in the background in online discussion groups, quoting from blogs and treating all web content as research material has been criticised as unethical since, even though content produced on the web is by its very nature public, not all Internet users always perceive it to be so.[54] Further, Kozinets strongly argues against any kind of covert observation as part of one's research because a researcher who wishes to conduct netnography ethically should always inform the participants of her/his presence[55].

Altogether 364 respondents were included in the final sample on the grounds that they lived in 12 different countries in the European Union area,[56] had completed tertiary degrees, were within the age bracket set for the study

---

52 This message generated 58 complete responses to the survey.

53 Information on the research was available in Finnish at www.ulapland.fi/EUtyo.

54 Murthy 2008, 840–841.

55 Kozinets 2010, 147–148.

56 There were no responses from Greece, and even though Sweden is the most popular destination of Finns moving abroad, there were only eight completed responses from there. These were omitted from the final sample because of the geographical proximity; a common language (Swedish is Finland's second official language) and a long history of migration between Finland and Sweden make the latter a special case.

(25–44) and had completed the whole survey. It has to be recognised that the publicising of my survey mainly via the Internet communities of Finns abroad did have an impact on the kind of people who were reached and who chose to take part in the survey. Certain groups are surely overrepresented as a closer breakdown of the respondent characteristics reveals. Thirty nine per cent of the respondents (143 individuals) were from the United Kingdom; this partly reflects the fact that it is one of the most popular destinations of Finns moving abroad, but it was also an indication that the snowball method worked efficiently in London. One may also suspect that those who have not lived abroad for very long are more active in the Finnish forums online than those who are more integrated into their current home countries. Moreover, there is a clear gender difference as 280 women (77%) and only 84 men (23%) responded to the survey.

However, despite the sampling bias of the method, which makes generalising to the overall expatriate Finnish population somewhat inappropriate, I was able to collect the labour market experiences of a large group of highly educated, contemporary Finnish migrants in 12 different countries. The Internet proved to be a useful tool for reaching this privileged group of migrants, for whom online interaction is a natural part of their life. But why should this exercise be called ethnography?

Encounters in a virtual field

If we adopt the proposition of Ulf Hannerz that ethnography is 'an art of the possible',[57] then it should not matter how the participants are found if the chosen method is the best one available for the aims of the study in question. Even though the Finns who chose to respond to my survey may not form a diaspora, they do share some of the characteristics of a community, of a cultural group that is distinct in several important ways. As first-generation migrants they share a common background in Finnish society,[58] a common *habitus*: the embodiment of cultural knowledge created during their childhood socialization.[59] Common features were also found in their experiences as expatriate Finns.

The participants in the study speak the same mother tongue[60] and are highly educated: 338 (93%) out of the 364 respondents had higher education degrees either from a university or university of applied sciences, and 26 (7%)

---

57 Hannerz 2003, 213.
58 A couple of the interviewees had lived abroad for some years when they were children. However, they had returned to Finland to finish their secondary schooling.
59 E.g. Bourdieu 1993, 86–88.
60 Finland has two official languages: Finnish and Swedish, which is the mother tongue of a small minority of around 6% of Finns. I did not ask about the mother tongue of the respondents, but as the survey was conducted in Finnish I assume that to be the mother tongue of most of the respondents, and all the open-ended responses were written in Finnish.

were finishing their studies at the time. Rather than being pushed abroad by unemployment or discrimination, they are voluntary migrants who have *chosen* to move abroad in order to experience something new, to look for work, to accept a company secondment or to take up a job offer.[61] Some could be identified as professional migrants or 'Eurostars', while for others the move is a *lifestyle choice*.[62] They have not been particularly affected by unemployment, as most had a good labour market position back in Finland. Only 15 (4%) of the respondents said they had been unemployed in Finland for over three months after graduation, and only 41 (21%) respondents said that they completely or somewhat agreed that they had been afraid of unemployment prior to moving abroad.[63] The same applies to work in the destination country: only 29 (8%) respondents had either been unemployed for over 6 months or had not found work at all.

All of the respondents have some previous international experience, the forms of which can be broadly classified into three categories: work, short exchange and longer exchange. Of the respondents, 249 (68%) had *worked* abroad as trainees, in summer jobs or doing voluntary work, 242 (67%) had been on a language course or other organised *short student exchange* and 201 (55%) of them had taken part in a *long student exchange*, either while in high school or at university. Some seemed to have seized almost every opportunity to go abroad since 65 (18%) of the respondents fitted into all three categories and 117 (32%) had been abroad in connection with two of them. In addition, 265 respondents (73%) had travelled in at least 10 different countries as tourists.

It can thus be argued that the respondents share some key characteristics that make at least some of their experiences mutually comparable. Most importantly, they all have the experience of looking for work and/or working in a situation where they belong to a minority and have to operate by the rules of a labour market that is largely unknown to them. To avoid jeopardising their careers when crossing national borders, they have had to try to negotiate the best possible value for their credentials and previous work experience and to make being different into an advantage rather than an obstacle to employment.[64] Working in a foreign language and in a multicultural environment has demanded adaptation and flexibility. Thus the existence of shared background characteristics and key experiences makes these expatriates into a community of sorts, even though they may have never met each other.

61 Koikkalainen 2009a.
62 On 'Eurostars' see Favell 2008, on lifestyle migration see O'Reilly & Benson 2009.
63 Not all of the respondents had had work experience in Finland. This question was relevant only to those who had studied in Finland: 167 respondents (46%) either skipped the question or had not worked in Finland at all after finishing their studies. Seventy four respondents (20%) had only foreign degrees, 90 (25%) had obtained degrees in both locations, having for example first passed a bachelor's degree in Finland and then continued directly to take a master's degree abroad.
64 Koikkalainen 2009a, 32–35, see also Csedö 2008.

The respondents were originally from different regions in Finland, had studied in numerous different universities in Finland and in their destination countries and had had diverse work careers either abroad or both in Finland and abroad. They included consultants, ICT workers, freelance journalists, self-employed language specialists, teachers, lawyers, bankers, accountants, project assistants, EU employees, managers, designers and health sector employees, to name but a few of their professions. In their open-ended responses they described the process of applying for work in a foreign country, the moments when they felt discriminated against, the joy of finally finding a job that felt like the right choice and the advantages of living in a sunnier, more exciting environment where people are less envious of one another than they are in Finland. For many, the moment of leaving Finland had signified a turning point in their careers, either because there were simply so many more job opportunities available or because the move had forced them to reconsider what they really wanted out of life. As I am a Finnish researcher studying Finns abroad, it is obvious that for me they do not represent a totally new and unknown exotic 'other'. My background makes me more similar to than different from the participants in the survey: I am educated, belong to the same age group and have also studied and lived abroad. In this kind or research, sharing some of the experiences of the group one is interested in is surely an advantage: if the expatriate Finns are to be taken as forming a community, then I myself have also been a part of that community.[65]

The survey data gave me a general albeit somewhat superficial understanding of how Finns working in Europe see their own positions on the labour markets of the destination countries. However, the survey did not give me as a researcher any 'personal engagement with the subjects [which] is the key to understanding a particular culture or social setting'.[66] Hence, I felt it was necessary to dig deeper into the lives of some of those who had participated in the survey. Would I be able to understand why the majority (76%) of the survey respondents describe moving abroad as a positive experience for their careers, even though the transition to the labour market of the new country had not been easy in all cases?[67]

The sociologist Dhiraj Murthy has argued that when 'ethnography goes digital, its epistemological remit remains much the same. Ethnography is about *telling social stories*'.[68] There are at least two different ways in which

---

65 The original survey data were collected before the global economic downturn. To assess whether the recession had a serious negative impact on the respondents, a short follow-up survey was sent in the summer of 2010 to the 269 respondents who had given their e-mail addresses. Even though many of those 194 individuals who responded did discuss the effects of the recession, a majority of them (63%) were still in fulltime employment, were working as freelancers or owned private businesses (12%).

66 Hobbs 2006.

67 Koikkalainen 2009a, 31.

68 Murthy 2008, 838, italics added.

I could continue gathering data for these social stories, using the opportunities that the virtual fields have to offer. In either case, the voices of the survey respondents should be heard and there should be interaction between the researcher and the participants in the study. Some researchers have gone so far in emphasising the collective nature of the research enterprise as to call the migrant participants or interviewees of the study, 'co-researchers'.[69]

In the first alternative, the participants who responded to the survey could be brought into contact with each other in an online focus group discussion[70] or a conference organised via the Skype software application. The discussions could centre on a variety of topics, such as employer attitudes towards foreign qualifications, the significance of language skills in searching for a job abroad, career plans or possible remigration. These would all be topics that participants living in different countries but sharing the expatriate experience could relate to.[71] In the second approach, Skype could be used to conduct individual interviews over the Internet. The interviews could take a similar form to an ordinary person-to-person interview and try to achieve a real sense of shared space despite the use of a computer as the medium that facilitated the interaction.[72] This is the option that I adopted because I wanted to hear the stories of individual migrants in different settings.

So far the literature on using Skype in qualitative research is somewhat limited, even though some researchers have found it a useful, safe, inexpensive and environmentally friendly tool for interviewing research participants.[73] The video capacity of Skype makes it possible to interact on a relatively personal level as the participants can see each other. In my case, Skype was a more suitable way of interviewing participants than multi-sited ethnography, for example, as the selection of participants did not have to be limited to those who happened to live in a location that I could visit.[74] The interviewees were selected from among the survey participants with the aim of gathering a purposive sample[75] that would be as diverse as possible. I examined this diversity in terms of migration motivation, year of mobility, educational background, field of study, career, country of residence, life situation and the kinds of positive and negative labour market experiences they wrote about in the open-ended questions of the survey. I interviewed altogether 18 Finns: six male and 12 female. At the time of the interviews they were living in Austria, Belgium, Denmark, France (2), Germany (2), Iceland, Ireland, Italy, Luxembourg, Portugal, Spain and the United Kingdom (5).

Skype can be used to call the Skype program on the computer of the person one is trying to reach or for calling a landline or mobile telephone.

---

69 Madison 2006.
70 See e.g. Turney & Pocknee 2004.
71 See Kozinets 2010: 48–49.
72 Kozinets 2010, 45–47, 110–111.
73 King & Horrocks 2010, 84-85; Hanna 2012; Cater 2011; Bertrand & Bourdeau 2010.
74 See also Hanna 2012; Bertrand & Bourdeau 2010.
75 Richie et al. 2006, 97.

While the first option was free of charge, for the latter calls I had to add credit to my Skype account with my credit card. The cost of the calls varied in price according to the length of the call and the type of telephone involved. A call made to a landline phone in Luxembourg cost just below two euros, while another call made to a mobile phone in the United Kingdom cost ten euros, for example. While it is true that many of my interviewees were regular Skype users and were thus very familiar with the technology, the possibility of making telephone calls with it makes it a convenient tool for reaching, in a rather inexpensive manner, also those who do not have access to Skype or prefer to be interviewed when they are at work, for example. Furthermore, the possibility offered by the Skype program for recording the telephone interviews was very useful. The interviews were recorded either as audio files or both audio & video files with a program called Call Recorder, a reliable yet inexpensive add-on to the basic Skype program itself.[76]

Skype proved to be a very reliable research tool since the program worked perfectly, and only once or twice was the interview interrupted by a technical problem during the call. The interviews were semi-structured and followed a predetermined topic guide.[77] The topic guides were rewritten individually for each participant, and information from that particular person's survey responses was included as background information. These data included information about their life situations, mobility history, reasons for migrating, job titles, countries of identification and future plans. The same set of questions was thus discussed in each case, even though there was some variation in the order in which the topics were addressed. At the end of the interviews the participants were asked to bring up any matters they thought had not been covered in relation to their experience of what it is like to live and work abroad.

These interviews provided valuable material for my study and also revealed both the advantages and the disadvantages of using this method. While Skype does allow you to see the person you are talking to as long as both participants have a web camera, you miss most of the information provided by the social setting where the interview takes place. If I had visited the homes of the interviewees, I could have seen how they live and even possibly met their families. Or if we had met at their workplaces, I could have observed the physical environments where they spend most of their working days. On the other hand, the relative anonymity of the virtual interview situation and the flexibility afforded by the possibility of arranging it whenever it was suitable for the interviewee were clear advantages in comparison with the scheduling problems involved in arranging a real life interview with people who lead busy lives.[78]

---

76 The price of the Call Recorder program for Mac in May 2011 was 19.95 USD. It can be purchased and downloaded from www.ecamm.com/mac/callrecorder/. Pamela is a comparable program for PCs. See www.pamela.biz/en.

77 Arthur & Nazroo 2003, 115–122 Fielding & Thomas 2008, 253–255.

78 See also Hanna 2012, 240.

The interviews only lasted from half an hour to slightly over an hour, even though the long list of subjects I had prepared suggested that the discussions could take longer. Using the computer as a medium of communication removes much of the social norms of face-to-face encounters, and the interaction tends to follow a question-answer format rather than resemble a natural discussion. On the other hand, it was clear that many of the interviewees used Skype on a regular basis to interact with their families and friends back in Finland, so they were comfortable drinking their morning coffee in front of the computer while chatting with me. Using this method with migrants who are less experienced with online communication might be more challenging as Skype conversations do take a bit of getting used to.

The interviewees did not receive any reward or payment for taking part in the interview. I asked them if they wanted a personal copy of the recording so that they could keep it as a memento of our encounter and review what was said afterwards if they had any second thoughts about taking part.[79] Eight interviewees were interested in getting a copy of the recording. For this purpose, another free Internet-based service called Dropbox had to be used because the file size of a video recording of a one-hour interview could be as large as 85 megabytes, far exceeding the acceptable attachment file size of most e-mail programs.[80] Each interviewee was given a pseudonym that is used in the study. A short biographical note was written on each interviewee as a part of the analysis of the data, and these biographies were sent to the participants for review. This also extended our contact from a one-time interview to an at least slightly longer relationship. In addition, I promised to keep them informed about the progress of my research and send them a link to my doctoral dissertation once it is available online.

The key to building an ethnography out of a survey and a set of interviews can lie in the way the research process is described and in how the end product of the research is written. One attempt to evaluate the quality of ethnographies was proposed by Laurel Richardson in a special issue of *Qualitative Inquiry*. Richardson defined five criteria for a good-quality ethnography: 1) Does the piece of writing make a substantive contribution to our understanding of social life? 2) Does the text succeed aesthetically? 3) How reflexive is the author of her role? 4) Does the text have an emotional or intellectual impact? 5) Does the text express a reality, an embodied sense of lived-experience?[81] These criteria do not exclude written texts based on virtual ethnography or prioritise some form of data-gathering over others. Hence the true quality of any research claiming to be ethnographic would lie

---

79 Participants in a study by Bertrand and Bourdeau (2010, 75) expressed worries about what was being done with the Skype recording afterwards.

80 The maximum size of an e-mail attachment in G-mail for example is 25 MB. I placed the interview video files in my Dropbox public folder, and the program generated a link to that specific file or document. This link was then sent via e-mail to the recipient, who accesses the file by clicking on the link. See www.dropbox.com.

81 Richardson 2000, 254.

in factors outside the data-gathering exercise, and the success of my virtual ethnography would be ultimately based on how well I manage to capture the experiences of Finns living abroad in the written text.

Conclusion

Several researchers have noted that the Internet is an interesting new research field for the study of social interaction. Internet-based research does have clear advantages: sending online questionnaires is cheap compared to sending out the same amount of paper copies, the ethnographer does not have to be absent from her/his family and home institution for years on end, and s/he can access the field whenever suitable from her/his office, home computer or conference trip abroad[82]. Armchair netnography thus has its advantages for the researcher, but a word of caution is also in order to ensure that the real-life ethnographic practice is not forgotten because of the ease of conducting virtual research. Kozinets suggests as a general rule that 'research on "online communities" should tend to have a primarily nethnographic focus. For research on a "community online", netnography should play more of a supporting or secondary role.'[83]

The history of ethnography can be read as an account of a research methodology that is able to adapt to different cultural and social settings both in the field itself and in the minds of the academics who engage in this form of research. Its story can be written from the perspective of various disciplines, and it can entail different signposts depending on which texts or turns are deemed most significant. As Kozinets has argued, '...its approach is continually being refashioned to suit particular fields of scholarship, research questions, research sites, times, researcher preferences, skill sets, methodological innovations and cultural groups.'[84] Ethnography bends but does not break, adapts and evolves to encompass different forms of research. Why should it not then also encompass that of studying the labour market experiences of scattered migrant groups by combining online survey and interview methods?

Highly skilled Finns move abroad to follow the lure of London or to seize a job opportunity in the EU capital Brussels. However, Finns move to many other cities in Europe as well, depending on their motivations, family situations and sometimes even the pure coincidence of being offered a job in a particular country or finding a partner from abroad. Trying to capture the diversity of this group with the traditional ethnographic approach, where the field is understood as a geographical location, would therefore be a challenge. Multi-sited ethnography has been conducted in many different ways – so my study could also be classified as multi-sited if the sites are understood

---

82 See e.g. Beaulieu 2004; Hannerz 2003; Hine 2000; Kozinets 2010; Murthy 2008.
83 Kozinets 2010, 65.
84 Kozinets 2010, 59–60.

as places of encounter[85] or as networks[86] and not as fixed locations. As this account of my research process has shown, the Internet as the new frontier of ethnographic fieldwork has a lot to offer as long as the research questions of the study match the methods used and the online approach is not chosen simply because it can save money and be more convenient for the researcher than some other type of fieldwork.

The aims of armchair netnography are radically different from those of armchair ethnology, but some of the criticisms targeted at trying to understand foreign ways and exotic 'others' from a distance also have to be taken into account in using modern technology in the virtual field. A balanced combination of both physical and virtual ethnography or netnography can give researchers a larger array of methods with which to take part in the lives of their research subjects and to tell their stories.[87] Christine Hine concludes: 'It appears that emphasis can usefully be placed on the production of meaning in contexts, where context is understood as both *the circumstances in which the Internet is used* (offline) and *the social spaces that emerge through its use* (online).'[88] Ethnographic methods can thus contribute to our understanding of the Internet both as culture and as a cultural artefact, and these need not be mutually exclusive categories.

However, it is clear that there is also a third dimension to how the Internet is useful for ethnographers at a very concrete level: it can be used to reach the hard-to-reach, which in my case meant the possibility to locate relatively small migrant groups scattered over different countries and localities. For such a study design, geographical distance becomes less important than before, and the Internet can be put to good use as a useful ethnographic tool that facilitates communication between these migrants and the researcher, each physically located in a different place. In my case, it has meant sitting in my office in Rovaniemi in northern Finland, but, thanks to Skype, learning from the lives and experiences of skilled migrants living in Spain, Austria and Luxembourg within the span of one working day.

Bibliography

Arthur, S. & J. Nazroo 2003: Designing Fieldwork Strategies and Materials. In: J. Richie & J. Lewis (eds.), *Qualitative Research Practice. A Guide for Social Science Students.* London: Sage.

Beaulieu, A. 2004: Mediating Ethnography: Objectivity and the Making of Ethnographies of the Internet. *Social Epistemology*, 18: 2–3, 139–163.

Bertrand, C. & L. Bourdeau 2010: Research Interviews by Skype: A New Data Collection Method. In: J. Esteves (ed.), *Proceedings of the 9th European Conference on Research Methodology for Business and Management Studies.* IE Business School Madrid, Spain.

85 See e.g. Falzon 2009.
86 See Wittel 2000.
87 Murthy 2008.
88 Hine 2000, 39, italics added.

Brinkerhoff, J. M. 2009: *Digital Diasporas. Identity and Transnational Engagement.* Cambridge: Cambridge University Press.

Bourdieu, P. 1993: *Sociology in Question.* London: Sage.

Bourdieu, P. 1986: The Forms of Capital. In: J.G. Richardson (ed.), *Handbook for Theory and Research for the Sociology of Education.* New York: Greenwood.

Cater, J. K. 2011: Skype – A Cost-effective Method for Qualitative Research. *Rehabilitation Counselors & Educators Journal,* 4: 2. http://uark.academia.edu/JanetCater/Papers/538835/Skype_A_cost_effective_method_for_qualitative_research. Accessed 25 April 2012.

Clifford, J. 1986: Introduction: partial truths. In: J. Clifford & G. E. Marcus (eds.), *Writing Culture. The Politics and Poetics of Ethnography.* Los Angeles: University of California Press.

Csedö, K. 2008: Negotiating Skills in the Global City: Hungarian and Romanian Professionals and Graduates in London. *Journal of Ethnic and Migration Studies,* 34: 5, 803–823.

Deegan, M. J. 2001: The Chicago School of Ethnography. In: P. Atkinson, A. Coffey, S. Delamont, J. Lofland (eds.), *Handbook of Ethnography.* London: Sage.

Denzin, N. K. 1997: *Interpretive Ethnography: Ethnographic Practices for the 21st Century.* London: Sage.

Ellison, N. B., Steinfield, C., & Lampe, C. 2007: The Benefits of Facebook 'Friends:' Social Capital and College Students' Use of Online Social Network Sites. *Journal of Computer-Mediated Communication.* 12: 4, 1143–1168.

Escobar, A. 1994: Welcome to Cyberia. Notes on the Anthropology of Cyberculture. *Current Anthropology,* 35: 3, 211–231.

Falzon, M-A. (ed.) 2009: *Multi-Sited Ethnography. Theory, Praxis and Locality in Contemporary Research.* Aldershot: Ashgate.

Fassman, H., U. Reeger, & W. Sievers (eds) 2009: *Statistics and Reality. Concepts and Measurements of Migration in Europe.* IMISCOE Reports. Amsterdam: Amsterdam University Press.

Favell, A. 2008: *Eurostars and Eurocities: Free Movement and Mobility in an Integrating Europe.* Malden: Blackwell Publishing.

Favell, A., M. Feldblum & M. P. Smith 2006: The Human Face of Global Mobility: A Research Agenda. In: M. P. Smith & A. Favell (eds.), *The Human Face of Global Mobility: International Highly Skilled Migration in Europe, North America and the Asia Pacific.* New Brunswick, NJ: Transaction.

Fielding, N. & H. Thomas 2008: Qualitative Interviewing. In: N. Gilbert (ed.), *Researching Social Life.* 3rd Edition. London: Sage.

Forsey, M. G. 2010: Ethnography as participant listening. *Ethnography,* 11: 4, 558–572.

Greenhalgh, C. 2007: Traveling Images, Lives on Location. Cinematographers in the Film Industry. In: V. Amit (ed.), *Going First Class? New Approaches to Privileged Travel and Movement.* The EASA Series Volume 7, Published in association with the European Association of Social Anthropologists (EASA), Oxford: Berghahn Books.

Hannerz, U. 2003: Being there... and there... and there! Reflections on multi-sited ethnography. *Ethnography,* 4: 2, 201–216.

Haverinen, A. 2009: Trobriand-saarilta internettiin – antropologisen kenttätyön haasteita virtuaalisessa ympäristössä. [From the Trobriand islands to the Internet – challenges of antropological fieldwork in a virtual environment] *J@rgonia,* 7: 6, 1–25.

Hine, C. 2000: *Virtual Ethnography.* London: Sage.

Hobbs, D. 2006: Ethnography. In: V. Jupp (ed.), *The SAGE Dictionary of Social Research Methods.* London: Sage.

Järvinen-Tassopoulos, J. 2007: *Suomalaisena naisena Kreikassa: arki, muukalaisuus ja nykyisyys ranskalaisen sosiologian näkökulmasta*, [Being a Finnish woman in Greece: everyday life, strangerness, and the present day viewed from the perspective of French sociology] SoPhi 106, Helsinki: Minerva Kustannus.

Karisto, A. 2008: *Satumaa. Suomalaiseläkeläiset Espanjan Aurinkorannikolla*. [Fairyland. Finnish retirement migrants on the sunshine coast of Spain]. Suomalaisen Kirjallisuuden Seuran Toimituksia 1190. Helsinki: Finnish Literature Society SKS.

King, R. 2002: Towards a New Map of European Migration. *International Journal of Population Geography*, 8: 2, 89–106.

King, N. & C. Horrocks 2010: *Interviews in Qualitative Research*. London: Sage.

Kiriakos, C. M. 2011: Finns in Silicon Valley: motivations and identities in relation to place. In: E. Heikkilä & S. Koikkalainen (eds.) *Finns Abroad. New Forms of Mobility and Migration*. Migration Studies C 21. Turku: Institute of Migration.

Koikkalainen, S. 2009a: Europe is My Oyster: Experiences of Finns Working Abroad. *Finnish Journal of Ethnicity and Migration*, 4: 2, 27–38.

Koikkalainen, S. 2009b: Työvoiman liikkuvuus Euroopassa [Mobility of labour in Europe]. In: M. Kinnunen & J. Autto (eds), *Tänään töissä. Sosiologisia näkökulmia työhön*. [Today at work. Sociological perspectives on work]. Rovaniemi: University of Lapland Press.

Koikkalainen, S. 2011: Highly skilled Finnish migrants in the European labor market: why do they move abroad? In: E. Heikkilä & S. Koikkalainen (eds.), *Finns Abroad. New Forms of Mobility and Migration*. Migration Studies C 21. Turku: Institute of Migration.

Kozinets, R. V. 2010: *Netnography. Doing Ethnographic Research Online*. London: Sage.

Turney, L. & C. Pocknee 2004: Virtual focus groups: New technologies, new opportunities, new learning environments. In: R. Atkinson, C. McBeath, D. Jonas-Dwyer & R. Phillips (eds.), *Beyond the comfort zone: Proceedings of the 21st ASCILITE Conference*. http://www.ascilite.org.au/conferences/perth04/procs/turney.html. Accessed 25 April 2012.

Madison, G. 2006: Existential Migration. Conceptualising out of the Experiential Depths of Choosing to Leave 'Home'. *Existential Analysis*, 17: 2, 238–60.

Marcus, G. E. 1995: Ethnography in/of the World System: The Emergence of Multi-Sited Ethnography. *Annual Review of Anthropology*, 24, 95–117.

Marcus, G. E. & D. Cushman 1982: Ethnographies as texts. *Annual Review of Anthropology*, 11, 25–69.

Marcus, G. E & M. M. Fisher 1986: *Anthropology as a Cultural Critique. An Experimental Moment in the Human Sciences*. Chicago: The University of Chigaco Press.

Murthy, D. 2008: Digital Ethnography: An Examination of the Use of New Technologies for Social Research. *Sociology*, 42: 5, 837–855.

O'Reilly, K. 2008: *Key Concepts in Ethnography*. Sage Key Concepts Series. London: Sage.

O'Reilly, K. & M. Benson 2009: Lifestyle Migration. Escaping to the Good Life? In: M. Benson & K. O'Reilly (eds.), *Lifestyle Migration. Expectations, Aspirations, and Experiences*. Studies in Migration and Diaspora. Farnham: Ashgate.

Piippola, S. 2007: Rethinking Identity in Crossing National Borders: The Case of Recruited Nurses from Finland in Sweden. In: Ö. Wahlbeck (ed.), *Ny migration och etnicitet i Norden*. Meddelanded från Ekonomisk-Statsvetenskapliga Fakulteten vid Åbo Akademi. Sociologi Ser A:554. Åbo: Åbo Akademi.

Puri, A. 2007: The web of insights. The art and practice of webnography. *International Journal of Market Research*, 49: 3, 387–409.

Recchi, E. & A. Favell (eds.) 2009: *Pioneers of European Integration. Citizenship and Mobility in the EU*. Cheltenham: Edward Elgar.

Richardson, L. 2000: Evaluating Ethnography. *Qualitative Inquiry,* 6: 2, 253–255.

Roff, S. S. 2005: The Return of the Armchair Scholar. *Journal of Scholarly Publishing,* 36: 2, 49–57.

Santacreu, O., E. Baldoni & M. C. Albert 2009: Deciding to Move: Migration Projects in an Integrating Europe. In: E. Recchi & A. Favell (eds.), *Pioneers of European Integration. Citizenship and Mobility in the EU.* Cheltenham: Edward Elgar.

Sinatti, G. 2008: The Making of Urban Translocalities: Senegalese Migrants in Dakar and Zingonia. In: M. P. Smith & J. Eade (eds.), *Transnational Ties: Cities, Migrations and Identities.* Comparative Urban and Community Research Series, Vol. 9. New Brunswick, NJ: Transaction publishers.

Smith, M. P. 2007: The two faces of transnational citizenship. *Ethnic and Racial Studies,* 30: 6, 1096–1116.

Smith, M. P. & M. Bakker 2008: *Citizenship Across Borders. The Political Transnationalism of El Migrante.* Ithaca, NY: Cornell University Press.

Snellman, H. 2003: *Göteborg – Sallan suurin kylä. Tutkimus Ruotsin lappilaisista.* [Gothenburg – the Largest Village of the Salla Parish]. Suomalaisen Kirjallisuuden Seuran Toimituksia 927. Helsinki: SKS.

United Nations 2009: *Trends in International Migrant Stock: The 2008 Revision.* Department of Economic and Social Affairs, Population Division (United Nations database, POP/DB/MIG/Stock/Rev.2008).

Vierimaa, S-M. 2011: Migrant Associations in a Transnational Advocacy Network. The Case of the Finnish Expatriate Parliament. In: E. Heikkilä & S. Koikkalainen (eds.) *Finns Abroad. New Forms of Mobility and Migration.* Migration Studies C 21. Turku: Institute of Migration.

Wittel, A. 2000: Ethnography on the Move: From Field to Net to Internet. [23 paragraphs]. Forum *Qualitative Sozialforschung/Forum: Qualitative Social Research,* 1, 1. http://www.qualitative-research.net/fqs-texte/1-00/1-00wittel-e.htm Accessed 25 April 2012.

Wendy A. Vogt

Ethnography at the Depot
Conducting Fieldwork with Migrants in Transit

It was a hot and humid late afternoon as I walked along the railroad tracks with a group of four male migrants I had met at the shelter earlier that day. There were hundreds of people, most of them from Central America, sitting and sleeping in small groups waiting for the next train to pass. Some people were laughing, making jokes, others trying to rest before they boarded the next freight train. On the horizon I could see a police truck with a pair of officers wearing black bulletproof vests standing in the back with their mounted shiny machine guns haphazardly pointed to the street. One of the men in my group whistled at a local girl dressed in a pleated navy skirt, white shirt, white socks and penny loafer shoes walking home from school. We walked towards two young boys sitting alone with their backs pressed up against an abandoned train wagon. As we passed them, they turned their eyes down to gaze at the ground. We sat just a few feet away from them when we stopped to talk to an older man, whom they called *tio* (uncle).

After a few minutes, a large man with an unbuttoned shirt and a gold chain necklace approached us. In one hand he carried a steaming bag containing a whole roasted chicken and warm corn tortillas, and in the other hand he gripped the top of a two-litre bottle of chilled coca-cola. At first I thought he was probably a local man taking food home for *comida* (lunch), and so it surprised me when he stopped where the two boys sat and started unpacking the food. The boys watched him closely and then without speaking a word grabbed the tortillas and stuffed them with the juicy chicken. They ate furiously. The man did not eat at all and instead began to make small talk with the people in my group. 'I'm from Honduras,' he said, 'and I'm on my way north.' Something was amiss though, as he lacked the ubiquitous backpack and baseball hat that the other migrants wore, and his jewellery distinguished him from most of the other men and women along the tracks.

One of the men in my group, Jesus, leaned over and whispered in my ear 'He is Mexican.' This, I learned during my fieldwork, was a way of informing me that he was not really a migrant, but a *pollero* (human smuggler). Earlier in the day we had watched several men leave a hotel in the centre of town;

Freight Train, Veracruz, Mexico 2009.

Jesus pointed them out to me and told me they were *Zetas* going out to survey the tracks for potential victims.[1] Even though I was sitting closest to the alleged *pollero* he turned to Jesus and asked him, '*¿Quien es ella?'* (Who is she?) Jesus replied, 'I think she is some kind of psychologist or something.' Still not looking at me, he asked, 'What is she doing here?' 'She is just talking to us,' he replied.

The man finally made eye contact with me and asked if I would like a chicken taco. '*No, gracias'* (No, thank you), I said. 'Are you sure? Here have one,' he said without a smile on his face.' '*No, gracias,'* I reiterated, realizing this was his way of letting me know he was watching me. I turned my attention back to the group I was with and saw that the other migrants were now smoking a joint and passing it around. It seemed that *tio* was in fact a local drug dealer. Politely, I declined the joint. At that point, I felt a sense of danger, and Jesus must have felt it too since he stood up and asked me if I was ready to go back to the shelter. I said yes, and we quickly walked back together leaving the others behind.

This experience occurred early on in my fieldwork with undocumented Central American migrants in transit in southern Mexico. In the span of a few minutes I had entered a militarised zone where children were trafficked, drugs sold, local women harassed, nationality was questioned and alleged

---

1 Los Zetas are a highly sophisticated cartel in Mexico largely made up of ex-military personnel and police officers. Los Zetas are involved in organized crime and drug trafficking and since 2007 have begun to prey on Central American migrants in Mexico.

Migrant Shelter, Veracruz, Mexico 2009.

organised criminals walked freely. A climate of illegality, distrust and fear permeated the air of diverted gazes and hushed voices. It was a zone of strained social relations that seemed to depend upon chaos and confusion. Yet, at the same time, people were laughing, eating and drinking as if this was any ordinary afternoon. And for them, it was. This chapter explores some of the theoretical and methodological issues I faced during fifteen months of ethnographic research along the migrant journey in southern Mexico.

In order to make sense of the chaotic and often dangerous conditions that define the journey and systematically investigate themes of violence with people in active transit, I constructed my field location at various points along the migrant journey where migrants congregate. I worked primarily in migrant shelters where migrants may spend a few hours, days or weeks, and I came to conceptualise such sites as depots. A depot may refer to a bus or train station, or it may more broadly refer to a transportation hub or storage facility for the loading and distribution of goods. Migrant shelters were depots in both senses: they were spaces where a highly fluid population of people constantly arrived and departed in the course of their journeys; and as undocumented and clandestine individuals navigating through dangerous territories, transit migrants in these spaces were also transformed into commodities where they were traded, bought, sold and distributed. Migrants in transit do not exist in a vacuum, and so I also worked with some of the individuals and communities who work in and live near migrant shelters in order to understand the local and long-lasting impacts of transitory movements. Migrant shelters offer concrete locations to interact with and 'reach the hard-to-reach'.

This essay illuminates how creative ethnographic methods with people in active transit open opportunities to capture the raw emotions, experiences and testimonies of individuals who are often ignored in migration studies. I argue that migration must be conceptualised not only as a descriptive term to define a fluid movement between nations, but also as a highly embodied experience of movement in space and place. Such an approach not only challenges traditional ideas of 'the field' but also offers a unique perspective from which to study the intersections of migration and violence within conditions of chaos. In what follows, I provide a brief background, review some of the broader theoretical contributions of ethnography with fluid populations and discuss my experiences in choosing a safe and productive field site. I will also discuss some of the challenges of research with clandestine and vulnerable populations including power differentials, positionality and ethical issues of representation.

Central Americans in transit through Mexico

Over the past thirty years, Mexico has become a major transit country for Central American refugees and migrants hoping to enter the United States. During the armed conflicts of the 1970s, 80s and 90s, people fled direct political violence in their home countries in search of asylum and safety on Mexican and U.S. soil.[2] Today, ongoing structural, political and social violence and economic insecurity throughout Central America continue to propel people from their homes. Long before Central American migrants reach the U.S.-Mexico border, they travel through some of the most impoverished regions of Mexico, where they ride on the roofs of cargo trains, engage in informal work activities and seek food and shelter in 'migrant houses' that have been established along the way by various religious and non-governmental organisations. Riding cargo trains presents an increased physical risk for the migrants as accidents resulting in severe injury, dismemberment and death are not uncommon. Those who choose not to ride on the train often depend on buses and minivans, which are increasingly subject to inspection at military and immigration checkpoints and thus involve an increased risk of detention and deportation.

Along the journey in Mexico, Central American migrants regularly encounter physical assault, verbal harassment, intimidation, extortion, disease, kidnapping, injury and death. Gendered violence against migrating women – rape, sexual harassment, economically coerced sex, forced prostitution and trafficking along with the ensuing trauma and psychological effects associated with such violent acts are particularly devastating and pervasive. Women are more at risk of acquiring sexually transmitted diseases and being contracted into sex work and/or domestic work where sexual violence is prevalent.[3] Men also experience sexual violence, often in the form of sexual

---

2 Garcia 2006.
3 Caballero et al. 2002.

humiliation, emasculation and rape. Finally, the local Mexican residents experience increases in fear and violence as their communities become politically, economically and socially reoriented around growing flows of transitory migrants and the increased presence of Mexican military, police, drug cartels and transnational gangs.

The journey for Central American refugees and migrants has always been perilous, but in recent years direct violence and aggression have become far more systematic and difficult to escape. A network of organised criminals and paramilitary forces has been extremely successful in developing methodical forms of kidnapping, extortion and violence targeted against migrants. In 2009, the Mexican National Human Rights Commission issued a report documenting nearly 10,000 kidnapping victims, most of them Central American migrants, over a period of six months.[4] My interviews with migrants confirmed abuse and human rights violations at the hands of several perpetrators, including transnational gangs (for example, *La Mara Salvatrucha*), *Los Zetas*, Mexican police and military, immigration officials, local people and other migrants. Amnesty International recently issued a report on the human rights abuses committed by the Mexican military, including torture.[5]

Since 2006 nearly 50,000 people have been killed in drug-related conflicts and violence in Mexico.[6] The number of undocumented Central American migrants who have died is unknown; as one Mexican priest explained to me, 'Mexico is a cemetery for Central Americans. A cemetery without crosses.' This was made all too clear in August 2010 when the bodies of 72 migrants, mostly Central Americans, were found tied up and executed on a ranch in the northern state of Tamaulipas. Since then, multiple mass graves have been uncovered in northern Mexico, and the victims were mainly migrants from Mexico and Central America. Such horrific massacres are only the tip of the iceberg of violence against migrants, yet they exemplify the dangerous terrain that individuals must navigate as drug and human smuggling have become intertwined in recent years.

Violence along the migrant journey against both migrants and local residents operates with impunity – that is, exemption from accountability or legal punishment – at the individual, local and national levels. Migrants and residents suffer in silence, without recognition or retribution for the abuses committed against them. Violence related to Mexico's war on drugs has captured the attention of the international media, policy-makers and human rights groups, especially as it threatens to 'spill over' into the United States. The majority of reports and accounts of this violence have tended to adopt a binary perspective with drug cartels on one side and the Mexican government and military on the other. I suggest that such analyses have overlooked the complexity and far-reaching impacts of this increased violence, in particular the silent conflicts and everyday forms of subordination committed against

4   Comisión Nacional de los Derechos Humanos 2009.
5   Amnesty International 2009.
6   This number includes killings between December 2006 and June 2012.

Central American migrants and the local communities they pass through. Ethnographic field research on, and an analysis of, the complex social world surrounding migrant journeys are long overdue.

Conceptualizing the migrant journey

In anthropology, the topic of migration has been approached at both micro and macro levels of analysis, ranging from neoclassical economic rational actor models to dependency and world-systems theories.[7] Anthropologists have sought to bridge these approaches by looking at 'both people and process' and recognizing the structural and historical contexts in which individuals make choices and act.[8] The majority of anthropological analyses of migration tend to focus on locally fixed communities of migrants or immigrants. In the 1990s scholars began investigating the fluid links, flows and circuits between transnational communities.[9] This scholarship grew out of an attempt to reject narratives of immigrant assimilation by focusing on the material, discursive and ideological circulations between migrant-sending and -receiving communities. Such analyses challenge bounded conceptualisations of identity and locality and instead explore how flows of people, information, capital, and identities are increasingly deterritorialised.[10] However, as Sidney Mintz reminds us, people are not working towards 'becoming transnational; they were creating forms by which to live'.[11] The language of flows, connectivity and deterritorialisation that frames much of the research on transnationalism often fails to account for the material realities of *how* people migrate.

Despite the turn to studying transnational processes in multiple locations, much of the literature on migration examines a linear progression of migration from departure to arrival, integration and finally assimilation, without examining the transit migratory process in its own right.[12] Most of the world's migrants do not simply board a 747 jet plane and land in their 'receiving community' hours later. On the contrary, migrants may live in a liminal state of transit for weeks, months or even years as they attempt to cross national borders, earn cash, secure shelter, eat and make incremental movements towards their destination. Therefore, I consider three aspects of the migrants' liminality: their legal status as paperless/unauthorised persons, their social status as largely disconnected from their core networks and family, and their physical status of being in between home and destination.

Several notable works that do address migrant journeys include Sarah Mahler's *American Dreaming*, Susan Coutin's *Nations of Emigrants* and

7   Kearney 1986.
8   Brettell 2003.
9   Kearney 2004; Basch et al.1994; Portes et al. 1999; Smith 2006; Rouse 1996.
10 Deleuze & Guattari 1987; Canclini 1995; Rouse 1996.
11 Mintz 1998, 119.
12 Papadopoulou-Kourkoula 2008.

Jacqueline Hagan's *Migration Miracle*.[13] Mahler and Coutin include chapters highlighting the journey narratives of people who had successfully migrated to the United States. Their approach echoes Roseman's strategy of collecting stories of people's movements that took place in the past.[14] My work differs to the extent that my informants do not yet have a complete narrative or story of their journeys as they are still very much in the process of living them. Hagan's work, which looks at the centrality of religion in migrant's lives, also shifts the focus to the journey and to practices in sending communities, unlike the majority of the literature that looks at the role of religion in immigrant communities.

While comprehensive approaches to migrant journeys are few and far between, there has been due scholarly attention to border regions and particularly the U.S.-Mexico border. This includes work on gender and the *maquila* (factory) industry, the borderlands as a space of cultural hybridity and the historical production of inequality and illegality at the U.S.-Mexico border.[15] Some significant work has also been conducted on Central American migrants in Mexico's southern border region.[16] My work seeks to add to this scholarship in order to elucidate how, for Central Americans and the communities they pass through, the fear, violence and danger that people experience exist not only in border regions but also in the spaces between.

A growing number of scholars have recently begun to investigate the spatial, sociological and demographic processes of transit migration and view 'transit spaces' as valuable for understanding inequalities and possibilities for mobility.[17] They have studied transit countries and zones such as Turkey, Greece and Morocco, where migrants temporarily reside and wait for entry into other countries. The focus of these works is on life during an 'indefinite migrant stay' in a transit country, not on the processes that accompany the physical and active movement of people. For example, in her important book on transit migration, Papadopoulou-Kourkoula conducts interviews with asylum seekers in refugee camps in Athens. Lyons and Ford look at the demographic impacts of internal and international migration on the Riau Islands transit zone in Indonesia.[18] Danis has studied religious networks among Iraqi Christians waiting in Turkey to enter Australia or Canada, and Akcapar has studied the important role of social networks and social capital among Iranian transit migrants in Turkey.[19] While these works look at step-migration processes, my work takes a fresh approach to transit migration by investigating the lived experiences of people actively in transit.

13 Mahler 1995; Coutin 2007; Hagan 2008.
14 Roseman, this volume.
15 Akers & Chacon 2006; Ngai 2004; Nevins 2002; Kopinak 1996; Fernandez-Kelly, 1983; Segura & Zavella (eds.) 2007; Canclini 1987.
16 Castillo 2003; Kovic 2008, 2010; Kovic & Kelly 2006; Vásquez 2006.
17 Collyer 2007.
18 Lyons & Ford 2007.
19 Danis 2006.

In sum, the bodily act of movement is a critical component of migration processes and one that is largely ignored in theoretical discussions of cultural, discursive and material flows. The social relations and experiences that occur *along* migrant journeys are not inconsequential, passing moments, but often shape people's lives in a multitude of ways. Moreover, as certain places such as migrant journeys are particularly susceptible to changes in the global economy and to increased securitisation and militarisation, they open new spaces for violence to operate. I argue that field sites along migrant journeys should be considered spaces of methodological and theoretical analysis in migration studies so as to provide a missing link with scholarly work that solely focuses on sending and receiving communities.

Fluid ethnography, the ethnography of fluidity

The analytic shift to studying processes along migrant journeys raises important questions for fieldwork with fluid populations. Anthropologists have advocated multi-sited ethnography as a way to study the links, networks and processes of both emigration and immigration in transnational sending and receiving communities.[20] Others have deconstructed questions of travel and the dichotomy between 'home' and 'the field' in ethnographic fieldwork.[21] The preoccupation in much of this literature has been with the movement of the researcher and not the research subjects. However, James Clifford states, 'Anthropology potentially includes a cast of diverse dwellers and travellers whose displacement or travel in 'fieldwork' differs from the traditional spatial practice of the field.'[22] Clifford's statement opens up the possibilities of non-traditional spatial practices of both researchers and informants. Instead of entering a static field location with informants *in situ*, what does it mean when informants are actively in transit and flow through a field location?

There is some work that sheds light on non-traditional fieldwork with transient or unstable populations. Research has been conducted with displaced and re-settled refugee and migrant communities, and there have been theoretical discussions of processes of deterritorialisation.[23] In her work on homeless people in New York City, Joanne Passaro rejects the idea of constructing a coherent 'homeless village' or conducting an ethnography of one shelter and instead combines a variety of activities in various sites to understand the experiences of homeless people.[24] In her work on Hutu refugees, Liisa Mallki's discusses the value of studying 'transitory phenomena' and 'accidental communities of memory' in addition to the 'normative' and

---

20 Glick Schiller 2003; Fitzgerald 2006; Smith 2006; Marcus 1995.
21 Clifford 1997; Gupta & Ferguson (eds.) 1997; Kaplan 1987; Weston 1997.
22 Clifford 1997, 208.
23 Kaplan 1987; Deleuze & Guattari 1987; Holtzman 2000; Malkki 1992, 1995; Valentine & Knudsen (eds.) 1995; Ager (ed.) 1999; Sommers 2000.
24 Passaro 1997.

'everyday' features of coherent communities that are the subject of most anthropological investigation.[25] While a study of violence along the migrant trail is in some ways a study of extraordinary events in individual lives, my work seeks to understand the ways in which such extraordinary and transitory phenomena can become part of people's everyday lived experience. This is particularly crucial in understanding the ways that transit migration impacts not only on the migrants themselves but also on the communities they pass through.

In view of my project's focus on fluidity, when I first began to think about my field site I imagined travelling along the journey with migrants from south to north, observing and sharing their experiences as they travelled between migrant shelters. During the exploratory phase of research, I travelled to the Guatemala-Mexico border and toured various shelters and train yards through the states of Chiapas, Oaxaca and Veracruz, speaking to migrants, shelter workers, activists and local residents and explaining my project and discussing the plausibility and possibilities of collaboration. However, after witnessing the complexity and chaos that define the various sites I visited, it soon became clear that studying people in transit did not mean that I needed to be in transit myself. On the contrary, I could establish myself in one or more fixed locations and through long-term research observe and study the physical and social movement of people across Mexico and the impacts it has on local populations. My approach was multi-sited and deeply embedded within a network of migrant shelters.

My work with undocumented Central American migrants looks at the daily experiences, movements and obstacles that migrants face with the objective of illuminating the complexity of what goes on in the weeks, months or years that may define an individual's migration journey. The everyday experiences of migrants in transit are deeply intertwined with local relations and national politics. They engage in a number of activities and interact with local people as they procure food, shelter, transportation safety, medical attention or legal resources. Such an approach offers a unique perspective on the notion of migrant flows and streams by documenting the everyday conditions of migrants actively in transit. Because I was positioned in the midst of the stream in locations I conceptualise as depots, I could observe and understand the recurring themes in people's lived experiences as they pass through. This, in turn, allowed me to iteratively develop new questions and probe more deeply into these themes as new people moved through my field site.

Like fieldwork with other transient populations, with migrants in transit the fieldworker may only have a few days or hours to speak and spend time with informants, which can hinder the possibility to build rapport and trust. I often met people and interviewed them the same day or the following day. Nearly every day I had to explain my presence and intentions anew to the migrants who passed through. In contrast to researchers who

---

25 Malkki 1997.

set up interviews with their informants in advance, giving them time to reflect on and construct their life histories, many of my informants had little time to think about their answers before I asked them. Although at first I thought this might detract from my ability to uncover deeper levels of social processes and relations, I now believe I was able to capture the raw concerns, emotions, thoughts and strategies of people in the midst of an extremely unknown and dangerous process. The element of fluidity and the perspective on people *en route* is something that sets this study apart from other work on migration and is critical for understanding the multitude of processes involved in human mobility and responses to violence.

Methods and the research site

Over a period of five years I developed relationships with, and conducted research at, several locations in southern Mexico, and in 2008-2009 I conducted a subsequent year of fieldwork primarily at the Casa Guadalupe shelter in Oaxaca, Mexico.[26] Casa Guadalupe is part of an organised network of migrant shelters that have been established in different locations throughout Mexico since the late 1990s. These shelters have dramatically changed the shape and logistics of the journey as they have become well known sites that not only offer food and rest but also serve as important centres that permit the migrants to navigate through risk and danger, meet potential travel companions and obtain legal and medical assistance.

Casa Guadalupe is not located directly on the railway tracks and is thus considered to be a relatively safe shelter where organised criminals and gangs have not (yet) infiltrated. As such, in recent years it has become a more popular shelter to pass through, particularly for those who wish to bypass some of the most dangerous sections of the journey where kidnappings are becoming the norm.[27] Migrants arrive at the shelter by bus and are often referred there by other migrants or by shelter workers who send particularly vulnerable migrants – including women, children and people who have suffered abuses and have made human rights denouncements – to the shelter.

Working within established migrant shelters was a critical research strategy for several reasons. Most significantly, it provided access to undocumented migrants – a group that is otherwise extremely difficult to locate and systematically recruit for participation in such a study. The fact that many vulnerable migrants pass through Casa Guadalupe meant that I was able to speak to a diverse subsection of people. Through my affiliation

---

26 As I note later, all names of shelters and individuals have been changed to protect the identities of my informants.

27 The infiltration of organized criminals was a major concern at the shelter throughout my research. Shelter workers were aware that human smugglers regularly posed as migrants and entered the shelter, but there was not yet a sense of imminent danger.

with Casa Guadalupe I met and spoke with hundreds of Central American men and women in the course of my fieldwork. I also met and interviewed shelter aid workers and volunteers, priests, public officials, local residents and Central American migrants who temporarily reside in Mexico.

At the time of my research, Casa Guadalupe was split into two locations, an office and the actual shelter where the migrants ate and slept. I conducted systematic participant observation at both locations. My participation at the office included the initial intake of migrants, providing advice on the risks of the journey and helping them to make phone calls to their families in their communities of origin or in the United States. Phone calls allowed people to update their worried family members about their situation and also to request money transfers when needed. I also accompanied sick, injured or pregnant migrants to a local clinic, where they received medical attention. At the office, I also worked with local Oaxacan community members who needed assistance in locating missing family members who had migrated to the United States. This work and searching for family members allowed me to understand the perspective of those who are left behind by migrants and some of the impacts it can have on individuals, families and entire communities.

Through long-term participant observation at the shelter of Casa Guadalupe, I was able to watch migrants' interactions with one another and participate in daily activities and conversations. My downtime at the shelter was spent sitting around and chatting, strategising possible routes, playing cards, rummaging through donated clothing and supplies, cooking and eating with migrants. While many shelters are very strict about only letting people stay for three days, Casa Guadalupe would often allow people to stay longer, particularly if they had medical issues, had no money or were victims of human rights violations. This allowed me to foster stronger relationships with individuals and engage in multiple conversations and interviews with them. The casual setting at most shelters was conducive to sharing stories and information with migrants in a two-way dynamic that is not always possible in more formal interviewing approaches.

I conducted both taped and un-taped semi-structured interviews with migrants, and owing to the context of violence and human rights abuses, some of these interviews naturally took the form of oral histories and/or *testimonios* (testimonies). As Jane Schneider notes, anthropologists must listen 'for the histories that others produce for themselves'.[28] Several scholars have advocated the use of oral histories as a mechanism in understanding and writing about migration processes from an 'insider's perspective'.[29] The methodology of *testimonio* is related to oral history, but it carries with it an explicit level of political engagement and 'bearing witness' to the realities of people's lived experience that may otherwise be erased from history.[30] Such an approach adds political weight to ethnographies of migration, particularly

28 Schneider & Rapp 1995, 7.
29 Brettell 2003; Gmelch 1992.
30 The Latina Feminist Group 2001; Mallon 2001.

through its emphasis on exposing histories of exclusion, exploitation and violence. I also ran focus groups, which were useful in cases where a group of people had experienced a traumatic event, such as a kidnapping or robbery, and could collectively discuss their experiences, both unique and shared, often building on each other's descriptions, perceptions and commentaries.

My position as a full-time volunteer allowed me to be embedded within an established institutional structure as well as to have access to, witness and understand what migration means for people in transit. I was able to conduct more 'traditional' long-term research with the people involved in running the shelters and local community members, and some of these people became key informants. I collected data on the inter-workings of the organisation – the main issues, concerns and challenges facing both migrants and aid workers. In addition to research at Casa Guadalupe, I made trips to several other shelters, participated in a variety of public events and conferences and collected archival materials. I witnessed a caravan of mothers from Central America who make an annual trip to Mexico to raise awareness about their children who have disappeared while crossing Mexico. I attended a shelter opening, where local women dressed in their traditional costumes made *tamales* (stuffed pastries) to symbolically welcome the Central Americans that would be passing through their community. As such, working within the migrant shelter network allowed me to witness and document not only the violence that people had experienced but also to study an emerging transnational social movement. On one trip to a shelter in Chiapas, Mexico a shelter worker told me, 'Wendy, you cannot study violence without also studying hope. They are part of the same thing.'[31] She was right, and my research expanded its focus to also understand processes of hope and empathy.

Upon my return to the United States I have maintained contact with several of my informants and shelter colleagues and friends through email and social networking websites, primarily Facebook. When I was in the field very few of my informants and colleagues were on Facebook, but today it is a major source of communication and activity related to the migrant rights movement in Mexico. Shelters and priests have their own Facebook pages. On Facebook people post articles, photos, announcements, press releases, and organise events related to migrant shelters and the migrant rights movement in Mexico. They also use email and Facebook to keep the online community aware of local happenings. Through email and Facebook I receive messages and press announcements about upcoming events, documentaries, conferences and marches. I also receive a fairly steady stream of news and photos documenting human rights violations and violence against migrants and shelters in local communities. In this capacity, Facebook has become an online archive of the major issues, events, and actions of concern to migrant rights workers.

31 Interview, February 2009.

Ethnographic research with clandestine and vulnerable populations

One of the greatest challenges in conducting research with undocumented people in transit is that they must live a clandestine existence, often in the shadows and on the margins of society, and thus do not want to speak openly about their citizenship status. Undocumented migrants do not share the same rights as citizens and are consequently particularly vulnerable to violence, exploitation and injury, often making them wary of strangers. Working as a full-time volunteer and incorporating myself into the daily activities of the shelter was important in that it allowed me to build a rapport with the migrants. While my primary role as an anthropologist was that of an observer, I myself was also observed by my informants. To see me cooking, helping them to make phone calls, accompanying sick migrants to the local clinic and giving advice on the risks of the journey allowed the migrants to see me as not only a researcher but also someone concerned about their well-being.

Throughout my fieldwork I took careful precautions to ensure the safety and anonymity of my informants, but my position as a shelter worker complicated this situation. I received their oral consent but did not have my informants sign any consent forms, as is customary in anthropological research. For research purposes, I did not collect any information that could potentially identify people's illegal presence in Mexico. However, it is standard practice for migrant shelters to document basic information about the people who enter the shelter, and some shelters have people sign forms and take fingerprints and photographs. At Casa Guadalupe all these practices were employed during the initial intake. It was thus one of my main responsibilities to conduct short interviews with migrants to find out their full name, nationality, religion, names and phone numbers of family members, their destination, if they have been abused or experienced human rights violations and any physical characteristics that would possibly help identify them in the case of disappearance or death. Personnel from other shelters regularly exchange such information in cases of missing migrants. Occasionally migrants would refuse to have their photo taken or to sign the intake form, and I suspect that they regularly used fake names to protect their identities.

I made it clear to all the people I interviewed for my research that their participation was voluntary and separate from their involvement with the shelter. In my own notes I did not record people's full names or other identifying information. I only tape-recorded interviews with a select group of people with whom I had established a significant amount of rapport and even so never used names in recordings. With migrants this meant that it generally took a few days, or in some cases weeks, before I would approach someone about doing a taped interview with me. I waited to conduct taped interviews with shelter aid workers until the end of my field experience. I felt the longer time spent in developing relationships and trust with informants allowed for more honest and in-depth interviews. All the names of people and shelters have been changed in my written work to ensure the anonymity of my informants and field sites. This is particularly important as some of my findings reveal contradictory aspects of individuals and shelter dynamics.

The vulnerable and clandestine existence that many of my informants embodied in addition to the makeshift and unpredictable nature of the journey meant that people constantly arrived at and departed from the shelter without notice, and therefore I had to employ a highly flexible research approach that adapted to daily events. In several instances, I arrived at the shelter prepared to conduct an interview or simply spend time with an individual only to find out upon arrival that they had left. Migrants' travel plans are often serendipitous and can change instantly with the unexpected arrival of a money order, meeting a new travel companion or becoming alienated or threatened by their current surroundings. We received some migrants who had been abandoned by their travel companions. In one case, a mother and her young daughter arrived at the shelter after they had bee robbed and abandoned in a remote village by the person hired to smuggle them across the country. The fact that migrants were not permanent residents in my field location also meant that they had a different relationship to, and experience of, violence than the shelter workers and local residents. It became clear that to truly understand the complexity of violence along the migrant trail, I would need to explore these differences.

Research amidst fear and violence

In the field of anthropology there is a rich tradition of conducting fieldwork amidst conditions of fear and violence.[32] Several anthropologists have discussed at length the methodological and personal challenges of working in such settings and at times the necessity to abandon entire projects.[33] Because transit migration through Mexico has become the site of unimaginable violence and profit, I was not immune to dangerous field situations, threats, deception and intimidation on the part of numerous different actors. A variety of measures were taken at many of the shelters to minimise the risks of human smugglers, traffickers, weapons and drugs entering them. The caution I needed to employ on a daily basis in my interactions at shelters and in local communities also applied to the ways I talked about and presented my research. During one interview with a priest, I inquired about the drug trade and whether it impacted on local dynamics in the community. He said that it certainly did, but that it was not something that was spoken about. 'Why not?' I asked naively. He replied bluntly, 'Because those who talk about it are killed.'[34] Mexico has one of the highest murder rates for journalists, and so as an anthropologist studying violence I needed to exercise extreme caution.

32 Daniel 1996; Feldman 1991; Das 2000; Green 1999; Kovats-Bernat 2008; Nordstrom & Robben (eds.) 1995; Scheper-Hughes & Bourgois (eds.) 2004; Sluka 2000.
33 Hannerz 2006; Kovats-Bernat 2002.
34 Interview, July 2006.

In navigating through the realities and politics of violence, I struggled with my desire to be on the 'frontlines' of dangerous situations because I assumed it would make for more compelling and exciting research. I envisioned riding on the tops of trains with migrants and accompanying them as they waited in train yards day and night. However, it quickly became apparent that my research would not only be safer but more robust and complex if I worked from within the established network of migrant shelters in Mexico. My goal was not to reproduce the journalistic snapshots of violence along the journey, but rather to investigate and illuminate some of the more subtle underlying social processes and contradictions that accompany mobility and ultimately reproduce inequality and violence.

Despite our location within the relative safety of shelter walls, the stressful and dangerous conditions that migrants experienced outside the shelter shaped my approach and interactions with them. Because most of my informants were still in vulnerable positions and had very little time to reflect upon or discuss their experiences in the middle of the journey, interviews were often very emotional and difficult. This was particularly true in discussing issues of gendered violence as many women did not want to speak openly about such experiences. I had to re-conceptualise my framework to get at the themes of gendered violence in more round-about and nuanced ways.

For example, people were very willing to tell me about *other* women they had met along the way who had been sexually assaulted. I suspect that this was an important survival strategy, and I therefore collected many more second-hand accounts of rape, torture and sexual slavery. My assumptions that women would be willing to speak about such violence to a stranger were rooted in my own feminist location, where women are encouraged to speak out about rape and shame is turned into 'empowerment'. This is not the case with many of the people I met, nor was it realistic to expect that people would openly and casually talk about such traumatic events while they were still at risk. I also realised I needed to broaden my understanding of gendered violence. Much of the fear and abuse suffered by male and female migrants was grounded in unequal gendered and sexual power dynamics involving the threat of rape, sexual humiliation, sexual assault of body parts and gendered derogatory comment and stereotyping.

My embedded role as a shelter worker allowed me to understand the complexities of shelter life, but I was also interested in the impacts of shelters and migration on violence in local communities. During visits to various shelters I always tried to speak to local residents about how their lives had been affected by transit migration in terms of violence, fear and economic concerns. The fluid movement of Central American migrants has had long-lasting effects on the daily lives of Mexican residents. While migrants shelters certainly are examples of hope and empathy, my research revealed that they are also highly contested spaces and local residents often have mixed and ambivalent feelings about the presence of Central Americans in their communities.

Early on in my research, I visited a shelter located in the state of Veracruz that was known for its extensive work with Central American migrants. When I arrived in the town, people seemed rather shocked to learn of my interest in the shelter and were hesitant in helping me to locate it. A nun I had met actually refused to tell me where it was, claiming that the area was full of *marijuaneros* (drug-addicts) and no place for a young woman to be in. When I finally found the shelter, I arrived only to find the doors closed and the building abandoned. I walked a few blocks down the road to where the train passed through and hundreds of migrants congregated. I spoke to two local men who sell jackets, gloves and bags of bread to passing migrants. I asked them about the shelter, and they told me that it had been closed after a migrant in the community raped a young girl and the neighbours protested, leading to the permanent closure of the shelter.

A very similar situation occurred a few years later in a community in Oaxaca state, where I conducted a significant portion of my research. A Central American man who lived in the community was accused of raping a six-year-old girl, and the local authorities threatened to burn the shelter down if the priest did not close its doors. I spoke to a young teacher from the neighbouring town, who explained her ambivalent feelings about the shelter. She remembered watching the local news with interviews of the local priest and the mother of the victim. She was unsure about the connection between the rape and the shelter, and while she sympathised with the plight of migrants, she was more concerned about the safety of her children.

Speaking to this woman and other local residents helped me to understand the multiple types of fear, violence and chaos that have seeped into Mexican communities as increasing numbers of migrants and people who prey on them pass through. While these histories shattered my neat narrative of violence and hope, they also led to critical insights into the complex ways violence is (re)produced. An ethnographic understanding of the journey must take into account these rippling effects of violence in local spaces.

Positionality, power differentials and representation

While I did my best to incorporate myself into the dynamics of shelter life, there were limits to my engagement, and these underscored power differentials both with migrants and with other shelter workers. Most importantly, my role as a U.S.-government-funded graduate student was to intellectualise processes of fear and violence, while my informants lived such processes in their everyday lives. My positionality as a young woman living alone in Mexico also differentially impacted on the way I related to male and female migrants. Approximately 80% of the migrants passing through the shelters are male, and people were not accustomed to seeing a foreign woman working in a migrant shelter. I was regularly asked about my marital status, if I had children and why my husband 'allowed' me to live in Mexico without him and *andar por la calle solita* (walk in the street alone). While

I could relate to the women I met on numerous levels, many were surprised that I was approaching thirty but did not yet have any children. I actually became pregnant while I was still in the field, and this changed the way many women interacted with me. Some women offered me intimate advice about breastfeeding and what foods to eat, and others treated me with a special level of respect and status. For example, I was once asked to give a woman my worn t-shirt so that she could wrap her newborn baby with it in the hope that it would cure the baby of colic.

Male migrants often joked with me about marrying them so that they could gain legal entry into the United States. I met a 16-year old male migrant from Honduras who had part of his ear bitten off in a fight and scabs on his scalp. There were no other women around the shelter that day, and so he asked me to help him to apply medicine to his wounds. He told me he was going to Texas, where his mother lived. She had left when he was only four years old, and he was on his way to find her. He said he wanted to find his *mama*, that is, unless I wanted to be his new *mamacita*, a term of endearment used between couples. While many of these interactions and comments were made in jest, at times they created awkward situations and highlighted the power differentials based on gender, nationality and class that constantly need to be negotiated during research. However, as anthropologists have noted, it is sometimes these awkward field situations that lead to the most productive insights.[35]

Through my position as a shelter volunteer and my alignment with the migrant rights movement in Mexico, I was in a unique position to study the complexities and contradictions of violence and hope along the journey. However, as Hale has argued with reference to 'activist research', this often drew me into the 'compromised positions of the political process'.[36] At times I found myself in the midst of the micro-politics of shelter life and tensions between and among migrants and shelter workers. I recall a group of men from Guatemala who refused to interact with the other men staying in their dorm room because they were from El Salvador, and Salvadorans were known for being gang members and drug addicts. Migrants confided in me about the unequal treatment they received from other shelter workers. One of my informants was a shelter worker who was later accused of smuggling a young woman. Another was accused of trying to recruit Central American women to work in the local sex industry. I was also privy to disputes between shelter aid workers.

Some of these cases were downright heartbreaking, but they illuminate the ways power seeped into daily life to create distrust and fractures within local communities, within groups of migrants and even within the migrant rights community. I needed to be cautious of my own positionality and maintain the intimate distance that is required of ethnographic research. I was careful to not be subsumed by such politics and instead try to use these

35 Hume & Mulcock (eds.) 2004.
36 Hale 2006.

difficult situations as analytical points of departure. Through a lens that does not focus on blaming 'bad' individuals but rather places such disputes and tensions within social, political, economic and historical contexts, I was able to understand more fully the ways power operates through and across social relations. Through situated and contextualised analysis, ethical questions of representation of the potentially negative findings of ethnographic research are partially resolved. It is ultimately up to the researcher to present her/ his findings in a way that does not compromise the safety or dignity of the people involved and adds insight into social processes.

Conclusion

Migrant journeys are critical and understudied spaces where social inequalities and multiple forms of violence are (re)produced. While there are certainly a number of challenges regarding safety, positionality and representation, ethnographic research methods are particularly appropriate for studying the fluid, serendipitous and often chaotic conditions of migrant journeys. Field sites located in migrant 'depots' allow researchers to capture the raw and immediate lived experiences of people in transit as well as to understand the multiple impacts of transit flows on local populations. Such an approach offers a systematic and relatively safe way to study the intersections between migration and violence.

As people become increasingly mobile globally in response to neoliberal policies, conflict, financial crises and poverty, it is essential that scholars conceptualise and study the world's many migrant journeys. With increases in securitisation and militarisation of border regions and transportation zones, the time it takes for people to cross transit countries like Mexico will only increase and become more dangerous. Undocumented migrants travel with few enforced legal protections and rights, creating the conditions for their exploitation and abuse. The manifold ways violence seeps into local communities can be equally devastating. As such, work on migration journeys not only fills an important theoretical and empirical gap in the migration literature but also highlights a global human rights issue.

Bibliography

Amnesty International. 2009. Mexico: New Reports of Human Rights Violations by the Military. London: Amnesty International.

Anzaldua, G. 1987. *Borderlands/La Frontera: The New Mestiza*. San Francisco: Aunt Lute Books.

Basch, L, N. Glick-Schiller & C. Blanc-Szanton. 1994. *Nations Unbound: Transnational Projects, Postcolonial Predicaments and Detteritorialized Nation-States*. London: Routledge.

Brettell, C. 2003. *Anthropology and Migration: Essays on Transnationalism, Ethnicity and Identity*. Walnut Creek, CA: Alta Mira Press.

Caballero, M., A. Dreser, R. Leyva, C. Rueda & M. Brofman. 2002. Migration, Gender and HIV/AIDS in Central America and Mexico. *Monduzzi Editore*.

Canclini, N. 1995. *Hybrid Cultures:Strategies for Entering and Leaving Modernity*. Minneapolis: University of Minnesota Press.

Castillo, M. 2003. Los desafíos de la emigración centroamericana en el Siglo XXI. *Amérique Latine Histoire et Mémoire 7*.

Chacon, J. & M. Davis. 2006. *No one is illegal: Fighting racism and state violence on the U.S.-Mexico border*. Chicago: Haymarket Books.

Clifford, J. 1997. Spatial Practices: Fieldwork, Travel and the Disciplining of Anthropology. In: A. Gupta & J. Ferguson (eds.) *Anthropological Locations*. Berkeley and Los Angeles: UC Press.

Collyer, M. 2007. In-Between Places: Trans-Saharan Transit Migrants in Morocco and the Fragmented Journey to Europe. *Antipode* 39: 4, 668–690.

Comisión Nacional de los Derechos Humanos. 2009. Informe Especial de la Comisión Nacional de los Derechos Humanos sobre los casos de Secuestro en Contra de Migrantes. Mexico City: Comisión Nacional de los Derechos Humanos.

Coutin, S. B. 2007. *Nations of Emigrants: Shifting Boundaries of Citizenship in El Salvador and the United States*. Ithaca and London: Cornell University Press.

Daniel, V. E. 1996. *Charred Lullabies: Chapters in an Anthropology of Violence*. Princeton: Princeton University Press.

Daniel, V. E., & J. Knudsen (eds.) 1995. *Mistrusting Refugees*. Berkeley: University of California Press.

Danis, D. 2006. Waiting on the Purgatory: Religious Networks of Iraqi Christian Transit Migrants in Istanbul. *European University Institute Working Papers* RSCAS N. 2006/25.

Das, V. 2000. *Violence and Subjectivity*. Berkeley: University of California Press.

Deleuze, G. & F. Guattari. 1987. *A Thousand Plateaus: Capitalism and Schizophrenia*. Minnneapolis: University of Minnesota Press.

Deleuze, G. & F. Guattari. 1987. *A Thousand Plateaus: Capitalism and Schizophrenia*. Minnneapolis: University of Minnesota Press.

Feldman, A. 1991. *Formations of Violence: The Narrative of the Body and Political Terror in Northern Ireland*. Chicago: University of Chicago Press.

Fernandez-Kelly, M. 1983. *For We are Sold: Women and Industry in Mexico's Frontier*. Albany: SUNY Press.

Fitzgerald, D. 2006. Towards a Theoretical Ethnography of Migration. *Qualitative Sociology* 29: 1, 1–24.

Glick-Schiller, N. 2003. The Centrality of Ethnography in the Study of Transnational Migration: Seeing the Wetlands instead of the Swamp. In: N. Foner (ed.) *American Arrivals: Anthropology Engages the New Immigration*, Santa Fe: School of American Research Press.

Gmelch, G. 1992. *Double Passage: The lives of Caribbean Migrants Abroad and Back Home*. Ann Arbor: University of Michigan Press.

Green, L. 1999. *Fear as a Way of Life: Mayan Widows in Rural Guatemala*. New York: Columbia University Press.

Gupta, A. & J. Ferguson (eds.) 1997. *Anthropological Locations*. Berkeley and Los Angeles: UC Press.

Hagan, J. 2008. *Migration Miracle: Faith, Hope, and Meaning on the Undocumented Journey*. Cambridge, Massachusetts: Harvard University Press.

Hale, C. 2006. Activist Research v. Cultural Critique: Indigenous Land Rights and the Contradictions of Politically Engaged Anthropology. *Cultural Anthropology* 21: 1, 96–120.

Hannerz, U. 2006. Studying up, down, sideways, through, backwards, forwards, away and at home: reflections on the field worries of an expansive discipline. In: S. Coleman & P. Collins (eds.), *Locating the Field: Space, Place and Context in Anthropology*. Oxford: Berg Publishers.

Holtzman, J. 2000. *Nuer Journeys, Nuer Lives: Sudanese Refugees in Minnesota*. Boston: Allyn and Bacon.

Hume, L. & J. Mulcock (ed.) 2004. *Anthropologists in the field: cases in participant observation*. New York: Columbia University Press.

Kaplan, C. 1987. Deterritorializations: The Rewriting of Home and Exile in Western Feminist Discourse. *Cultural Critique* 6 Spring, 187–198.

Kearney, M. 1986. From the Invisible Hand to Visible Feet: Anthropological Studies of Migration and Development. *Annual Review of Anthropology* 15, 331–361.

Kearney, M. 2004. *Changing Fields of Anthropology: From Local to Global*. Lanham: Rowman & Littlefield Publishers, Inc.

Kopinak, K. 1996. *Desert Capitalism: Maquiladoras in North America's Western Industrial Corridor*. Tucson: University of Arizona Press.

Kovats-Bernat, C. 2002. Negotiating Dangerous Fields: Pragmatic Strategies for Fieldwork amid Violence and Terror. *American Anthrolpologist* 104:1, 208–222.

Kovats-Bernat, C. 2008. Sleeping Rough in Port-Au-Prince: An Ethnoggraphy of Street Children and Violence in Haiti. *American Ethnologist* 35: 4, 4043–4046.

Kovic, C. 2008. Jumping from a Moving Train: Risk, Migration and Rights at NAFTA's Southern Border. *Practicing Anthropology* 30: 2, 32–36.

Kovic, C. 2010. The Violence of Security: Central American Migrants Crossing Mexico's Southern Border (photo essay). *Anthropology Now* 2: 1, 87–97.

Kovic, C. & P. Kelly. 2006. Fronteras seguras, cuerpos vulnerables: migracion y genero en la frontera sur. *Debate Feminista* 33: 17, 69–83.

Lyons, L. & M. Ford. 2007. Where Internal and International Migration Intersect: Mobility and the Formation of Multi-Ethnoc Communities in the Riau Islands Transit Zone. *International Journal on Multicultural Societies* 9: 2, 236–263.

Mahler, S. 1995. *American Dreaming: Immigrant Life on the Margins*. Princeton, NJ: Princeton University Press.

Malkki, L. 1992. National Geographic: The Rooting of Peoples and the Territorialization of Natonal Identity among Scholars and Refugees. *Cultural Anthropology* 7: 1, 24–44.

Malkki, L. 1995. Refugees and Exile: From 'Refugee Studies' to the National Order of Things. *Annual Review of Anthropology* 24, 495–523.

Malkki, L. 1997. News and Culture: Transitory Phenomena and the Fieldwork Tradition. In: A Gupta & J. Ferguson (eds.), *Anthropological Locations*. Berkeley and Los Angeles: UC Press.

Mallon, F. 2001. Bearing Witness in Hard Times: Ethnography and Testimonio in a Postrevolutionary Age. In G. Joseph (ed.), *Reclaiming the Political in Latin American History: Essays from the North*. Durham: Duke University Press.

Marcus, G. E. 1995. Ethnography in/of the World System: The Emergence of Multi-Sited Ethnography. *Annual Review of Anthropology* 24, 95–117.

Mintz, S. 1998. The Localization of Anthropological Practice: From area studies to transnationalism. *Critique of Anthropology* 18: 2, 117–133.

Nevins, J. 2002. *Operation Gatekeeper: The Rise of the 'Illegal Alien' and the Making of the U.S.-Mecixo Boundary*. New York: Routledge.

Ngai, M. 2004. *Impossible Subjects: Illegal Aliens and the Making of Modern America*. Princeton: Princeton University Press.

Nordstrom, C. & A. Robben (eds.) 1995. *Fieldwork under Fire: Contemporary Studies of Violence and Survival*. Berkeley: University of California Press.

Papadopoulou-Kourkoula, A. 2008. *Transit Migration: the missing link between emigration and settlement*. In: Z. Layton-Henry & D. Joly (eds.), *Migration, Minorities and Citizenship*. Houndsmills, Hampshire: Palgrave Macmillan.

Passaro, J. 1997. 'You can't take the subway to the field!': 'Village' Epistemologies in the Global Village. In: A. Gupta & J. Ferguson (eds.), *Anthropological Locations*. Berkeley and Los Angeles: UC Press.

Portes, A., L. E. Guarnizo & P. Landolt. 1999. The study of transnationalism: pitfalls and promise of an emergent research field. *Ethnic and Racial Studies* 22: 2, 217–237.

Rouse, R. 1996. Mexican Migration and the Social Space of Postmodernism. In D. Gutiérrez (ed.), *Between Two Worlds: Mexican Immigrants in the United States.* Wilmington, DE: Scholarly Resources Inc.

Scheper-Hughes, N. & P. Bourgois (eds.). 2004. *Violence in War and Peace: An Anthology.* Oxford: Blackwell.

Schneider, J. & R. Rapp, ed. 1995. *Articulating Hidden Histories: Exploring the Influence of Eric R. Wolf.* Berkeley: University of California Press.

Segura, D. & P. Zavella (ed.) 2007. *Women and Migration in the U.S.-Mexico Borderlands.* Durham: Duke University Press.

Sluka, J. 2000. Introduction: State Terror and Anthropology. In J. Sluka (ed.) *Death Squad: The Anthropology of State Terror.* Philadelphia: University of Pennsylvania Press.

Smith, R. 2006. *Mexican New York: Transnational Lives of New Immigrants* Berkeley: UC Press.

Sommers, M. 2000. *Fear in Bongoland: Burundi Refugees in Urban Tanzania.* New York: Berghahn Books.

The Latina Feminist Group. 2001. Introduction. In *Telling to Live: Latina Feminist Testimonios.* Durham: Duke University Press.

Vásquez, L. & A. R. García. 2006. *Migrantes por la puerta sur.* Oaxaca de Juarez: Coordinación Estatal de Atención al Migrante Oaxaqueño.

Weston, K. 1997. The Virtual Anthropologist. In A. Gupta & J. Ferguson (eds.), *Anthropological Locations.* Berkeley: UC Press.

Fran Meissner & Inês Hasselberg

Forever Malleable

The Field as a Reflexive Encounter

Locating the field: an epistemological concern

In recent social science debates on the practice of fieldwork, one overarching concern has been that complex social phenomena, in an interconnected world, need to be studied with research methods that can generate data which make this complexity more accessible to academic debate.[1] Of concern in this paper are the assumptions and expectations of 'the field' in research with migrants, or more precisely with people who have moved. These are connected to issues of professional and disciplinary authority, of distancing and otherness, and of course to the development of a workable field site.[2] As has repeatedly been established, the field is no longer easily found,[3] and it must be critically understood and reviewed. As an epistemological construct, it is thus not necessarily spatially bound but depends upon the delineation of the social phenomenon under investigation. In migration studies, more often than not the social phenomenon being studied is mobile, scattered and/or fragmented.[4] As such, migration is a particularly rich field for the development of innovative research methods and has been cited as one area of research that has shifted the conception of the field as a 'village site' to something more malleable.[5] Further, it is argued that migration provides an excellent way to highlight the contours of social change.[6] Despite this, migration scholars point out that migration research need not be characterised as exceptional.[7] One aspect that can be seen as specific to the field of ethnic and migration studies is its recent self-criticism

---

1 Erikson 2007; Coleman & Collins 2006; Falzon 2009.
2 Gupta & Ferguson 1997.
3 Amit 2000; Passaro 1997; Gupta & Ferguson 1997.
4 Wendy Vogt in this volume gives a very good account of the fluidities of migration.
5 Marcus, 1995.
6 Van Hear, 2010.
7 Bilger & Van Liempt 2009; Dahinden & Efionayi-Mader 2009.

and continued challenging of assumptions that easily become entrenched in the process of studying people who move. Issues such as methodological nationalism[8] or groupism[9] are but two examples of this. One can argue that these debates foreground, if not an exceptional, then a specific topic-related reflexivity. This challenges researchers to think outside the box in their attempts to study migration and its social implications.

In this chapter we want to critically review how the complexities of the field develop and become apparent during fieldwork and how these sometimes unexpected complexities influence the way researchers negotiate and perceive the delineation of their field. We will do this by reflecting on the fieldwork involved in two migration research projects and foregrounding the role that access to research participants and research locations plays in this process.

We will first introduce each of the research projects and show how their focus shifted during fieldwork; secondly we will discuss these aspects of access and location by drawing on relevant literature and highlighting similarities and differences between the two projects. This is done to emphasise how the (pre-research) idea of the field contrasts with the field that we are able to access and investigate. Finally, in conclusion, we will argue that the 'location' of the field is processual, that *ante factum* reflecting on what may and may not be the demarcating, but still fuzzy, lines of the field can be a useful exercise to better understand the social phenomena under investigation, and that this important exercise adds a further dimension to the reflexive engagement of social science research. The field always remains malleable. What must be recognised is that not only is it constructed for a particular research project, but also that the execution of the research project develops along with the process of finding its field.

The research projects

The two research projects analyzed in this article were conducted as doctoral-level studies, each by a single researcher. Both projects, at the time of writing, were in the early analysis and data review phase. First, we briefly outline the aims of these projects and how we delimited the field during research design. Next, we move on to explore in more detail the two aspects of conducting research pointed to above – access and locations. The first project, by Inês Hasselberg, focuses on the deportation of long-term migrants from the UK. Fieldwork took place in London from January to December 2009. The second project, by Fran Meissner, focuses on super-diversity in urban areas and is a two-sited research project carried out in London (UK) from September 2009 to March 2010 and in Toronto (Canada) from June to November 2010.

---

8   Glick Schiller & Caglar 2009; Wimmer & Glick Schiller 2002.
9   Brubaker 2002; Wimmer 2009.

An ethnography of deportation from Britain

The first project we draw on aims to explore the impacts of British deportation policies on the ground. In taking London as the site of field research, the project was designed to look at the deportation and deportability of long-term migrants in the UK,[10] at the ways this measure affects those who are threatened by it and those who are left behind, and at the responses and strategies devised to cope with and react to deportation. For the deporting state, the removal of the unwanted ends when they cross the border, but for those who are removed and their families this experience is lived continuously.[11] The absence left by the migrant's deportation and the ways in which this absence is construed and lived were the main issues this research proposed to address.

A theoretical framework was developed and a methodology devised as part of the research design. Emphasis was given to qualitative research techniques: the methods chosen included semi-structured interviews with deportees, their families and others involved; focus group discussions; life stories and courtroom ethnography. Defining the field, however, proved to be more challenging: How can one delimit the field when the population studied is not only geographically scattered but can hardly be described as a group, let alone a community? While it is obvious that people tend to empathise with others going through the same difficulties, this alone does not necessarily establish them as a group. How can one carry out field research in a setting where there is nothing immediately available to observe and no one identifiable to talk to?[12]

Taking guidance from Joanne Passaro's[13] work with homeless people in the USA, several strategies were devised to delimit and access the field. Hasselberg chose to engage as a volunteer in an NGO that works closely with foreign criminals and could thus give her an understanding of deportation from the perspective of an imprisoned migrant and, most importantly, act as a gatekeeper to potential research participants. The set of strategies also included a courtroom ethnography. The Asylum and Immigration Tribunal (AIT) is an instance of contestation where a foreign national can appeal his/her deportation, and hence a significant location where the experience of facing deportation is manifested. It was also a site where research participants could be identified and approached. Focus groups were another element in the research design, as by fostering discussion among participants, they

10 For the purposes of the deportation study, 'long-term migrant' refers to a foreign national who has resided in the UK for at least five years – the period of time the British Government considers necessary for a foreign national to have established an existence in the country, i.e. when s/he may apply for citizenship. For the diversity study, length of stay was not a primary concern; rather, the focus was on whether an individual had moved to London or Toronto.
11 Peutz 2006.
12 See Morgan 1997 and Hirvi, this volume, for an exploration of this question.
13 Passaro 1997.

could offer other insights and bring out issues that the researcher might not know to ask about.[14]

RESEARCHING URBAN DIVERSITY THROUGH NETWORKS

The second project we draw on aims to contribute to the academic debate on super-diversity in urban areas.[15] The study focuses on London and Toronto and sets out to evaluate super-diversity in these two cities by analyzing the ego-centric social networks of individuals who originate from a particular geographic area with relatively few co-migrants living in the same city. The questions at the heart of this research project are: What social contacts do migrants from such numerically small groups form after migration to a super-diverse city? Would the social contacts of the respondents turn out to be embedded in an ethnic network, or would their networks be as ethnically diverse as the city? Would the analysis of their contacts yield insights about other factors in the respondents' networks, such as the ages, employment backgrounds or migration trajectories of their friends? Assuming that the social contacts people maintain impact on how they experience and negotiate their everyday life, do these networks then also reflect how a person talks about her/his city and how diversity in that city is experienced?

Drawing on Brubaker's[16] notion of ethnicity without groups,[17] the specific 'group' approached for this research was loosely framed as people originating from the South Pacific, a cohort that in both London and Toronto was reported as having no more than 2000 individuals from one of the regional nationalities living in each city, with some nationalities accounting for less than 20 individuals.[18] The original research design was based on four methods, mixing quantitative and qualitative data collection. First, the study was to use participant observation to gain the trust of respondents and to better understand the 'setting' of diversity in both cities. Second, an online survey, also available in paper format, was designed to reach a larger cohort of respondents and, in the absence of detailed statistics, to get a better idea of the population composition of South Pacific people in London and Toronto. Third, Meissner planned to draw a sample of survey respondents to participate in an ego-centric network interview and finally to draw another subsample from this group for an even more in-depth live history interview.[19] The field was assumed to be the two cities in general, and the spaces within them that had significance for the respondents and for understanding 'diverse diversity'.

---

14 Atkinson 1998; Plummer 2001.
15 See Vertovec 2007.
16 Brubaker 2002.
17 While not necessarily adopting his constructivist standpoint, the project tried in this way to avoid prior assumptions about group membership.
18 See Finella 2006 for London and Statistics Canada 2007 for Toronto.
19 These were supposed to be focused life history interviews, with an emphasis on the migration and post-migration experience rather than being complete life history interviews.

The practicalities of 'doing it' – the logistics of being in the field

In the process of carrying out fieldwork, the premises of each of the studies and the strategies for conducting research had to be changed and re-appropriated as part of the interaction between informants and researchers. Both projects were designed as exploratory studies, leaving room to change the methods during data collection. This also meant significant changes to the notion of 'the field' each project engaged with. In the diversity study conducted by Meissner, these included fundamental shifts in the notion of who was included in the 'group' being studied and how the comparative objective of focusing on two field sites was conceptualised. Inserting herself as a complete outsider into pre-existing networks became in itself an important aspect of understanding how conviviality was practised and more intense social contacts maintained by the respondents. The shift in the study's focus was primarily due to difficulties in finding a sufficient number of respondents willing to participate in the relatively lengthy (two-hour minimum) ego-centric network interviews that the study relies on. This also meant that the more in-depth life-story interviews had to be amended into shorter semi-structured interviews and that the survey, rather than serving as a sample frame, had to be analyzed with attention to who participated and who did not. As a consequence, the notion of the 'small group' which underlies the research took on somewhat different meanings in the two cities. In London, Meissner could gain access to a large network of smaller groups – almost all the respondents who agreed to participate in the study are connected through their social networks, meaning that they know people who know other respondents. In contrast, in Toronto she was able to gain access to multiple small networks of people – meaning that the people from the different clusters of individuals who were interviewed did not know each other or have acquaintances through which they could contact other individuals from the other clusters. This meant that the self-understanding of being a small group was much more pronounced amongst the respondents in Toronto.

In the deportation project conducted by Hasselberg, applied field research meant that focus groups and life-story interviews were very difficult to put into practice. Similarly to the diversity project, it was found that the time commitment such interviews demanded was too much to ask from participants who were already giving so much of their time to the researcher. Focus groups proved unviable for two reasons. First, the homes of the participants were spread over the city, and it was extremely difficult to get enough people together at one time and in one location. Second, participants felt uneasy about the presence of others. Facing deportation is a long, tiring process and often by the time participants were interviewed they were no longer talking about their situation to anyone, including their spouses. Deportation had become a silent everyday presence in their lives. After many efforts, however, one focus group was set up. More than anything, it revealed how lonely deportation can be and the extent to which deportees are disenfranchised from debates about their situation. The difficulty in accessing participants was in fact a major obstacle throughout the fieldwork. In the end, the reluctance of gatekeepers to establish contact and of research participants to facilitate snowballing led Hasselberg to broaden the spectrum of sites where she worked as a volunteer in order to gain access, and to shift the primary focus of analysis away from examining how deportation impacts on those left behind towards the experience of deportability – issues that will be dealt with in more detail below.

Although these two projects differ substantially in their topics and theoretical interests, both serve as good examples of shifting notions of what constitutes the field under investigation and of how methods often have to be adjusted and creatively re-imagined in order to be practicable within the research context. Next, we reflect on the two themes that are most prevalent in the shifting idea of what constitutes the field under investigation: gaining access to respondents and finding locations to carry out the research. This allows us to examine specific instances that highlight how conducting research relates to constructions of the field.

Gaining access: on reluctant gatekeepers, tapping into networks and dead-end snowballing

The focus of the deportation study is a classic 'hidden population' because its respondents cannot be identified through any regularly available databases or agencies and because the circumstance of facing deportation is socially stigmatised.[20] The diversity study also deals with a population which in principle is difficult to sample owing to the relatively small number of potential respondents.[21] In more quantitative approaches to studying these types of difficult-to-access populations, various approaches are employed. However, most rely on the remuneration of respondents or on researchers building on previous research with similar populations.[22] In neither of these studies were such approaches possible. In the cities that served as field sites, no prior research on the same populations was available and both researchers had to gain access through creatively imagining their field and identifying access points. They considered finding gatekeepers and building trust and rapport to be the most effective means of gaining access.[23] As the following discussion will show, the difficulties in delimiting a field that was accessible to the researcher meant that the scope and focus had to be adjusted. This was not a one-off effort developed during the initial stages of field research: finding access points was a continuous process, which impacted greatly on the gathering and analysis of data and on the research project itself.[24]

20 See Singer 1999 and Atkinson & Flint 2001 on hidden populations.
21 Lepkowski 1991; Schensul 1999.
22 See Statistics Canada 2004 for a collection of essays on the topic.
23 Singer 1999; see also contributions in Smith & Kornblum 1996.
24 Burgess 1991; Hammersley & Atkinson 1995.

Literature on researching hidden and hard-to-reach populations tends to rely heavily on access via snowballing and gatekeepers.[25] However, this approach can be unsuccessful. For the deportation study, which was imagined as a qualitative anthropological study, gatekeepers were expected to play an important role in identifying respondents. The diversity project – based on a mixed-method approach and more concerned in its design with accessing as representative a sample as possible – developed the notion of its field by relying heavily on building networks of trust with an initial set of respondents, who then used chain referral. In this section, we discuss how these ideas about accessing gatekeepers and building trust and rapport did not yield the expected outcome and how this shifted the research focus and our perceptions of the field. What is emphasised is that a study always depends on the people a researcher is able to gain access to – a point that we will elaborate on in our conclusion.

The reluctant gatekeeper

Identifying and accessing informants was predictably a major challenge for the deportation project. Whereas Hasselberg expected to find people currently facing deportation at the AIT site, how could the families of those already deported be identified? They would already have been through the system, so locating them was fully dependent on gatekeepers such as NGO staff, legal practitioners and informants. Prior to fieldwork she had already established contact with an NGO working closely with foreign criminals. This NGO agreed to act as a gatekeeper and had even already identified possible informants. Hasselberg also engaged as a volunteer with this organization, which deepened the relationship and enhanced the trust between her and the NGO workers. Other civil rights groups were also contacted prior to field research. Further, she expected that conducting ethnographic field research at the AIT would facilitate encounters with law practitioners and other civil rights advocates who could eventually act as gatekeepers and thus diversify the sample.

As expected, the AIT did prove to be a site where many gatekeepers could be approached, in particular migration legal workers and migration advocates who work directly with deportees and thus have extensive contacts. They were excited about this research project, urging Hasselberg to share her findings with them as soon as possible – they hoped that they would be able use the findings in their advocacy of their clients.[26] All assured the researcher that they could put her in contact with several potential research

25 Atkinson & Flint 2001; Singer 1999.
26 Although, of course, findings were shared in informal conversations and written exchanges, what the case workers were looking for were written findings in the form of publications or a final thesis – documents that would be credible in court. For obvious reasons, at the time of the research, Ines Hasselberg was not able to provide these, although it is her intention to do so in the future.

participants. However, when it came to actually facilitating contact, these gatekeepers were surprisingly reluctant to do so. Altogether only three research participants were recruited through gatekeepers.

This unwillingness to establish contacts was not unique to gatekeepers. Hasselberg's own informants, whom she knew well after several meetings, were also reluctant to divulge contacts and facilitate snowballing. Perhaps more surprisingly, this same reluctance was also found among her friends and colleagues, who hearing about the project would volunteer the names of one or two acquaintances who would be 'perfect' for the project, but who in the end never did approach these individuals on her behalf.

Issues of trust are often cited as the reason for this reluctance.[27] After all, deportation is a very sensitive matter entailing questions of conviction, legal status and family relations. Moreover, the increasing securitisation of borders and criminalisation of migrants[28] may lead to higher levels of stigmatization,[29] exacerbating migrants' mistrust of strangers.[30] However, some people were actually close acquaintances of the researcher and trusted her judgment and work ethics. Trust (or the lack thereof) cannot in itself account for the disinclination to introduce people to the researcher after demonstrating such enthusiasm for her work. In the case of gatekeepers, the vulnerability of informants might better explain this reluctance. Most people participating in this project, whether deportees or those close to them, had been thoroughly interrogated several times, whether by the Home Office, solicitors, barristers or immigration judges. To put them in contact with the researcher was to submit them to another questioning session, having them retell their stories yet another time. This, understandably, may be too much to ask of an acquaintance, even a close one. When it comes to the informants' reluctance, and the consequent failure of the snowballing strategy, another issue might be added: it is possible that informants were afraid that the researcher would accidently leak information about their own cases to their acquaintances, despite her reassurances that their confidentiality would not be breached.[31]

Given the sensitive nature of the subject that the deportation project deals with, the difficulty in accessing and identifying informants was compounded by the suspicion that an outsider, like the researcher, faced when approaching gatekeepers. Although considerable efforts were put into building trust, this experience revealed how trust alone was not sufficient to motivate gatekeepers to facilitate contact with respondents. From this two interconnected consequences arose for the project. First, the need to identify additional field sites where informants could be accessed in person, a subject which is explored in the next section. Second, because access to the families of those already deported was totally dependent on gatekeepers, and the

27 Bilger & Van Liempt 2009; Burgess 1991; Singer 1999; Rossman & Rallis 1998.
28 Peutz & De Genova 2010.
29 Dahinden & Efionayi-Mader 2009.
30 Bilger & Van Liempt 2009.
31 Jacobsen & Landau 2003.

gatekeepers failed to act as such, Hasselberg focused her efforts mainly on those informants she could identify and contact, i.e. those facing deportation at the time of research. Consequently, at the early stages of fieldwork, the project solidified around the experience of facing deportation, moving away from the initial focus on absence and post-deportation experiences. This is not to say that the absence of deportees no longer forms part of this project – it does, in more ways than one – but rather the primary focus shifted from absence to deportability.

Weaving Diverse Waves – Diversifying the Sample, Gatekeepers and Networks

Although Meissner's project did focus on a more conventional 'group', which in principle could be sampled on the basis of official census data, it was not possible to gain access to a sampling frame because of the numerical size of the national sub-groups and applicable data protection regulations. Instead, she opted to try to diversify her sample by identifying as many entry points to the proposed population of study as possible. Drawing on insights from snowball[32] and network sampling[33] as well as from respondent-driven sampling,[34] the intention was to recruit as many different individuals as possible to be initial respondents (seeds) and through snowballing achieve a sizable number of respondent waves – interviewees who were identified by respondents already interviewed; in other words, people identified by the initial respondents would be the first wave, respondents identified by first-wave informants would be the second wave, and so on. It was hoped that by conducting interviews with sufficient waves of respondents, the study would gain reliability, based on the argument that the sample characteristics eventually approximate the population characteristics.[35] The population was broadly defined as people originating from the South Pacific Islands now living in London or Toronto. This intention was hampered in both these cities, albeit by two very different factors, which are discussed next. Similarly to the deportation project, Meissner with her diversity project, opted to use participant observation not only as a tool for data accumulation but primarily to gain the trust of respondents.[36] In both London and Toronto, through pre-fieldwork internet research, different groups and individuals were identified as potential gatekeepers.

Upon arrival in London, Meissner tried to follow up every lead to sites where she might be able to meet potential respondents. In her emails to gatekeepers, she stressed her wish to speak to 'Polynesians' living in London, which was one of the many identifiers used for her research population. To

---

32 Goodman 1961.
33 Granovetter 1976.
34 Heckathorn 1997; Volz & Heckathorn 2008.
35 Volz & Heckathorn 2008.
36 Hammersley & Atkinson 1995.

her surprise, one gatekeeper urged her to participate in a regularly held New Zealand Māori group, which eventually led her to include NZ Māoris as part of her sample. By nationality, most NZ Māoris are New Zealanders, and at the time of the 2001 census there were close to 30,000 New Zealanders living in London[37] – a criterion not complying with the notion that these migrants are from a numerically small group. There is some uncertainty as to how many NZ Māoris live in London but, based on information from within the group, including NZ Māoris in the study as a small(ish) sub-group seemed viable.[38] This inclusion was also motivated by slow progress in contacting other Pacific Islanders living in London. The point here, however, is that this inclusion is in line with the notion that groupness should not be a pre-prescribed idea but should emerge from the field research.[39]

During sustained participation in gatherings of NZ Māoris and Pacific Islanders, Meissner established trust and rapport by demonstrating a strong commitment to her project and her potential respondents. Many of her informants identified this commitment as an important motivator in their decision to talk to her. It is clear that the researcher's continued dedication is what led to the willingness of some potential respondents (but not of all those approached) to participate in the survey and the ego-centric interviews. Ego-centric network interviews are a type of interview that is relatively time-consuming and requires respondents not only to answer questions about themselves but also about the people they know. However, even though Meissner was participating in multiple groups, only the NZ Māoris and one other Pacific Island dance group were meeting regularly enough to validate the relevance of continued commitment and trust-building as a necessary precondition for interviews. Overall, 24 respondents were identified through groups that met regularly (16) and other related events (8).

When Meissner tried to snowball from these initial seeds, the interviewees became gatekeepers. They were asked to provide her with names and contact details for, or to at least facilitate contact with, other potential respondents. The hoped-for number of contacts per respondent was not achieved, and many respondents generated only one or two contacts. Other than a reluctance to divulge contact details, this low rate was due to a single somewhat unexpected reason: many of the potential contacts named were individuals whom the researcher had either already interviewed or approached for an interview.

---

37 Macintosh 2005.

38 During her early fieldwork, Meissner talked to different participants in this group to establish the number of Māoris living in London. The estimates given ranged from 300 to a few thousand. After further reviewing the statistics and combining the percentage of self-identifying Māoris living in New Zealand (Source: Statistics New Zealand) with the number of New Zealanders living in London (Source: Macintosh 2006), Meissner now estimates the number of Māoris in London at approximately 4000. However, there are obvious problems with this crude oversimplified approximation which will be addressed in more detail in her PhD dissertation.

39 Brubaker 2002; Wimmer 2008.

Of those potential respondents who were identified by seeds, ten actually agreed to participate, and only one individual can be counted as a second-wave respondent, not a sufficient number of waves to argue for the sample representativeness of the data based on the number of waves. By contrast, in Toronto, it was not possible to access respondents via an established network of different groups or at public events, and the researcher once again had to adapt her strategy for the second field site.

Internet research and contacts made through different social networking sites allowed the researcher to tap into four almost distinct networks of people that could roughly be delineated along country-of-origin lines – Tongans, Samoans, Fijians and NZ Māoris. There were few individuals who knew people from more than one of these small networks, and for a number of respondents participation in the project was motivated by the possibility that the researcher would facilitate contact with other Pacific Islanders living in Toronto. This fragmentation of the population under study meant that Meissner faced similar problems in Toronto to those experienced by Hasselberg with the deportation project in London. How is it possible to carry out participant observation and gain trust if there is nothing readily identifiable to observe or participate in? The disjuncture between the availability of field sites for participation in one research location and their absence from the second location will be discussed in the next section. For gaining access to respondents through networks, this meant that although seeds came from different sources and were generally able to put Meissner in contact with other respondents, the expected number of waves was not generated because the contacts provided for the second wave had already been pointed out by the seeds. This was compounded by the fact that within the research population living in Toronto there were many individuals who decided not to participate in the research, an issue that Clara Sacchetti in this volume reflects on critically from a feminist perspective.[40] Ultimately, this meant that in Toronto, as in London, the sample of respondents recruited was far below the number originally hoped for. In total 22 ego-centric network interviews were conducted in Toronto, and 36 in London. The implication for 'the field' of this study was that more emphasis was given to participant observation. This entailed a stronger engagement with the question of what it means 'to be from the South Pacific' in London and Toronto although the intention of the study was to move clearly beyond an ethno-focal understanding of diversity.

In both case studies, gatekeepers and snowballing were of limited use, and, as has been illustrated, this 'setback' had consequences for the development of the field in each project. What these experiences do show in a roundabout way is that gaining access is, in practice, a two-way process: it builds on the efforts of the researcher in recruiting respondents but also on the respondents' willingness and drive to participate in the project. This was illustrated in both projects through the use of communication technology.

---

40 Sacchetti, this volume.

Both researchers set up research websites designed to inform and 'recruit' respondents,[41] but, as Saara Koikkalainen aptly demonstrates in this volume, these virtual presences also form part of the field the researcher negotiates. Hasselberg was able to recruit two respondents in this way, and although Meissner was not able to directly recruit respondents via her website, she found it beneficial to point to her website as a form of validation of her research and to inform respondents who otherwise might have not been interested in participating. We further develop this point in the conclusion, and in the next section discuss how the locations where research takes place assume particular importance in delimiting the epistemologically construed field. Here we want to reflect on the question of what to do when the research population is hidden and/or scattered *and* gatekeepers and snowballing fail to grant the scope of access needed. We conclude by reflecting on the theoretical and practical implications for migration research.

Locating location

As we have seen in the case studies presented here, a reluctance to identify others in precarious situations and the different dimensions of networks in two field sites are two ways in which gaining access to a research population can alter how research questions are investigated. In fact, a number of recent studies with migrants from hard-to-reach populations admit to failed snowballing.[42] It is thus surprising how little is written on alternative approaches to accessing research populations.[43]

Drawing on Amit, the question in this case has to be: 'Where do we "hang out" when the processes which we are studying produce common social conditions or statuses [...] but not necessarily coterminous collectivities?'[44] One possibility is for the researcher to carry out research in locations that the research population is expected to frequent at one point or another.[45] This site-oriented approach, eventually used by the authors of this paper, is a common option.[46] However, its success is not guaranteed, as the Toronto experience of the diversity project shows. Furthermore, one criticism of seeking out 'likely' locations concerns the potential bias created by who is not in the chosen locations, those potential respondents who remain on the margins and thus are not captured by the research.[47] Additionally, it has been argued that research locations are spaces of differential power relations

---

41 Hasselberg: http://www.sussex.ac.uk/Users/iah20/; Meissner: http://www.sussex. ac.uk/Users/fm77/theresearch.html.
42 Bilger & Van Liempt 2009; Staring 2009.
43 See e.g. Duncan et al. 2003 on the use of internet based surveys; and Singer 1999 and Staring 2009 on the site-oriented approach.
44 Amit 2000, 15.
45 Singer 1999.
46 See also Passaro 1997; Staring 2009; Empez 2009.
47 Wimmer, 2008; Singer 1999; Staring 2009.

not only among potential respondents and between the respondent and the researcher but also between the respondent, the researcher and any third parties.[48] The locations where research is conducted in a spatially 'unbound' research project thus become an important theoretical concern. Nonetheless, fieldwork practice translates into the imperative that the researcher has to go somewhere, a physical or cyber location, to talk to someone. It follows then that the researcher always has to make a decision on which localities and instances are part of the field, so that identifying and accessing such locations may present further challenges and lead to changes in the delineation of the field, as we show below.

On expanding and diversifying research locations

Passaro's experience became even more valuable as a guide for the deportation project when Hasselberg needed to seek additional sites for research. Passaro, as an anthropologist, felt compelled to create her own 'homeless village' where participant observation was possible. Instead, however, she opted in her own words, '...to choose sites that would afford me positionalities at varying points along a participant-observer continuum'.[49] Adopting flexible and creative ethnographic approaches, Passaro volunteered for, and got involved in, a series of different campaigns and organizations that allowed her to study homelessness from different perspectives.

With Passaro's experience in mind, Hasselberg a few months into her fieldwork realised that she could not rely on gatekeepers or snowballing and devised other strategies in order to increase her direct access to informants. Direct access would mean focusing more on those people currently facing deportation and on their families and less on the families of those who had already been deported, since the latter do not go to specific locations in their role as family members of deportees, thus making it impossible to locate them without gatekeepers. The researcher then had to spend more time at sites that possible informants were bound to frequent – sites that Barthia calls the theatres of state power over migrants' bodies:[50] the AIT, prisons, and detention and reporting centres.[51] The AIT is a tribunal that is open

48 Gupta and Ferguson 1997, 35–36.
49 Passaro 1997, 156.
50 Barthia 2010.
51 Broadly speaking, in the UK, a foreign national with leave to remain is deportable if convicted to a sentence of 12 months or longer. Upon serving the sentence, the immigration services might detain the migrant in an Immigration Removal Centre (mostly known as detention centres) while his or her deportation file is processed. The migrant may apply at the AIT for bail, which may be granted under certain conditions. Reporting to the Home Office (at designated reporting centres) monthly or weekly is usually part of the bail conditions. These conditions remain in force until the migrant is either detained again for removal or has his deportation appeal at the AIT granted. Thus prisons, detention centres, reporting centres and the AIT are all locations where one is likely to find someone facing deportation.

to the public, which made it possible to conduct research there. In fact, the majority of research participants were first approached there. Additionally, it proved to be a site where rich observation data were obtained. Other facilities, however, have restricted access. Access to reporting centres is limited to those reporting and their legal representatives, but because the queues and the time spent waiting in them are long, the researcher was able to 'hang out' by the entrance door and observe migrants queuing to report, occasionally chatting with them. Although only two were interviewed for the project, the one-off informal chats with many other migrants at this location were very informative.

Permission to conduct research in detention centres and prisons may be granted, but the process is long and the time allocated for field research is limited. The researcher was, however, able to access migrants in detention centres and prisons by working as a volunteer in different organizations. This meant that she did not go to these sites in her capacity as a researcher but rather as a volunteer. Her conversations with prisoners and detainees were determined by what they wanted to talk about. The research agenda was never pursued, and no informants were recruited during these visits. All the same, valuable information that informed the research was obtained even if it was not directly used in it. Volunteer work with detainees and prisoners thus resulted in unusable data – the people she visited, their stories, hopes and concerns are not part of the data used to support the arguments presented in the final work. Nevertheless, as a volunteer the researcher was able to gain a better understanding of the experience of deportability and this allowed her to better formulate questions to her informants about the role of prison and detention in their experience of deportation – questions that the researcher would not have asked without this experience.[52]

Accessing people in these theatres of state power can be very intimidating. People are often very distressed and suspicious of official presence, and this lowers the participation rate. In order to counterbalance this and to diversify the sample, the researcher volunteered to work with two other organizations that provide services (legal advice, benefits advice, etc.) and support for migrants. Neither organisation had a state or official presence, and each offered a very welcoming and relaxed setting. Here the researcher was able to interact with people who, although still facing deportation, were no longer in the appeals process or under any official form of surveillance such as reporting.

Although initial contact with informants was established at these institutions (prisons and detention centres were excluded), interviews were always carried out at places designated by the respondents: their homes, the gym, a quiet café, the park and so on. These locations where informants felt comfortable formed part of their daily lives and gave the researcher a further

---

52 This is by no means infringes the rights of the inmates she visited in prison and detention or compromised her work as a volunteer, which she took very seriously. The assumption of different roles in research has important ethical implications, which were considered by Hasselberg in conducting her research.

insight into how deportability is experienced. Overall, by expanding and diversifying the research sites and her positionalities, the researcher gained an understanding of deportability from different perspectives and was able to obtain the necessary data to pursue the project.

From locating a group to location as context

As the case of the deportation study demonstrates, the locations where research is conducted remain a significant part of what constitutes the field. In Meissner's diversity study, research locations also played an important role in how the scope and focus of the research was realised. She based much of her pre-fieldwork considerations of which locations to use on ongoing discussions in ethnic and migration studies scrutinising the pitfalls and assumptions that research with migrant groups has to address.[53] She strove to avoid these by focusing her research on the social networks of individuals rather than predefining a complete network of people from the South Pacific. Even so, when push came to shove, potential respondents had to be identified somehow, and the researcher had to establish 'likely' locations where informants could be contacted. Although the researcher tried to avoid prior assumptions about how the migrants to be interviewed might congregate in the same places, the majority of research locations were in some way associated with her respondents' migration background. This was despite the intention to use the research process to reveal more general locations where social interaction took place.

This ethnic framing of locations aside, the different accessibility of observable social interactions in the two cities had an unforeseen outcome. In principle, replicating the methods used in London was supposed to produce a directly comparable field in Toronto.[54] However, even though the interview questions stayed the same, the locations did not. In London, following a slow start, Meissner was faced with an 'overload' of possible research locations, primarily at festivities and dance group performances after including NZ Māori and NZ-born Pacific Islanders in her research. In Toronto, she was only told about smaller-scale events that primarily included family members and close friends. Thus in London participant observation at larger public events was a regular occurrence and took up approximately as much time as actually setting up and conducting the ego-centric and semi-structured interviews. In Toronto much more field data derived from setting up and conducting interviews. Attending 'likely' field sites, on the other hand, was not conducive to establishing contact with potential respondents. Consequently, in the diversity project, 'recreating' the London field in Toronto in order to produce comparable data was not

---

53 Brubaker 2002; Wimmer 2008; Glick Schiller & Caglar 2009.
54 After other obvious differences between the two cities had been taken into consideration.

feasible, and the research locations in the two cities differed substantially, as did the roles Meissner had to assume in them.

To give one example of this, it is helpful to reflect on the physical accessibility of field locations. In London, research locations were mainly centrally located.[55] In Toronto, the 'events' that the researcher could attend primarily took place in people's private houses, which barring those of three respondents, were located at least a one-hour journey from the city centre. In addition, the respondents in Toronto were dispersed across different suburban areas. Relying on public transport to get to field locations was not always feasible, and the researcher frequently had to rely on respondents to pick her up by car from the nearest bus stop or subway station. This had important implications for the respondent-researcher relationship. 'Being given a lift' became an opportunity to turn the ride into a field location, where more informal discussions with the respondents were possible and in the best cases trust and rapport could be developed.

Thus, similarly to the deportation project field, the locations had to be identified as such. They had to be sought out and tested for their usefulness in providing insights that would help answer the research questions. The two-sitedness of the diversity project made this especially important as the focus of the post-fieldwork analysis had to be shifted towards contrasting rather than comparing the two field sites. What can be clearly seen in these two case studies is the importance of not taking the locations of field research for granted. Even when a specific location appears to be particularly good for accessing respondents, other factors may lead the researcher to discard them as field locations. Meissner, for instance, when faced with the choice of two simultaneously occurring field opportunities often discovered *post factum* that the one she did not attend would have yielded access to a larger number of potential respondents than the one she did attend. Hasselberg, to give another example, chose not to approach detainee's families who were waiting to visit their loved ones at the detention centre because of the ethical implications of approaching them in a small waiting room where others could hear her conversations with these potential informants. Research locations may have to be changed or simply expanded, according to the challenges and opportunities encountered during fieldwork. Locations are thus a crucial element in the reflexive process of conducting fieldwork, impacting greatly on what constitutes the field.

Conclusion

In the introduction to this paper, we stated that the field always remains malleable, and through our two case studies we have shown how this malleability is part and parcel of the research process. It was also pointed out

55 This was despite the fact that some respondents also lived further out of town. Meissner generally only went to the less central areas of Greater London for interviews and some rare events that were held in these more residential areas.

in the introduction that studying migration-related social phenomena should not be seen as exceptional, but that in exploring fieldwork practice migration can best be understood as a specific lens that allows for critical reflections on how the field of a research project is defined. We thus have purposely not pointed to specific instances in which it mattered that our respondents moved from one country to another at some point(s) in their lives. This is done appositely in this issue by Wendy Voigt, who explores the challenge of focusing research on transient and mobile people. Further, Deirdre Meintel and Géraldine Mossière, also in this volume, discuss how studying migrants brings with it specific inter-subjectivities that impact on the possibility and scope of participant observation. Here, we have instead opted to mix and mingle methodological literature with migration literature to present two fieldwork narratives that help to foreground how the field is developed during fieldwork. We have argued throughout that although the conception of the field as a geographically bounded space has long been considered obsolete, researchers planning and designing their studies nonetheless have expectations about what their field will be and how fieldwork methods can help them to answer their research questions. Despite these ideas, the field, as an epistemologically informed concept, rarely coincides with the field the researcher then has to negotiate in praxis.

In this paper, we have used two research projects, one focusing on deportation from the UK and one focusing on super-diversity in urban areas, to show how this imbalance between the idea of the field and its day-to-day manifestations interact. We have focused on issues of gaining access to respondents and on identifying locations in which fieldwork could be carried out. This discussion showed that one of the main challenges in conducting ethnographic research on elusive and scattered populations is the difficulty of identifying and accessing informants.[56] As has been demonstrated, the field is largely determined by whom the researcher is able to talk to or to observe and otherwise engage with. This shows that the question of who decides to participate is an important aspect of how the field emerges from the research – an issue also discussed critically in Clara Sacchetti's paper in this volume.

Furthermore, we can identify two aspects that introduce bias in trying to diversify the different perspectives the researcher needs in order to better understand the social complexities being studied. One concerns the aptitude of certain respondents to part take in the research, an aspect that has been discussed only marginally in the literature.[57] We recognise that this aptitude is also dependent on the topic of the research and the available resources to recruit respondents but want to argue that additionally different individuals have different levels of willingness to partake in research out of their own volition. As our discussion of the question of trust and response rates has shown, this aptitude of some people to participate over that of others is an important aspect of sample selectivity. In addition to querying who are the

---

56 See also Hirvi in this volume.
57 Bilger & Van Liempt 2009 and Staring 2009 are good exceptions.

non-participants, researchers should therefore also ask who the individuals that do participate in the research are? In concluding this paper we want to emphasise this by asking: Why do some people help researchers by giving their time and others do not? The answer to this question has to be recognised as an important factor in the shaping of the field.

The second point, as we discussed, concerns locations as research sites that are found but at the same time also chosen. They frame the research not only through their accessibility but also through their visibility to the researcher. By arguing that access to respondents is a multi-way process, we recognise that this is also the case with locations and their accessibility to the researcher. This is another aspect that merits further investigation. Overall, we conclude that being open about the things that 'go wrong' in the field makes understanding the research process clearer and has to be understood as part and parcel of the complexity of the social relations that are the basis of field research and how we conceive of 'the field'.

Bibliography

Amit, V. 2000: *Constructing the Field: Ethnographic Fieldwork in the Contemporary World*. London: Routledge.

Appadurai, A. 1996: *Modernity at Large Cultural Dimensions of Globalization*. Minneapolis: University of Minnesota Press.

Atkinson, R. 1998: *The Life Story Interview*. London: Sage Publications.

Atkinson, R. & J. Flint 2001: Accessing Hidden and Hard-to-Reach Populations: Snowball Research Strategies. *Social Research Update*, 33.

Basch, L. G., N. G. Schiller & C. Szanton Blanc 1994: *Nations Unbound: Transnational Projects, Postcolonial Predicaments, and Deterritorialized Nation-States*. Amsterdam: Gordon and Breach.

Bhartia, A. 2010: Fictions of Law: The Trial of Sulaiman Oladokun, or Reading Kafka in an Immigration Court. In: N. De Genova & N. Peutz, (eds.), *The Deportation Regime: Sovereignty, State and the Freedom of Movement*. London: Duke University Press.

Bilger, V. & I. Van Liempt 2009: Methodological and Ethical Dilemmas in Research among Smuggled Migrants. In: I. Van Liempt & V. Bilger (eds.), *The Ethics of Migration Research Methodology: Dealing with Vulnerable Immigrants*. Brighton: Sussex Academic Press.

Brubaker, R. 2002: Ethnicity without Groups. *Archives European Sociology* XLIII: 2, 163–189.

Burgess, R. 1991: Sponsors, Gatekeepers, Members and Friends. In: Shaffir, W. B. and A. S. R. (eds.), *Experiencing Fieldwork: An Inside View of Qualitative Research*. London: Sage.

Coleman, S. & P. Collins 2006: *Locating the Field: Space, Place and Context in Anthropology*. Oxford: Berg.

Cook, J., J. Laidlaw & J. Mair 2009: 'What if There is no Elephant? Towards a Conception of an Un-sited Field'. In: M. A. Falzon (ed.), *Multi-Sited Ethnography - Theory, Praxis and Locality in Contemporary Research*. Franham: Ashgate.

Couper, K. & U. Santamaria 1984: An Elusive Concept: The Changing Definition of Illegal Immigrant in the Practice of Immigration Control in the United Kingdom. *International Migration Review*, 18: 3, 437–52.

Dahinden, J. & D. Efionayi-Mader 2009: Challenges and Strategies in Empirical Fieldwork with Asylum Seekers and Migrant Sex Workers. In: I. Van Liempt & V. Bilger (eds.), *The Ethics of Migrant Research Methodology: Dealing with Vulnerable Immigrants*. Brighton: Sussex Academic Press.

Duncan, D. F., J. B. White & T. Nicholson 2003: Using internet-based surveys to reach hidden populations: Case of non-abusive illicit drug users. *American Journal of Health Behaviour*, 27: 3, 208–218.

Empez, N. 2009: The fieldworker as a social worker: dilemmas in research with Moroccan unaccompanied minors. In: I. Van Liempt & V. Bilger (eds.), *The Ethics of Migrant Research Methodology: Dealing with Vulnerable Immigrants*. Brighton: Sussex Academic Press.

Falzon, M. 2009: *Multi-Sited Ethnography: Theory, Praxis and Locality in Contemporary Research*. Farnham: Ashgate Publishing.

Goodman, L. A. 1961: Snowball Sampling. *The Annals of Mathematical Statistics* 32: 148–170.

Granovetter, M. 1976: Network Sampling: Some First Steps. *American Journal of Sociology* 81: 6, 1287–1303.

Gupta, A. & J. Ferguson 1992: Beyond "Culture": Space, Identity, and the Politics of Difference. *Cultural Anthropology*, 7: 1, 6–23.

Gupta, A. & J. Ferguson 1997: Discipline and Practice: 'The Field' as Site, Method and Location in Anthropology. In: A. Gupta & J. Ferguson (eds.), *Anthropological Locations: Boundaries and Grounds of a Field Science*. Berkeley: University of California Press.

Hammersley, M. & P. Atkinson 1995: *Ethnography: Principles in Practice*. London: Routledge.

Hannerz, U. 1996: *Transnational Connections: Culture, People, Places*. London: Routledge.

Heckathorn, D. D. 1997: Respondent-Driven Sampling: A New Approach to the Study of Hidden Populations. *Social Problems*, 44: 2, 174–199.

Holmes, D. R. & G. E. Marcus 2005: 'Refunctioning Ethnography: The Challenge of an Anthropology of the Contemporary'. In: N. K. Denzin & Y. S. Lincoln (eds.), *The Sage Handbook of Qualitative Research (Vol. 3)*. London: Sage.

Jacobsen, K. & L. B. Landau 2003: The Dual Imperative in Refugee Research: Some Methodological and Ethical Considerations in Social Science Research on Forced Migration. *Disasters*, 27: 3, 185–296.

Lepkowski, J. M. 1991: Sampling the Difficult-to-Sample. *The Journal of Nutrition*, 121: 3, 416–423.

Mackintosh, M. 2005: London: The World in One City. *Data Management and Analysis Group*. London: Greater London Authority.

Malkki, L. 1997: News and Culture: Transitory Phenomena and the Fieldwork Tradition. In: A. Gupta & J. Ferguson (eds.), *Anthropological Locations: Boundaries and Grounds of a Field Science*. Berkeley: University of California Press.

Marcus, G. E. 1995: 'Ethnography in/of the World System: The Emergence of Multi-Sited Ethnography'. *Annual Review of Anthropology*, 24: 95–117.

Maxwell, J. A. 2005: *Qualitative Research Design: An Interactive Approach*. London: Sage Publications.

Morgan, D. L. 1997: *Focus Groups as Qualitative Research*. Thousand Oaks: Sage.

Passaro, J. 1997: 'You Can't Take the Subway to the Field!': 'Village' Epistemologies in the Global Village. In: A. Gupta & J. Ferguson (eds.), *Anthropological Locations: Boundaries and Grounds of a Field Science*. Berkeley: University of California Press.

Peutz, N. 2006: Embarking on an Anthropology of Removal. *Current Anthropology*, 47: 2, 217–41.

Peutz, N. & N. De Genova 2010: Introduction. In: N. De Genova & N. Peutz (eds.), *The Deportation Regime: Sovereignty, State and the Freedom of Movement*. Durham: Duke University Press: 1–29.

Plummer, K. 2001: *Documents of Life 2: An invitation to a Critical Humanism*. London: Sage Publications.

Portes, A., L. E. Guarnizo & P. Landolt 1999: The Study of Transnationalism: Pitfalls and Promise of an Emergent Research Field. *Ethnic and Racial Studies*, 22: 2, 217–37.

Rossman, G. B. &. S. F. Rallis 1998: *Learning in the Field: An Introduction to Qualitative Research*. London: Sage Publications.

Schensul, J. J. 1999: Mapping social networks, spatial data, and hidden populations. In: J. Schensul & M. J. LeCompte (eds.), *Book 4 of the Ethnographer's Toolkit*. New York: Altamira Press.

Schiller, N. G. & A. Çağlar 2009: Towards a Comparative Theory of Locality in Migration Studies: Migrant Incorporation and City Scale. *Journal of Ethnic and Migration Studies*, 35: 2, 177–202.

Singer, M. 1999: Studying Hidden Populations: Mapping Social Networks, Spatial Data and Hidden Populations. In: J. Schensul. & M. J. LeCompte (eds.), *Book 4 of the Ethnographer's Toolkit*. New York: Altamira Press.

Smith, C. D. & W. Kornblum 1996: *In the Field: Readings on the Field Research Experience*. London: Praeger.

Staring, R. 2009: Different methods to research irregular migration. In: I. Van Liempt & V. Bilger (eds), *The Ethics of Migrant Research Methodology: Dealing with Vulnerable Immigrants*. Brighton: Sussex Academic Press.

Statistics Canada 2004: *Symposium 2004 – Innovative Methods for Surveying Difficult-to-reach Populations*, http://www.statcan.gc.ca/pub/11-522-x/11-522-x2004001-eng.htm. Accessed 10 January 2011.

Statistics Canada 2007: 'Detailed Country of Citizenship (203), Single and Multiple Citizenship Responses (3), Immigrant Status (4A) and Sex (3) for the Population of Canada, Provinces, Territories, Census Metropolitan Areas and Census Agglomerations, 2006 Census – 20% Sample Data. *2006 Census of Population*. Ottawa: Statistics Canada.

Statistics New Zealand 2011: Ethnic groups in New Zealand. *QuickStats About Culture and Identity*, http://www.stats.govt.nz/Census/2006CensusHomePage/QuickStats/quickstats-about-a-subject/culture-and-identity/ethnic-groups-in-new-zealand.aspx. Accessed Febuary 11 2010.

Van Hear, N. 2010: Theories of Migration and Social Change. *Journal of Ethnic and Migration Studies*, 36: 10, 1531–1536.

Vertovec, S. 2007: Super-diversity and its implications. *Ethnic and Racial Studies*, 30: 6, 1024–1054.

Volz, E. & D. D. Heckathorn 2008: Probability Based Estimation Theory for Respondent Driven Sampling. *Journal of Official Statistics*, 24: 1, 79–97.

Wimmer, A. 2008: Elementary strategies of ethnic boundary making. *Ethnic and Racial Studies*, 31: 6, 1025–1055.

Wimmer, A. 2009: Herder's Heritage and the Boundary-Making Approach: Studying Ethnicity in Immigrant Societies, *Sociological Theory*, 27: 3, 244–270.

Wimmer, A. & N. Glick Schiller 2002: Methodological nationalism and beyond: nation–state building, migration and the social sciences. *Global Networks*, 2: 4, 301–334.

CREATING COMMUNITIES

LISA WIKLUND

Creative Cosmopolitanism
New Fields of Work Require New Fieldwork

It has sometimes been said that the true symbols of modernity were those cities that were on the verge of turning from national capitals into international metropolises. In those vibrant, pulsating locations, the essence of modernity has been seen as something that could be found in the here and now – modernity was to be lived in every passing moment. Perhaps even more importantly, these crowded settings seemed to come with the promise that modernity would also be observed, and in one way or another communicated, by a vigilant, attentive and freshly urbanized human mind.[1] The French poet, writer and critic Charles Baudelaire found the best interpreters of modernity among the artists. In his essay *The Painter of Modern Life,* he salutes the artist Constantin Guys. Guys has not been particularly celebrated as an artist either in his own time or today – in fact he is probably best known for the connection with Baudelaire. However, Baudelaire found him like no-one else capable of capturing big city life through his rapidly executed charcoal-on-paper drawings. 'In trivial life, in the daily metamorphosis of external things, there is a rapidity of movement which calls for an equal speed of execution from the artist,' Baudelaire states.[2]

The urban scenes of postmodern life, much like the classical settings of modernity, have certainly not been without their interpreters. Sometimes, however, they have taken on a less optimistic perspective. In his essay *America,* the French sociologist and philosopher Jean Baudrillard finds New York to be 'the city that is heir to all other cities at once', in many ways barbaric and primitive – entirely without the long cultural history that he perceives in European capitals. Baudrillard shares with the reader his annoyance with phenomena such as breakdance, graffiti and even the New York Marathon, all of which he experiences as empty performances with one single aim: to demonstrate mere existence. 'Why do people live in New York?' is his

---

1 See Holm 2005.
2 Baudelaire 1995, 4.

rhetorical question, to which he gives the blunt response: 'There are millions of people in the streets, wandering, carefree, violent, as if they had nothing better to do – and doubtless they have nothing else to do – than produce the permanent scenario of the city'. Turning his spleen on graffiti ('They simply say: I'm so-and-so and I exist!') and breakdance ('You might say that in curling up and spiralling around on the ground like this, they seem to be digging a hole for themselves within their own bodies'), Baudrillard is clearly not enchanted with the artistic utterances so often worshipped and celebrated as vital elements of cosmopolitan life.

Baudrillard's record of a city where 'no-one looks at you, caught up as they all are in their passionate efforts to carry off their own impersonal roles'[3] to some extent illustrates the methodological challenges to urban ethnography that this chapter will focus on, albeit hopefully in a rather less rebarbative manner. Having said this, I will now introduce what is to be examined here: the contemporary organization of artistic expression as labour. There are numerous methodological considerations to be taken into account in researching how the young people of my study organize their work life. This chapter will examine how the rather ephemeral structures by means of which work and life are managed can be captured ethnographically. It can be considered an exploration of the ethnographer's potential for being what Baudelaire found Constantin Guys to be – a sharp-eyed and alert interpreter of fast-moving, fleeting urban life. How everyday life with its 'rapidity of movement' calls for 'an equal speed of execution from the artist' is transferable, I will argue, to how the ethnographer is required to change some of her/his techniques so as to sometimes resemble the art of drawing rapid charcoal lines on paper – in both cases, the challenge is to ensure that the subject itself is still captured in all its rich detail.

I will begin by presenting the main premises of my argument in this chapter, which claims that a globalized world is contributing to changing the conditions for ethnographic fieldwork. Then I will present the background to my particular field, followed by reflections on how the specific characteristics of ethnographic research can be regarded as going through changes. I will then discuss the implications of multi-sited fieldwork with regard to both the informant's influence and the researcher's role in creating the field. I will conclude by discussing how geographical decisions still have an impact on the research produced.

The implications of globalization for fieldwork

The field of labour has been changing along with new conditions for work and employment. This, to a great extent, is connected with changes in the global economy and the ways in which companies are rearranging and adjusting to these changes, a trend that has been widely debated and

---

3 Baudrillard1988, 19–21.

discussed in recent years.[4] How do these changing conditions for labour in a global or cosmopolitan setting imply changing conditions for ethnographic fieldwork?

My research focuses on the conditions for work and life in what could be described as a creative cosmopolitan environment. I have conducted my fieldwork primarily in the neighbourhood of Williamsburg in Brooklyn, New York, investigating how young people from different parts of the world come together to work in a creative environment, taking freelance jobs in fashion, music, art, photography, etc. My research centres especially on young Japanese people working in this environment. My approach highlights the encounter between new ways of organizing labour and a far more traditional field of labour, in this case the hierarchical Japanese career ladder, which is still strongly founded on life-long company employment. A similar conflict is manifested in the fact that Williamsburg, a traditional immigrant neighbourhood, is now dealing with a totally different type of work immigration, one that is in some respects the opposite of the traditional type in that it is entirely voluntary and undertaken by people from relatively privileged social backgrounds who deliberately choose a lifestyle with much lower material standards and even self-imposed poverty.

It is not possible to use the concept of cosmopolitanism without reference to the debate about globalization. The word 'cosmopolitanism' has a longer history than the word 'globalization', but the two concepts are intimately linked and to some extent describe the same phenomena; indeed, sometimes the words are used more or less synonymously.[5] The process of globalization thus holds a central position in my investigation and therefore needs to be examined more closely in this context. It is nowadays rare for the term 'globalization' to be used without reservations. Ulrich Beck has dubbed the concept 'the most used, abused, most often defined, probably the most distorted, fuzzy and politically effective slogan in recent years'.[6] Zygmunt Bauman has described it as 'a buzzword that quickly turned into a slogan, a magical incantation, a password to open the gates to all present and future mysteries'.[7] It has also been claimed that the word was barely used, even in the academic world, before 1980 but that it is now no longer possible to open a newspaper without seeing it.[8] As a result of the fatigue caused by its overuse, it has occasionally been ironically referred to as 'the g-word'.[9]

Globalization theory is a central part of postmodernist theory, itself a system of ideas that has not gone unquestioned. Primarily, the debate has

---

4   See e.g. Beck 2000; Florida 2002; Sennett 2006.
5   For a detailed discussion and an historical context to the concept of cosmopolitanism, see e.g. Breckenridge, Pollock, Bhabha & Chakrabarty (eds.) 2002; Fine 2007. The relation between cosmopolitanism and globalization is further discussed in my dissertation, Wiklund forthcoming.
6   Beck 2000.
7   Bauman 2000.
8   Eriksen 2007, 1; Giddens 2000.
9   Beck 2000, 31; Rantanen 2005, 67.

concerned whether what has been called the postmodern or late modern society should be regarded as something completely different and new, or whether it is really just an extension of modernity. Objections to globalization theories have specifically sought to assert, for example, that global interaction was already very extensive at the turn of the century. However, criticism of the concept is also found among those who acknowledge the existence of a postmodern society. For example, postmodern theorists like Ulrich Beck and Zygmunt Bauman are primarily critical of the consequences of making globalization into an almost 'magical' concept that assumes a quasi-supreme power with the possible aim of concealing financial interests, among other things. In any event, there seems to be a fair degree of consensus that the concept of globalization is very difficult to encapsulate and that it can accommodate several different dimensions.[10]

No general discussion of the possible implications of globalization will be taken up here. However, I will argue that some of the effects of globalization can unquestionably be experienced in conducting fieldwork. One can regard the most obvious impacts of globalization on the project described here as the following:

1. Globalization processes are connected with a blurring of geographical borders, which has direct consequences for carrying out fieldwork.
2. The economic aspects of globalization affect the realm of freelance work. Researching certain types of work and freelance careers that are organized in new ways requires specific methodological techniques.

The field of Williamsburg

At the Bedford Avenue subway stop in Williamsburg in the spring of 2008, one could see an advertisement for a new luxury building project in the area. The text on the board read: 'Manhattan is so five minutes ago'. The double meaning of the phrasing indicated the fact that it takes no more than five minutes to get to Manhattan by subway and also alluded to the area's relatively new status as presumably trendier than Manhattan. Williamsburg in Brooklyn is a neighbourhood historically characterized by labour immigration, where numerous different ethnic groups, including Italians, Puerto Ricans, Dominicans and a large group of Hasidic Jews, are represented.[11] The area began to change when young people, many of them artists and creators, started to move into the neighbourhood in the late nineties because of the still relatively low rents. Although prices have risen in recent years, it is still possible to live more cheaply in Williamsburg than in Manhattan. The labour immigration in question is of a radically new kind that does not imply the primary purpose of the former type of labour

---

10 Eriksen 2007, 2; Beck 2000, 37.
11 Snyder-Grenier 2004, 262.

immigrants: to attain a higher material and financial standard of life. The current settlers are young people from other parts of the United States and from many different parts of the world. They differ significantly from the other immigrants living in the area in terms of the type of work they are doing. Rather than baking bread, driving taxis or selling vegetables, they are photographing street fashion on Bedford Avenue sidewalks, arranging parties in disused factories – or are seen working on their laptops in coffee shops.[12]

The interviews with the informants were filled with descriptions of how much they worked and how little money they earned. The trials and tribulations of labour were clearly not connected with the hardships of sweeping floors or serving hamburgers. Their lamentations were rather about trying to get American fashion magazine editors to answer their e-mails. On the other hand, the will power and tenacity can be said to typify all of Williamsburg's immigrants, both old and new. As Bonnie Menes Kahn puts it in her book *Cosmopolitan Culture*, two things characterize a cosmopolitan city: tolerance of strangers and intolerance of mediocrity.[13] It can be argued that New York in general and my informants' work environment in particular are characterized by this maxim. There are jobs, even for someone who is relatively inexperienced in her/his professional field, but competition is also very hard since there is a plethora of freelance photographers, designers, stylists, etc. who are all willing to work for low (or no) wages. The informants often describe New York as a great city if you have the energy to work hard, but not a good city to be worn out, tired or temporarily without creative inspiration. As one young woman stated: 'If you don't keep your energy up, the city will eat you alive.'[14]

12 Richard Florida has coined the concept 'the creative class', which he defines in his book *The Rise of the Creative Class*, where he states: 'If you are a scientist or engineer, an architect or designer, a writer, artist or musician, or if you use your creativity as a key factor in your work in business, education, healthcare, law, or some other profession, you are a member.' The basic definition of this new class, as well as of other classes is, according to Florida, economic, and because creativity is the driving force behind economic growth, the creative class, in terms of power, is society's new dominant class. Only by understanding this new class can we begin to understand the massive and seemingly unconnected changes taking place in our society and handle our future in the most intelligent way, Florida argues. One of the key points he makes is that this group of people will increasingly influence the organization of cities, particularly because companies are moving to places where these people want to live. The creative class appreciates features such as a busy street life and cities that have a high 'bohemian index', 'gay index' and 'melting pot index', which together constitute a 'diversity index'. The members of the creative class are interested in the 'organic street culture' found in urban neighbourhoods. Williamsburg seems to fit this description well. The question of to what extent the district's residents belong to 'society's dominant class' or whether they should rather be regarded as extras posing as the 'organic street culture' is further explored and discussed in my dissertation. See Florida 2002.
13 Kahn 1987.
14 Interview with Emi, May 10, 2008. All names of informants are pseudonyms.

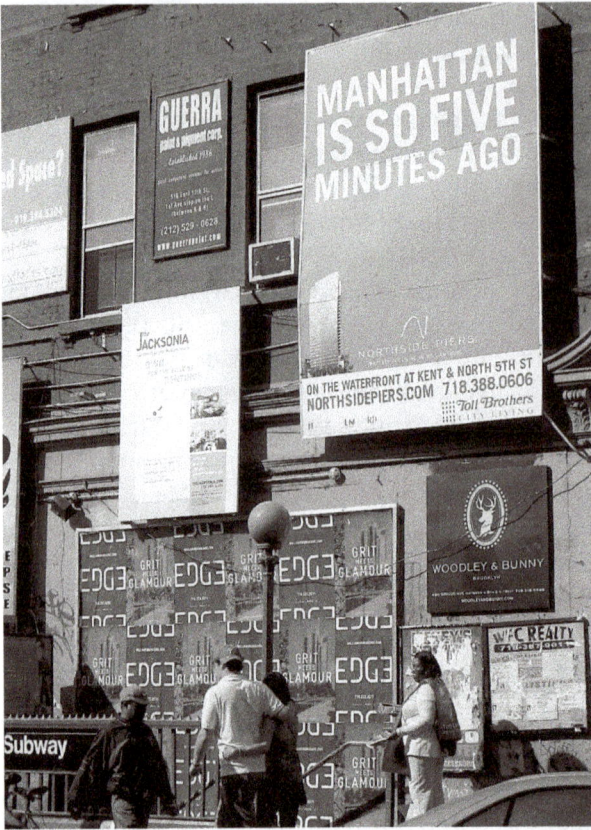

*Bedford avenue
subway station,
Williamsburg, 2008,
Lisa Wiklund.*

The young population of Williamsburg has in recent years been regarded with some scepticism in the American media; nicknames such as 'trustfunders' and 'trustafarians' suggest that despite a dogmatic and alternative lifestyle, they are highly privileged young people who really live well off their parents' money. In 2009, under the heading 'Parents Pulling the Plug on Williamsburg Trust-Funders' *The New York Times* described how the economic crisis has meant that parents can no longer afford to pay their children's housing costs. The article offers comments on the trend by area brokers and landlords as well as by young musicians, artists and writers with varying financial arrangements.[15] This depiction, however, met with some opposition. The following week *The New Yorker* wrote an article in response: 'Beyond Hipsters: Williamsburg's Tough Economic Realities',[16]

15 Haughney 2009.
16 Halpinn 2009. The word 'hipster' first appeared in the 1940s and had a revival in the 1990s and 2000s. Williamsburg has been regarded as a core neighbourhood of the new generation of 'hipsters'. The word signifies young persons with alternative or 'hip' life styles and an interest in art, music and contemporary culture. The hipster has been regarded both as apolitical and progressive. Historical parallels can be drawn with depictions of 'the bohemians'. The various definitions and uses of the term are further explored in my forthcoming dissertation.

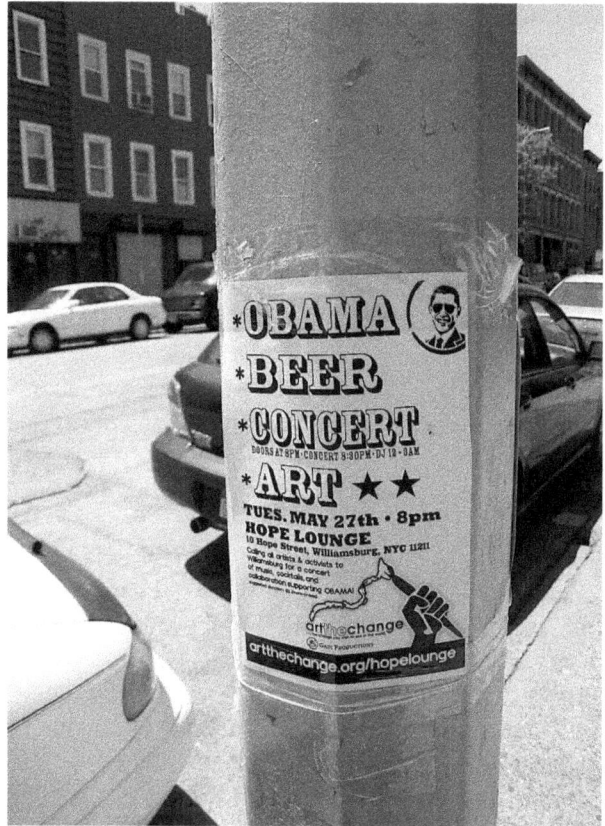

Poster announcing a support event for the Obama-campaign, Williamsburg 2008, Lisa Wiklund.

which presents statistics showing that the vast majority of the residents have a very difficult financial situation. Barely three percent of the households have an income of over 200,000 dollars a year: 'The reality of Williamsburg, beyond the mythical trust-funders, is that it is a community of people mostly struggling to get by, with a few wealthy residents grabbing headlines – the way New York has always been.'[17]

It is certainly true that some of the informants received some type of financial support from their parents, but far from all of them did. It is in any case legitimate to claim that they all had forsaken comfort, a steady income and a material standard of living for other values. The expression 'money-job' appeared frequently in the interviews. In order to be able to pay the bills most of the informants had additional jobs, besides work that was consistent with their artistic goals. In order to get money for rent and food, many of the informants worked in bars, restaurants or shops. Some also took 'money-jobs' that were more related to their creative aspirations but which they still primarily regarded as necessary sources of income. A common example was 'street-photographing' for Japanese magazines. This meant taking pictures of typical young Williamsburg-residents wearing characteristic

17 Halpin 2009.

'street fashion'. These types of jobs did not enjoy a very high reputation, but the Japanese magazines paid fees – as opposed to the American alternative magazines, where it was prestigious to be published, and for which many of the informants were working for free.[18] This way of organizing work led to the formation of something that looked like a barter economy. It entailed, for example, assisting friends with their art projects, sometimes perhaps in the hope that it would help your personal career in the future, but in many cases only with the assurance that the other person would do the same for you, a sort of code of honour that was symptomatic of the scene. The voluntary choices of the informants resulted in living situations characterized by economic uncertainty, material constraints and practical difficulties. These complications also affected my ethnographic endeavour to capture the informants' organization of work.

Researching work

Traditional ethnographical methods for studying labour may have been applicable to the 'old' Williamsburg.[19] It might in some ways be easier to follow a factory worker or baker than a freelancer, or there may at least be more time-tested ethnographic methods available, suitable for this. However, the question of how to study the new world of work has for some time been one that has aroused considerable interest. Barbara Czarniawska, a researcher in organization theory, believes that there is '…an urgent need for a mobile ethnology: ways of studying the work and life of people who move often and quickly from place to place'. She calls her method *shadowing*, which in short means 'following selected people in their everyday occupations for a time'. [20] Czarniawska seeks to distinguish shadowing from traditional field-techniques, in particular from participant observation. Shadowing, she argues, is a less participatory and thus an easier method because it does not require simultaneous action and observation. It is also, she argues, really the only option for organization studies because for most ethnographers it is impossible to participate in complex work situations in an office where specific knowledge and skills are required. However, she points out that in spite of the theoretical aim to do so, it can be difficult to distinguish shadowing from participant observation in field practice.[21]

---

18 This was to some extent a consequence of the fact that some of the informants had visas that did not permit them to work in the USA. However, even those who were allowed to take employment with American companies sometimes worked for free.

19 Of course, no clear division between the 'old' and 'new' Williamsburgs can be easily made since the neighbourhood, as I have shown, still consists of numerous different groups of residents.

20 Czarniawska 2007, 17.

21 Ibid, 56–57.

Street fashion photographing for Japanese teen magazine, Tokyo, 2008, Lisa Wiklund.

An ethnographic stance broadly agreed on is that all direct observation is, in some sense, at some point, hard to distinguish from participant observation.[22] However, the degree of participation 'is seldom constant during the field work', and 'the researcher can alternate between being a participant observer and just an observer'.[23] I would argue that it is likely that the degree of participation increases if the field is vague or indistinct in some sense. For example, shadowing in the sense of non-participant observation is probably easier to implement if, like Czarniawska, one stays put in an office for several hours a day (even if this involves different offices scattered across the globe). But my informants did not work in offices; their daily routines consisted mostly of work carried out before their laptops at home or in coffee shops; they had several odd 'money-jobs' with irregular schedules, or were temporarily unemployed. Thus, it was obviously more difficult to follow them around without participating in some way. The observations consisted of detached sessions lasting a few hours at a time and were spread out geographically. It was impossible for me to remain an invisible shadow because I had to be involved with my informants in order to find out, for example, what would happen next so that I would know whether I would

22 As noted by Czarniawska 2007, 55.
23 Öhlander, 1999, 74, my translation.

*Artist loft,
Williamsburg,
2008, Lisa Wiklund.*

be able to accompany my informant or not. Therefore, what I was doing was clearly not shadowing; rather it would be possible to regard this kind of participant observation as a practice resembling a sort of *mirroring*, in the sense that the somewhat vague and sketchy characteristics of the field required me to imitate some loose and spontaneous modes of action, which I will elaborate on in the following.

Following freelancers

'We seem to worry about "the field" these days,' the Swedish anthropologist Ulf Hannerz states. He concludes that perhaps anthropologists always did, but argues that the 'field was probably a rather fixed entity to worry about, a "tribe", a village, some place you could get to know by covering it on foot.'[24] It has been hard to ignore the discussion in recent years about translocal or multi-sited fieldwork. It is of course possible to argue that these forms of fieldwork are not entirely new and that almost all fieldwork in some way is, and always has been, multi-sited. Not even Malinowski's classic study of the Trobriand Islanders – which is usually contrasted with today's translocal

24 Hannerz, 2006.

118

Coffee shop with free Wi-Fi, Williamsburg, 2008, Lisa Wiklund.

ethnography – was in reality completely local. In fact, he studied a network of *Kula* men who, in their pursuit of valuable shells, moved between a dozen islands over a relatively large region.[25] However, it would not be wrong to argue that the tendency to study more than one place has been increasing, which makes the methodological implications associated with this trend a relevant question for ethnography.

The conception of the field as a 'rather fixed entity' thus no longer holds true for the ethnographer: as Vered Amit states, '…today, the people whom they are trying to study are increasingly likely to be as mobile as the ethnographers trying to keep up with them, if not more so.'[26] This new order of things seems to call attention to how the researcher still can be able to pursue the 'total experience' of fieldwork.[27] 'Fieldwork through immersion' has long been an ethnographical ideal. The idea of 'immersion' could be defined as 'an involvement so deep that the supposed risk was one of "going native" (hardly anybody did)', as Ulf Hannerz points out.[28] This could be considered a search for 'authenticity', 'truth' and other concepts that have been abandoned for some time now by most researchers in the cultural field.

25 This is pointed out in Björklund 2000, 105.
26 Amit, 2000, 12.
27 Ibid, 15.
28 Hannerz 2006, 34.

The sarcastic appellations 'fieldwork by appointment' and 'quick and dirty ethnography'[29] nevertheless still echo the ideal of 'immersion' and axioms such as 'Good anthropology will always take time'.[30] The anthropologist Michael M. J. Fischer claims that 'the complexities of our times require ethnographic skills'.[31] Equally true then is the fact that our times require the ethnographic skills to be of some complexity. This is why ways of organizing fieldwork where the researcher have no prospects of 'immersing' her- or himself in the field – possibly because s/he is in fact trying to trail it, or is even active in the construction of it – can no longer be regarded as irrelevant anomalies. Rather, they might be the alternative that is needed to capture the world we live in, and therefore they need to be examined and developed. 'Fieldwork by appointment' was, in a rather strict sense of the phrase, sometimes actually what my fieldwork resembled most. However, in an endeavour to study people who to a great extent organize their own lives through appointments, it is not an entirely bad idea for the researcher to do the same. This is the particular style of participant observation that I have chosen to call *mirroring*.

The work lives of the informants included endless choices, changes of plan, last minute cancellations, broken agreements and so on. In order to keep up with the informants, it was necessary to adapt to a manner that was equally flexible. The following incident may serve as an example. One night I teamed up with a photographer named Emi. She was assigned to take photos of 'cute American boys' and write about their outfits for a Japanese magazine, a typical 'money-job'. Emi suddenly terminated the assignment because she decided she could not find any cute boys at the club where we were supposed to look for them. Instead she spent the night taking photos for her private art project, which was dedicated to portraying men with big beards. The original job was postponed, and she let me follow her when she took it up again the next night at another club. Everything about the assignment and how it developed seems to illustrate the impossibility of trying to control the outcome of the situation. The work my informants did had no resemblance to nine-to five-jobs, so to be able to carry out research my schedule had to be as flexible as theirs. This seems, in one sense, fairly basic. However, the inability to plan days and nights and the need, often at short notice, to prioritize and re-prioritize the options for fieldwork can be complicated and requires a lot of energy, some creative thinking and a very adaptable calendar. This kind of fuzzy structure needs to be reckoned with in order to plan for the unplanned. Mirroring has advantages as well: in one way it could be seen as an approach to the old ethnographic recommendation that the researcher should adapt to the life of those s/he wishes to study in order to personally try to experience – to the extent possible – the same things as the informants, which in this case was the rather large amount

29 See e.g. Melhuus et al. 2010, 13; Robben & Sluka 2007, 212.
30 Fischer 2009, xiii.
31 Ibid.

of stress and uncertainty that was a natural part of everyday life for the informants.

Since the researcher's time in the field is limited, some strategic thinking is, however, necessary. It is important to realize that the fieldwork often involves a long wait to meet the right people and that the researcher in many cases depends on them in order to get in touch with others. Therefore it is good, if it is feasible, to keep several options open in order not to spend more time waiting than actually doing fieldwork.[32] This was especially true of my fieldwork. It is, to say the least, complicated to carry out a labour study when it is almost impossible to know whether the informants will have jobs the following day, or even whether they will be in town, since they might well go somewhere else for work or other reasons. This, again, puts the ethnographer in the position of mirroring the field. Just as the informants had freelance assignments, the opportunities for my fieldwork were arranged in the same way. In the same manner as my informants had to hunt for jobs, I had to hunt for informants. Just as they made contacts at parties and through friends and acquaintances, so did I. I deliberately chose the option of having enough informants to follow to enable me to stay in Williamsburg rather than have to follow fewer informants around wherever they went. This choice was made because of my intention to study the specific scene of Williamsburg, but the mobility of the informants meant that who I got to spend time with turned out to be rather random and not possible to plan ahead. This is also pointed out by Laura Hirvi, who discusses the fact that the field site cannot really be defined beforehand but rather emerges in the fieldwork process and is a result of endless small choices and decisions that the researcher is confronted with during the fieldwork.[33]

Creating a community

The anthropologist Arjun Appadurai has coined the term 'trans-localities' to refer to places that are characterized by people of different national origins who pass through them rather than stay there permanently. The challenge of building local communities in these places is that there is an inherent instability in the social relations.[34] New York generally, and certainly the environment of young creators and performers of all kinds in Williamsburg, can be seen as an example of such a trans-locality. The fact that most people there have wide social networks, where individuals are exchangeable, can be regarded as an expression of the existing social instability. Such a situation can lead to loneliness, but it also seems to generate a desire to help and be there even for strangers or neighbours whom one does not know particularly well.

32 See e.g. Kaijser 1999, 31.
33 Hirvi, this volume.
34 Appadurai 1996, 192.

This was proved true again and again in my fieldwork by the fact that it was very easy to form new relationships and establish contacts with people. This was an advantage since the informants did not really form a 'community' which a researcher could 'enter'. They had loose, if any, relations with each other even though they were all Japanese living in a relatively small neighbourhood, belonging to more or less the same crowd and sharing the same friends and work contacts. Although they often knew each other by name, there was a conscious desire not to get too involved with other Japanese persons. One girl claimed in an interview: 'There's something almost chemical about Japanese people living here sometimes. We don't like each other.'[35] This kind of almost 'reversed diaspora' – people of the same ethnic origin avoiding each other rather than forming a group – is further examined in my PhD dissertation[36], but what I wish to present here is an obvious example of how the researcher can sometimes be responsible for creating a community where there is none. On the basis of a similar experience, Vered Amit states:

> My 'field' would be defined in terms of a social category that I have singled out rather than a self-conscious social group, whose members are interacting with one another on an ongoing basis, independently of my intervention. Such a shift renders the ethnographer an even more central agent in the construction of the field.[37]

My role in the construction of the field was without doubt central since I could be held more or less totally accountable for the creation of a community of Japanese young people engaged in creative careers in Williamsburg. My main material consists of participant observations and interviews carried out in New York. Apart from New York, I have also conducted fieldwork in Japan. In terms of carrying it out, one of the core challenges for multi-sited fieldwork is how to limit the study geographically and still be able to follow the field. Interviews that have the characteristics of biographical narrative have special idiosyncrasies that the researcher needs to be aware of. How individual biographical narratives enter into a dialogue with other people's stories and are affected by numerous different contexts is an established research topic. Over the years this topic has been examined and discussed, not least within the Swedish ethnologic community. The endeavour to examine what people actually do, not just what they say they do, is a basic ethnological principle. It has been argued that, because there are different 'life-scripts' that vary between different cultural contexts, it is crucial that researchers take into account the fact that a person's interpretation of her/his own life is based on the context in question and is therefore a combination of 'life, expectations and self-understanding'.[38] The scholarly discussion

---

35 Interview with Mai, May 3 2008.
36 Wiklund, forthcoming.
37 Amit 2000, 14.
38 Frykman 1992, 243, my translation.

has also referred to the fact that interviewees sometimes try to 'help' the researcher by representing personal traits and actions as typical of their time and group, and in that way already in the interview situation start to convert themselves from unique individuals into examples of a more general pattern. Consequently, such interviews should not be used as primary source material without reflection.[39] It has been argued that it is therefore necessary to have an idea of people's cultural contexts before you can use their biographies.[40]

My research trip to Japan was motivated by such arguments. The decision to go there was based on the desire to carry out fieldwork in both of the different geographical and cultural environments that characterize the stories that emerged in my interviews with the informants. In Japan, I was accompanied by an informant called Mai. I also emailed my other informants in Williamsburg and asked them to tell me about places in Tokyo that were special to them, or that they thought could tell me something about their home country. Visiting places that for various reasons fascinated the informants or were significant for them gave me a chance to try to see Japan from their point of view. The young Japanese persons in the study were in various ways analytically interesting for researching the scene of creative work; the main reason was that they came from an environment characterized by a traditional attitude to many aspects of life, including employment and careers. Their lives in Williamsburg are consequently more complicated than those of the many young people from other parts of the world who populate the district, mainly because their option to return home after a few years is fraught with problems. The informants' decision to leave the Japanese employment system means that it will be very difficult for them to return and get a 'proper' job, i.e. one suited to their college education, which in most cases was not related to their current occupations. The female informants also claimed that they were already too old to get married in Japan and therefore could not be part of the Japanese way of life.[41] The fieldwork in Japan included meeting up with some of Mai's old schoolmates who were already housewives, and their opposites, young professionals who worried about finding time to start a family.

---

39 Ehn 1992, 207–217, my translation.
40 Löfgren 1992, 261, my translation.
41 The anthropologist Merry White (1988: 105) describes how stigmatized and isolated a returnee can be after a few years abroad and how absence from Japan in itself is enough to challenge national norms: 'Belonging does not just depend on active involvement, it *is* that daily interaction itself, and there is no acceptable substitute for being there [...] When Japanese leave Japan, their membership is suspended. Every year they are away, reentry as members of the group – reestablishment of relationships to the satisfaction of those at home – becomes more difficult. It is particularly difficult if after reentry they betray their exposure to foreign ways, which reminds others of the severing of bonds.'

The informants often compared their lives in Williamsburg with their lives in Japan and how work was organized there. They had a clear view of the work ethic being much stronger in Japan, which they saw in part as a good thing. But mostly the informants expressed sharp criticism of both the Japanese labour market and the education system. The latter was accused of being designed not to encourage critical thinking but only to train students for entry to prestigious universities, which later would lead to employment in a large company. The problem with the labour market in Japan most often referred to by the informants was the rigid hierarchical system. The places they wanted to show me in Japan were often characterized by their desire to show Japan as a society obsessed with status, material values and money. Because of this, I attended a 'host club', a modern version of the traditional Japanese 'hostess clubs', which are bars where men pay to talk to hostesses. The clients of a host club are instead mostly unmarried businesswomen looking for a relaxing break. Motoko, one of my informants from New York, had made a photo story for the Japanese edition of an international fashion magazine in one of Tokyo's main host clubs and recommended me in an email to go there in order to 'explore the madness of Japan'. Such instances of participant observation provided a basis for discussions and questions later on and also served to create a context for the interviews already conducted. In this way, my informants were in some sense present during my stay in Tokyo, even though physically they were not.

When ethnography is broken up into short periods of time, I would argue that it becomes more important to let the informants have as much influence as possible since their contribution to the researcher's orientation in a somewhat diffuse field is so important. Paradoxically, this can be difficult to accomplish since, as I argued earlier, it is harder for the researcher to abstain from participation when the fieldwork is arranged in the manner described above. One concrete technique was to let the informants decide the settings for the observations. The approach of letting the informants lead the way in a limited geographical field (cities or neighbourhoods) should, however, be combined with a careful consideration of *which* geographical settings are of most analytical value in studying persons who move around a lot. If this is not done, the contextual relation to the informants' lives might get lost – which could entail the real threat that the fieldwork would stop being ethnography and become nothing but a series of appointments.

The globalization of fieldwork and the return of geography

There is an old saying, most often seen in London guidebooks and English language textbooks that if you stand at *Piccadilly Circus* long enough you will eventually bump into every person in the world. In the same manner, I argue, it is possible – and perhaps preferable – to study cosmopolitanism without moving too much. The blurring of geographical borders does not imply that it is imperative for every contemporary ethnographic study to include various long journeys across the globe. In fact, it should perhaps

Shibuya crossing, Tokyo, 2009, Lisa Wiklund.

suggest just the opposite. Conducting fieldwork in a cosmopolitan setting, among people moving freely between world metropolises, could of course involve unlimited time spent following informants around. The prime focus, however, must be on the aim of the research. In this case, it was to study the artistic scene in Williamsburg as an example of a centre for young people engaged in creative freelance work.

Although many of the informants moved a lot – they had exhibitions in Berlin, photo shoots in Los Angeles, visited friends in London, etc. – I decided not to follow them on these long-distance trips. This was motivated by my aim to ensure that the observations would be as concentred as possible since, as this chapter has described, they were already scattered enough as it was. In researching a fast-paced world, there may be some point in resisting the urge to follow everything that moves, assuming that the same phenomena could just as well be studied from one geographical setting. The trip to Japan, on the other hand was, as described above, motivated by the aim to experience the environment that contrasted with my informant's lives in Williamsburg. Since this context was crucial for the analysis and a recurring theme in the interviews, an essential element of my study would obviously have been missing if the fieldwork in Japan had not been included.

However, the decision not to follow the informants is, as I have argued, not valid in the local setting. In the limited field of one neighbourhood, Williamsburg, or city, Tokyo, the strategy was rather to be as flexible and spontaneous as possible in trailing the informants – in order to let them construct the field within these given geographical boundaries. Geography, even in a globalized world, is not obsolete. This is very clearly demonstrated by Williamsburg and other so-called 'hip' neighbourhoods around the world. The same types of scenes in, for example London and Berlin all point to the paradox that – despite a postmodern, wireless and, as is sometimes said, location-independent world,[42] there seem to be some cities that continue to be important human venues. The high concentration of people in the same field of work in a few cities – and even neighbourhoods – points to a different truth from the one that claims that the freelance world of work is characterized by placelessness. Human interaction can never be 'globalized away'. This is why ethnography should not give up on the field in the geographical sense of the word but rather embrace the advantages of using it as a basis for analysis. Even the people in my study, who regard themselves in one sense as 'citizens of the world' and not especially rooted, have – no matter how temporarily – a place they call home. Ethnography's task could perhaps be defined in part as the endeavour to explain the everyday meaning of such rather ephemeral terms as 'cosmopolitanism'. The easiest way to capture this might not be to try and trail the fast-moving people who define these modern circumstances but rather to slow down and stay put in the particular urban scenes constituted by them.

Bibliography

Amit, V. 2000: Introduction: Constructing the field. In: V. Amit (ed.) *Constructing the field. Ethnographic fieldwork in the contemporary world.* London/New York: Routledge.

Appadurai, A. 1996: *Modernity at Large: Cultural Dimensions of Globalization.* Minneapolis: University of Minnesota Press.

Baudelaire, C. 1995: *The Painter of Modern Life and Other Essays.* London: Phaidon Press Limited.

Baudrillard, J. 1988: *America.* London: Verso.

Bauman, Z. 2000: *Globalization: The Human Consequences.* New York: Columbia University Press.

Beck, U. 2000: *The Brave New World of Work.* Malden, Mass.: Polity Press.

Beck, U. 2000: *What is Globalization?* Malden, Mont.: Polity Press.

Björklund, U. 2000: Att studera en diaspora. Den armeniska förskingringen som fält. In: U. Hannerz (ed.), *Flera fält i ett. Socialantropologer om translokala fältstudier.* Stockholm: Carlsson.

Breckenridge C. A., S. Pollock, H. K. Bhabha & D. Chakrabarty (eds.) 2002: *Cosmopolitanism.* Durham & London: Duke University Press.

Czarniawska, B. 2007: *Shadowing and Other Techniques for Doing Fieldwork in Modern Societies.* Malmö: Liber.

Ehn, B. 1992: Livet som intervjukonstruktion. In: C. Tigerstedt, J. P. Roos & A. Vilkko (eds.), *Självbiografi, kultur, liv. Levnadshistoriska studier inom human- och samhällsvetenskap.* Stockholm: Brutus Östlings Bokförlag Symposion.

Eriksen, T. 2007: *Globalization. The Key Concepts.* Oxford/New York: Berg.

Fine, R. 2007: *Cosmopolitanism.* London & New York: Routledge.

---

42 See for example Eriksen 2007, 36.

Fischer, M. 2009: Foreword. In: James D. Faubion & George E. Marcus: *Fieldwork Is Not What It Used to Be. Learning Anthropology's Method in a Time of Transition.* Ithaca & London: Cornell university press.

Florida, R. 2002: *The Rise of the Creative Class: And How It's Transforming Work, Leisure, Community and Everyday Life.* New York: Basic books.

Frykman, J. 1992: Biografi och kulturanalys. In: C. Tigerstedt, J. P. Roos & A. Vilkko (eds.), *Självbiografi, kultur, liv. Levnadshistoriska studier inom human- och samhällsvetenskap.* Stockholm: Brutus Östlings Bokförlag Symposion.

Giddens. A. 2000: *Runaway World: How Globalization Is Reshaping Our Lives.* New York: Routledge.

Halpin, M. 2009: Beyond Hipsters: Williamsburg's Tough Economic Realities. In: *New York Magazine*, 22/6 2009.

Hannerz, U. 2006: Studying Down, Up, Sideways, Through, Backwards, Forwards, Away and at Home: Reflections on the Field Worries of an Expansive Discipline. In: S. Coleman & P. Collins (eds.) *Locating the Field. Space, Place and Context in Anthropology.* Oxford/New York: Berg.

Haughney, C. 2009: Parents Pulling the Plugs on Williamsburg Trust-Funders. Parental Life-Lines, Frayed to Breaking. In: *The New York Times*, June 8th 2009.

Kahn, B. M. 1987: *Cosmopolitan Culture. The Guilt-Edge Dream of a Tolerant City.* New York: Atheneum.

Kaijser, L. 1999: Fältarbete. In: Kaijser, L. & M. Öhlander (eds.) *Etnologiskt fältarbete.* Lund: Studentlitteratur.

Löfgren, O. 1992: Mitt liv som konsument. Livshistoria som forskningsstrategi och analysmaterial. In: C. Tigerstedt, J. P. Roos & A. Vilkko (eds.), *Självbiografi, kultur, liv. Levnadshistoriska studier inom human- och samhällsvetenskap.* Stockholm: Brutus Östlings Bokförlag Symposion.

Rantanen, T. 2005: Giddens and the 'G'-word. An interview with Anthony Giddens. In: *Global Media and Communication* Vol. 1:1. London: SAGE Publicatios.

Sennett, R. 2006: *The Culture of the New Capitalism.* New Haven: Yale University Press

Snyder-Grenier, E. M. 2004: *Brooklyn: An Illustrated History. Critical Perspectives on the Past.* New York: Brooklyn Historical Society.

White, M. 1988: *The Japanese Overseas: Can They Go Home Again?* Princeton University Press.

Öhlander, M. 1999: Deltagande observation. In: L. Kaijser & M. Öhlander (eds.), *Etnologiskt fältarbete.* Lund: Studentlitteratur.

Deirdre Meintel & Géraldine Mossière

Going through the Back Door
Studying Ethnicity via Religion

Introduction

In a team study of contemporary religious groups in Quebec, we have looked at a number of congregations whose members include many immigrants to Canada. Although a minority of the groups in our study are monoethnic – for example, the Tamil Catholics from Sri Lanka studied by Melissa Bouchard[1] – most of those that are made up principally of immigrants attract members of different national and ethnic origins; moreover, they usually include at least a few members of the social majority (native-born Anglo- and Franco-Quebecois). Religious groups such as these offer a particularly interesting slant on the process of resettlement and the experience of migration. At the same time, such congregations constitute a site where interethnic relations unfold in ways that are likely to play out differently than in contexts where immigrants are in the minority.

When viewed through the prism of religion, ethnicity, migration and resettlement appear in a somewhat different light than when the point of departure is, say, ethnicity or integration. We find, for example, that for the immigrants involved in the groups we studied, religious affiliation is usually more important than ethnic or national origin. Moreover, immigrants (and sometimes those of a particular national origin or region of the world) are in the majority in these religious settings; social interaction tends to be regulated by religious norms as well as broadly cultural ones and is likely to involve one or more languages besides French or English, the two official languages of Canada. Religious groups also offer their own definitions of interethnic relations and how migrants should participate socially and politically in the wider society. While supporting the transmission of the home language and culture to the next generation, many such congregations also offer help in adapting to the new sociocultural environment.

Extended fieldwork in religious groups sheds new light on migrants' experiences in the host society with regard to matters like deskilling,

---

1 Bouchard 2009.

unemployment and race prejudice. Besides the practical help that such congregations offer newcomers, religion provides symbolic resources that allow migrants to give new value to the experiences of migration and settlement and the difficulties they bring. Moreover, we shall argue, religious groups, as 'moral communities', offer symbolic support of a particular kind that reinforces the social resources they provide.

We argue that participant observation in religious groups where *religion* is the primary object of study involves different types of fieldwork relationships from those that usually prevail in research carried out on migrants in their society of residence. Research that is focused on religion usually involves long-term participant observation, something that is less common in studies of immigrants, where many studies are based exclusively on interviews (often only one with each informant). Moreover, studying religion usually obliges researchers to situate themselves in conscious ways. Though one's ethnic background may well be a factor in research on migration or ethnicity, it is rarely the subject of extended reflexivity on the part of the researcher. In studies of religion, by contrast, researchers are usually obliged to situate themselves in relation to the religion of those they study and indeed, in relation to religion in general, and to explain their positioning to the research subjects as well as, often enough, to colleagues.

Before going into further detail on these points, we first describe our own respective backgrounds in studies of religion and of migration and ethnicity. Then we describe the methods used in the study that inspired the reflections presented here.

Situating the researchers and the research

Géraldine Mossière has done extensive research on a mostly Congolese Pentecostal congregation in Montreal, beginning in 2003 and continuing on a part-time basis into the present.[2] In 2008 she did fieldwork on three Pentecostal Church congregations located in the homeland: the Democratic Republic of Congo (DRC). She explored the economic and social ties linking them to the Montreal congregation, which provides them with substantial financial support.[3] Between 2006 and 2008 she also studied female converts to Islam in France and Quebec.[4]

The Pentecostal church that Mossière has studied was founded by a Congolese pastor, who after an unsuccessful attempt to build a church in Belgium, where he studied theology, moved to Quebec and founded the Communauté Évangélique de Pentecôte (CEP) there in 1992. Starting with only a few participants in his living room (mainly his own family and his children's friends), the new congregation spread westward to other parts of Canada, where some of its members have moved. It has also sponsored

2   Mossière 2007a; 2007b; 2006.
3   Mossière 2010a; 2008b.
4   Mossière 2010b; 2008a.

eight affiliated churches and prayer groups in the DRC, the homeland of the majority of its members. Through contributions and tithes, the church has acquired a large building in a multi-ethnic and multi-religious neighbourhood in the north of Montreal. The congregation includes approximately 430 first-generation immigrants. Some have immigrated recently from the DRC or from other African countries[5] as political refugees, fleeing civil war and political retaliation. Others are younger and better off, notably those who left the homeland at a young age and spent time in French-speaking Europe (Belgium, France, or Switzerland) before immigrating to Quebec. The church also attracts Haitian men and women from an earlier wave of immigration. The Haitian-born have varied migration trajectories: some came for economic reasons, others to join their families or pursue university studies. Almost all the members of the congregation were raised in the Christian tradition, and fieldwork data reveal that most members from Africa had been converted to Pentecostalism in their country of origin by European and American missionaries. The Haitian members usually came to Canada as Catholics and then decided to convert, often after discovering a particular Pentecostal church. In most cases, the members came to know of the CEP through their social networks, and some had attended various other churches before staying with this one. The members' family profiles are quite diverse, ranging from young singles, students and single mothers to families and divorced or widowed men and women. Nearly half the members are less than 30 years old, and the majority are women. Almost all of this population knew French upon arrival in Quebec, half claiming it to be their mother tongue. The Congolese predominate among the members, and governance is concentrated in the hands of the pastor's family along with a few of the more highly educated Congolese. As head of the congregation, the pastor maintains personal ties with everyone in it, while his wife and daughters are responsible for ministries such as that of *mamas*.[6] In the long term, his son is the most likely candidate to take over his role as religious leader.

Deirdre Meintel came to the field of religion after long experience of research on ethnic issues, including emigration from the Cape Verde Islands,[7] immigrant women's domestic and paid labour,[8] family relations and identity issues among immigrants' young adult children,[9] ethnically (and sometimes religiously) mixed unions,[10] and so on. Originally, her research among Montreal Spiritualists,[11] which began in 2000, was motivated partly by the wish to find a Montreal site for doing 'real field work' rather than the 'research management' on ethnic themes that she had found herself

5   Angola, the Democratic Republic of Congo, Congo, the Ivory Coast, Cameroon, Burundi, Rwanda, Benin.
6   *Mama* is the appellation usually used in the DRC in addressing women elders. It displays both affection and respect.
7   Meintel 2002a.
8   Meintel 1984.
9   Meintel & Kahn 2005; Meintel 1992.
10 Meintel 2002b.
11 Meintel 2011; 2007a; 2007b; 2003.

doing. In other words, in her research on ethnic and migration issues, she had ended up supervising numerous assistants who carried out the actual research. Moreover, these studies were mostly based on interviews, save for the cases where student assistants carried out participant observation as part of their thesis research. Typically, the interview method is adopted in studies of migrants and ethnicity, in great part for reasons of cost- and time-efficiency, and probably also because anthropologists are in the minority in this field compared with sociologists and political scientists.[12] Through her personal network, she came into contact with a Spiritualist congregation whose members were mostly born in Quebec and raised Catholic and who, in many cases, still identify as Catholic. This research in turn led to a much broader study in which the two authors have collaborated since 2005.

Fieldwork methods

Our collaborative research[13] aims at documenting the new religious diversity that has appeared in Quebec, as it has developed in the aftermath of the Quiet Revolution (which began in the 1960s) as well as the meaning of religion in the everyday lives of the Quebecois today. Although the study concerns the whole of the province, the present analysis is based mainly on data that have been collected in Montreal, the province's largest and most multicultural city. Over the past three years, observations have been carried out on religious groups that represent (1) religions established in Quebec since the 1960s (e.g. Baha'i and Neo-shamanism, including Druidism and Wicca); (2) new forms of religious practice in long-established religions (the case of some Jewish and Catholic congregations); (3) religions imported by immigrants (including Islam, Hinduism, certain forms of Buddhism); (4) congregations of long-established religions that include a substantial proportion of immigrants among their members. Thus far, observations have been carried out on a total of 100 groups; of these, 38 have been studied in-depth through extended participant observation and interviews with members and leaders. Research assistants have observed religious rituals and other religious activities like neighbourhood prayer groups as well as social activities involving members of the group, such as communal meals and picnics, funding events and courses sponsored by the group. They have also interviewed members who vary in terms of gender, age, profession, matrimonial status and level of commitment to the group. The interviews

12 Fortunately, many of the assistants also did participant observation for master's or doctoral theses on the groups they studied.

13 The research is supported by the Fonds de recherche sur la société et la culture (Québec) and by the Social Sciences and Humanities Council of Canada. Co-researchers represent four different universities and include Marie-Nathalie Le Blanc, Josiane Le Gall and Claude Gélinas, all anthropologists, as well as Khadiyatoulah Fall, a linguist, and François Gauthier, a specialist in religious studies. Géraldine Mossière is the coordinator and Véronique Jourdain the assistant coordinator of the project.

cover the individuals' personal and religious trajectories, the role of the religious group in their everyday lives, their level of economic, social, and ideological commitment to the religious community and, when relevant, religious activities pursued outside the group's purview.[14]

The methodology of the research is strongly influenced by approaches termed variously 'experiential', 'phenomenological' or 'experience-near'.[15] Our research tools give an important place to the voice of the actors, their subjectivity and embodied experiences. At the same time, we seek to limit the biases of such an approach by the use of standardised interview and observation formats (adjusted as needed for each group), a common analytical grid for research reports and careful supervision of the work of assistants by several researchers. Meintel and Mossière devised these tools for the team study on the basis of their own extensive fieldwork in a Spiritualist church (Meintel) and in a Pentecostal congregation (Mossière). Their research was integrated into the project.

Although the members of these religious groups are often geographically scattered in the same way as the Finnish expatriates examined by Saara Kokkalainen, their involvement within a common religious space offers an opportunity to consider them as a social group. While anthropologists now make considerable use of resources offered by the new technologies of communication (the Internet), they also contend that fieldwork is no longer delineated by fixed boundaries, which emphasises the use of interviews over participant observation.[16] Our method of approaching migrants within their congregations, however, makes traditional fieldwork methods still relevant, at least for studying those who are active in religious groups. As a matter of fact, many of them consider the congregation as a social space of belonging and see their fellow believers as their families, just like the Japanese workers studied by Lisa Wiklund in New York, who regard their neighbourhood as their home.[17]

Immigrant Congregations

This paper focuses on the religious groups in our research that attract mainly immigrants. Forty-eight (48) such groups have been studied, and of these 30 are composed mostly of a single ethnic group (Vietnamese, Moroccans, Tamils from Sri Lanka and so on). Sixteen (16) of the 30 are formed around religions that are closely tied to one particular national/ethnic origin; e.g. Indian Hinduism or Senegalese Muridism. Twenty-three (23) groups attract

---

14 Abridged digital versions of published reports from the project are available at www.grdu.umontreal.ca/fr/publications-workingpapers.html.
15 The last-mentioned term is taken from Wikan 1991. This broad current includes many authors. See e.g. Csordas 2001; Csoradas 2002, Desjarlais 1992; Dubisch 2005; Goulet 1998; Goulet 1993; McGuire 2008; Turner 1994; Turner 1996.
16 See Hirvi, this volume; Wiklund, this volume.
17 Wiklund, this volume.

members from a common geographic area, e.g. Latin America, and two groups include mostly congregants from Africa or from the Caribbean. Finally, 60 other groups are composed of immigrants and non-immigrants from different backgrounds, where no particular ethnic group predominates; these involve religions that claim to be universal, including evangelical Christianity and Baha'i.

In our research on these groups, we find that many congregations where immigrants are in the majority are organised in such a way as to give a central place to the needs of newcomers, both religious and practical. There are a number of Catholic churches, for example, where immigrants are able to find religious expression in their own language, musical forms and prayer styles, e.g, those where Tamil Catholics worship. In most cases, the religious groups in our study have considerable influence over how their immigrant members adapt to Quebec. Usually they provide symbolic resources, and often practical, material help, to assist newcomers. Religious leaders often serve as cultural brokers and mediate interaction with the institutions and norms of the host society.

While a few congregations are monoethnic or nearly so, usually for reasons of language (e.g. the Tamil Catholics just mentioned), most serve as sites of *interethnic* relations; that is, members are rarely from a single country of origin but rather from a broader region of the world. For example, most Spanish-speaking Evangelical congregations include immigrants from various Latin American countries, as well as their Canadian-born children. Moreover, like most immigrant religious groups in our study, they include at least a few members of the social majority (white, Francophone, Quebec-born); some are married to immigrant members of the group, others not. Often these are individuals in ethnically mixed unions who came to the group through their immigrant spouse.

Religion, Resettlement and the Religious Community

As several researchers have shown to be the case with immigrant religious groups in the United States,[18] the immigrant congregations in our study frequently offer services to their members beyond religious ones. Newcomers receive material, social and affective support as well as practical advice and help in finding housing and employment and accessing government services. For example, members of the Senegalese Murids (brotherhoods) in Montreal receive new arrivals for extended stays in their homes while helping them to get established in a job and find a dwelling.[19] French and English language classes, tutoring for children, help in dealing with the state bureaucracy for refugees are offered by various congregations in our study. Mossière's study of a Congolese/Haitian congregation shows that the pastor of the church functions as a veritable cultural broker, helping his parishioners

18 Yang & Ebaugh 2001; Ebaugh & Chafetz 2000, 71–79.
19 Traore 2010.

to understand Quebecois mores regarding, for example, gender and parent-child relations.[20] This pastor, like several Congolese Catholic priests in the city, helps paragovernmental agencies to find Congolese families to care for unaccompanied minors arriving as refugee claimants from the country of origin.[21] While helping migrants to adapt to the new country, many religious groups also offer classes and activities that transmit the language and culture of the home country to the Canadian-born children and grandchildren of immigrants: for example, the courses in martial arts and the Vietnamese language given at a the Buddhist pagoda studied by Anaïs Détolle[22] or the classical Indian dance classes given at a Hindu Temple.[23] All these examples show how the religious communities created by migrants serve as a support for new arrivals and help their members to make their way in the host society while also in some cases acting as vehicles of transmission for minority cultures.

While important, these extra-religious functions of immigrant congregations should not obscure the importance of the religious resources they offer to their members. In fact, we would argue that the strength of the social ties in these congregations and the efficacy of their extra-religious services derive in great part from the religious bond between the members. In his research on a Muslim group in our study, Yannick Boucher shows that the mosque functions as a community centre, thus becoming more than just a sacred space devoted only to worship and prayers.[24] Solidarity and feelings of belonging are generated on the basis of religious beliefs and symbols held in common and the shared experience of migration. His work shows how the religious group helps replace community ties fractured by migration and plays a major role in the settlement process of members in the receiving society. According to one of the founding members, the mosque provides a

> ...social space for mutual help. For example, when some of us go to pick up *halal* meat, we all go to the slaughterhouse together. People share... The best help is from belonging, when you share the same objective of transcendence, where you are recognised for who you really are. This is the best help. You maybe didn't eat that evening, but nonetheless you feel satisfied after being together, because it's worth so much more, it recharges your batteries.

The social and economic functions of the religious group are reinforced by the normative dimension of the community. As the words of Boucher's informant indicate, the comfort offered by religious sociality to new migrants is partly due to shared religious values, a common relationship with transcendent sacredness.[25] The immigrant religious groups in our study

20 Mossière 2006.
21 Fortin 2007.
22 Détolle 2009.
23 Betbeder 2009.
24 Boucher 2009.
25 Boucher 2009.

tend to develop social communities based on common values, symbols and practices as well as deep feelings of belonging. Religious rituals often constitute key moments in the life of the group and reinforce the members' sense of community. Co-experience of the sacred fosters the creation of a community of shared meanings, affective ties and, in many cases, ecstatic experiences. In Pentecostal congregations, for example, ritual techniques using music, hymns, sermons and personal accounts of conversion by members engender deep emotional sharing among those present. Often such narratives articulate the religious experience with the pain and tribulations of migration, as is illustrated by examples from Aranza Recalde's work (2009) in our project presented below. In this sense, conversion narratives sometimes become a sacralised form of storytelling (cf. Roseman, *infra*), a way of talking about migration as well as one's encounter with the Divine.

We observe the importance of spiritual healing techniques and rituals in a wide variety of religious groups, including many of those with immigrant clienteles. Tamil Catholics, for example, have requested charismatic healing ceremonies so that the priest responsible for the group[26] occasionally invites charismatic clergy from Sri Lanka to visit and perform such rituals.

Religion and Transnationalism

Though transnationalism is often presented in economic terms, our study shows that religion is sometimes the central element in the transnational practices that link immigrants to the home country and other national contexts, something Peggy Levitt has also noted.[27] The international circulation of priests and religious leaders, as in the Tamil case just mentioned, is common. For example, the Murids studied by Diahara Traore for our project remain in constant contact with sheikhs (leaders) who travel between Senegal and Murid associations in Montreal, New York and other parts of the world.[28] This helps establish links between Murid groups in different countries as well as rivalry in fundraising efforts for Touba and Porokhane, Muridism's sacred cities in Senegal;[29] indeed sheiks are known to encourage marriage between single devotees who live in different cities, even different countries. The Latin American Pentecostal groups in Montreal that we have studied remain in close contact with Hispanic congregations elsewhere in the Americas. The Congolese Pentecostals studied by Mossière also belong to transnational networks based on shared Christian beliefs as well as a common language, French. For example, the pastor was proud to tell

---

26 Missions are based on language and national/ethnic origin rather than geography; a number of such missions exist in the Montreal diocese, for Koreans, Chinese, Filipinos and other groups.
27 Levitt 2008.
28 Traore 2010.
29 Touba is the city of origin of the founder of Muridism, Sheikh Amadou Bamba; Porokhane is that of his mother, Mam Diarra Bousso.

Mossière that he posts his weekly sermons on the French-speaking Christian website *TopChrétien*,[30] from which he receives many encouraging messages from members all over the world. Moreover, the CEP has a socioeconomic development project in the DRC, for which the pastor draws funding and management skills from other Pentecostal congregations located in various parts of North America.

Relations with the Host Society

Many of our findings run counter to the stereotypical views of immigrant religion that are often found in the mass media, where religion and religiosity are presented as markers of difference between immigrants and non-immigrants. In Quebec, such notions are further reinforced by the belief, largely erroneous,[31] that the host society is generally irreligious. Rather than posing an obstacle to social and economic integration, the religious groups frequented by immigrants generally inculcate norms of hard work, the value of education and, often, abstemious lifestyles; furthermore, most encourage participation in the wider society.

The mutual aid and support migrants find in religious groups are not considered a substitute for public institutions and government services but rather complement the resources provided by the state, and members often transmit information about these to new arrivals.[32] Moreover, religious norms often reinforce behaviour seen as conducive to success in the new society. The Congolese pastor of the Pentecostal congregation studied by Mossière counsels his flock to avoid 'Satan's trap' of easy credit and to gain the strength to do so from religious observance. Exhorting his followers to stay away from welfare, he declaims: 'That is not your place; go back to school. God doesn't want you on welfare!'[33] The message is much the same in a Salvadorian evangelical church in our study; economic success is seen as the fruit of honourable work, a sign of divine favour.[34]

Adaptations of religious practice to the wider society are common among the groups we have studied. A Muslim scholar in Quebec, Khadiyatoulah Fall[35] argues that Islam has its own notion of 'reasonable accommodation' (the term currently used in Quebec to describe how social pluralism should be attained) expressed in the concept of '*Arrouhsatou*' (compromise), which allows the adaptation of religious practice to the social and physical environment. For example, the ritual sacrifice of sheep for the Muslim feast

---

30 www.topchretien.com
31 Our research finds much evidence to the contrary (Meintel, forthcoming), though often people prefer to describe themselves as 'spiritual' rather than religious. Meintel, in press.
32 Boucher 2009.
33 Mossière 2006.
34 Recalde 2009.
35 Fall has been a member of our research team since 2010. Fall 2007.

of Aïd el-Kebir is sometimes complicated, especially in regions where there are few Muslims. Instead, many send remittances to their families back home in order to have the ritual performed there.

Hindus modify rituals such as cremation, which in India, would be performed along a riverbank, to conform with Quebec law. For example, certain Hindu festivals involving sacred fireworks are supervised by police and firemen because of the crowds involved and the danger of fire. Cremation, which would be performed by a priest on a riverbank in India, is executed by funeral home in a crematorium in Quebec. The religious doctrines of new groups are sometimes presented by their leaders and members as converging with the dominant values in the host society. For example, Hindu philosophy advocates a vision of the world in which all life forms take their meaning through interactions between each other. Accordingly, Hindus in Montreal have presented their religion as a holistic philosophy of life rather than as a religious creed.[36] Hindus, like the Tamil Catholics studied by Bouchard, also develop new places of pilgrimage in Canada; Montreal Hindus, for example, are likely to visit a temple in Val Morin, a rural town in Quebec, for retreats, prayer and to celebrate a major religious festival held in the summer.[37] Tamil Catholics have adopted certain local Catholic pilgrimage sites such as the shrine to Our Lady of Lourdes in Rigaud Quebec.[38]

In a number of cases, political participation in the new society is encouraged by the religious group. For example, Serge Maynard studied a Muslim group in our research project that was mainly comprised of Moroccan immigrants and whose members are encouraged to let go of the 'myth of return' (to Morocco) and rather contribute to the society where they are living by volunteering, being active in their neighbourhoods and political participation.[39] Similarly, Hindu leaders give lectures about local cultural diversity, while temples organise their members to participate in public events like blood donation campaigns or marches to encourage kidney donations.[40] Mosques in Montreal have held 'open door' days, this so as 'to get to know our neighbours and give our neighbours an opportunity to know us better', according to the President of the Muslim Council of Montreal, Salam Elmenyawi.[41] The Vietnamese pagoda in our study invites government officials to important rituals, and its leaders express gratitude to Canada on these occasions for accepting Vietnamese refugees.

Certain religious groups such as the one studied by Recalde put more emphasis on shielding members from what are perceived to be the moral dangers of Quebec society (drinking, sexual promiscuity, etc.) than on civic

---

36 Betbeder 2009.
37 Bouchard 2009.
38 On occasion, Tamil customs such as picnicking on the sacred site in large numbers and inviting their Hindu friends to take part in services has caused some conflict with local religious authorities.
39 Maynard 2009a; 2009b.
40 Betbeder 2009.
41 Scott 2010.

participation.[42] Such groups are likely to see Quebec as a field of potential converts. Many others, such as the Pentecostals that Mossière studied as well as Latin American Evangelical groups currently under study in our project, encourage schooling as well as participation in the wider society while fostering values such as modest dress, family values and so on. Most immigrant religious groups support family models that are at variance with dominant trends in Quebec, which include high rates of cohabitation without marriage, children born out of wedlock and marital separation; this is in keeping with findings from some of Meintel's earlier research on migrant families showing that both immigrant parents and their children who have grown up in Quebec prefer the family patterns of the group of origin.[43] The respect for elders, sexual restraint (especially for women) and greater familism of the group of origin are typically contrasted with prevailing mores in Quebec.

Though leaders may seek to orient how the religious group is positioned in the wider society, members sometimes differ widely in how they see relationships with the dominant group. Some Muslims in one of the Montreal mosques studied by Maynard consider their lifestyles and beliefs to be too different from those of non-Muslims to allow social mixing, while a minority at the same mosque expresses more openness.[44] The range of positions individuals take towards the dominant society is to some extent a matter of subjective attitudes to religious identity and personal beliefs and practices.

One of the practical issues immigrant groups face in dealing with the wider society is that of obtaining spaces of worship. This, it must be said, is a problem even for groups whose members were mostly born in Quebec, as is the case with the Spiritualist congregations studied by Meintel. Affordable space that is suitable for religious activities is hard to find, particularly in Montreal.[45] Congregations often have limited resources because their members are also of modest means. Many try to rent buildings near subway stations for the benefit of their members who use public transport. Negative stereotyping makes finding a suitable space all the more difficult for immigrant religious groups. When, for example, Tamil Catholics sought to buy a Catholic parish church from a congregation whose declining numbers made it necessary to sell the building, the remaining parishioners vetoed the sale. Congolese Pentecostals and North African Muslims have also faced objections by owners or neighbours. Traffic difficulties and noise are common objections; however, it is likely that other factors are at work.

42 Recalde 2009.
43 Meintel 1992.
44 Maynard 2009a; 2009b.
45 Germain & Gagnon 2003.

Interethnic Relations in Religious Contexts

Most of the immigrant religious groups in our study include members of several, if not many, different national and ethnic origins. However, the groups generally have the flavour of a particular region of the world in their religious practices and social activities. In the pagoda studied by Détolle, Buddhism is linked to cults of ancestor worship traditional to Vietnam.[46] Visitors are welcomed, are free to participate as they wish and are even invited for a vegetarian meal after the religious celebrations. At the same time, traditional Vietnamese values of discretion, modesty, respect for elders and dignity prevail and make for a culturally different religious milieu than that of other Buddhist groups in our study, where native-born Quebecois predominate. The same pagoda is also the place of worship of a number of Chinese-born Buddhists, who, in spite of the difference in language, participate in rituals and enjoy cordial relations with the Vietnamese majority. Often, however, as Judith Nagata has noted, language is influential in defining the social boundaries of the religious group.[47] Tamil Catholic services are usually held in the Tamil language, and those of a Vietnamese Catholic congregation under study are in Vietnamese even though a few non-Vietnamese spouses may be present.

Even in groups where rituals and social interaction are carried out in languages little known beyond a particular ethnic group, the usually include a few Quebecois spouses or other converts born in Quebec, as for example in the Senegalese Murid studied by Traore, where the main language is Wolof.[48] Immigrant religious groups typically provide an experience of fellowship with individuals of different origins, even sometimes, as in the Vietnamese pagoda studied by Détolle, between people who speak different languages.[49] Wan and her husband, both Chinese-born, do not speak Vietnamese, the language used at the pagoda, and yet are very active there. Wan says: 'It cannot be described by language like this. But we have the feeling. With some people we feel very close without saying anything.'

Most immigrant congregations are made up of members from various countries who share general cultural similarities, a common language and come from the same general region of the world. For example, there are many Latin American Spanish-speaking churches in Montreal like the Central American Spanish-speaking Evangelical church studied by Recalde, whose members come from Guatemala, El Salvador and Honduras.[50] Similarly, Hindu temples bring together immigrants from various regions of the Indian subcontinent, serving as a focal point of social participation and forming contexts where common transethnic cultural values, symbols and religious practices are emphasised over those that are specific to a particular

---

46 Détolle 2010.
47 Nagata 1988.
48 Traore 2010.
49 Détolle 2009.
50 Recalde 2009.

region or ethnic group. Anne-Laure Betbeder's research on four temples in the Montreal area shows that this encompassing pan-Hindu vision continues to expand in the second generation, so that temple environments tend to grow ever more inclusive over time.[51]

Immigrant congregations generally support ethnic identifications that are somewhat broader than those their members held before migrating. In some cases, members and leaders assert the primacy of religious affiliation over ethnic differences. This is the case, for example, with the Muslims who frequent the mosques in our study. Similarly, Evangelicals often mention that their fellow church members are from diverse ethnic backgrounds. Although immigrant believers may identify by ethnicity, social class or level of education, their religious affiliation constitutes a source of pride and a positive form of distinctiveness and helps to shape their relations with the non-immigrant majority.

Nonetheless, we have found one case where ethnic differences outweigh religious ones, and where divisions in the congregation are emerging. This is the case of a regional mosque in our study where the use of Arabic for sermons (downloaded from Mecca every Friday) and the lack of participation by North African members in the Murid feast of the Grand Magal[52] has led to disaffection on the part of Sub-Saharan African members. As they are also uncomfortable with what some of them see as an inflexible, dogmatic approach to Islam on the part of the North Africans, they have recently formed a separate prayer group. We have also learned of mosques in Montreal (not included in our study) where divisions between West Africans (usually Wolof-speaking) and Arabic-speaking North Africans have emerged.

The interethnic relations experienced in the religious group sometimes help migrants to overcome the experiences of racism they have encountered in the wider society by emphasising religious identity over ethnic origin. Marie-Rose is a Haitian-born nurse who arrived in Quebec as a teenager. She remembers her arrival in Montreal as a difficult time, especially at school, where she experienced race prejudice and felt isolated from other students. Of Catholic background, some fifteen years ago she converted to a Pentecostal church studied by Mossière.[53] Now in her fifties, she feels at peace with herself and believes that God has transformed her:

> He changed my life, I am no longer the same person, and I don't see life the same way any more. I am becoming more mature through the church. [...] I no longer see this one as Black, that one as White, now we are human beings. I have White friends, we talk on the phone and so on.

---

51 Betbeder 2009.
52 The Grand Magal is an annual Murid celebration that remembers the exile of the founder (Cheikh Mamadou Bamba) by French colonial authorities in 1985.
53 Mossière 2007b.

Another Haitian woman in the same congregation, Claudette, had also experienced racism in the past but says that now that is no longer the case and that she has a number of White friends and acquaintances. Speaking of a woman in the congregation (a White Quebecoise born in the province), she says:

> You don't know if she's White or Black or what, we see in her a sister, there's no colour that bothers us where we'd say, 'Oh, she's White', no. At the church – I don't know if it's like that in other churches, but it's like that it's sister Monique, sister Claudette, and that's all.'

Conversion, or the adoption of a new religious identity, by non-immigrants often involves becoming part of a religious community where migrants from other parts of the world predominate. Many women converts to Islam whom Mossière has met in Quebec describe their relationships with Muslim-born people in terms similar to those expressed by one of her informants: 'Good thing I found Islam before I met Muslims!'[54] The women usually marry Muslim-born men from North Africa in the hope that their husband will teach them proper Muslim practices as well as the Arabic language, the language of the Qur'an.[55]. However, many converts come to question their husband's Muslim heritage when they discover that their partner's religious practices and values are mixed with elements from their cultural backgrounds. According to the women, this conveys an erroneous image of Islam. Issues of sexism become problematic when converts associate their husbands' expectations with the customs of the latters' countries of origin, while the men see them as Islamic prescriptions regarding gender roles. At the same time, the men are often less fervent in their observance of Islam than their wives. This discrepancy between visions of Islam has led a significant number of the women to get divorced and to marry another, more observant, Muslim-born man.

Reframing Difficult Experiences

Besides the social and economic support offered to new arrivals by religious groups, the symbolic resources they provide are of particular value to new migrants who experience hardships such as deskilling and unemployment, which are often part and parcel of the migrant experience. For example, Maynard met well-educated Muslim immigrant men who used periods of extended unemployment to intensify their activities in the service of

54 Mossière 2008a.
55 We do not find the same tendency among Evangelical Protestants. For instance, Haitian members who convert to Pentecostalism in the Congolese congregation studied by Mossière do not appear to find the religion of Africans born into the faith as more authentic than their own.

their religious group.[56] Wan came to Canada in 2001 with her husband, an accountant. He was unable to work in his field initially because he knew no French. It was in this context that he, and later she herself, discovered Buddhism and the (mainly Vietnamese) pagoda, to which they now give all their spare time.[57] Though he later found work as an accountant, once Wan found her own well-paying position in business, her husband decided to devote his time to child care (they have a young daughter) and the practice of Buddhism at the pagoda.

In Evangelical churches, migrants often develop a religious reading of their difficult experiences in the host country. Antonio, an immigrant from El Salvador whom Recalde interviewed, believes that it was God who inspired him to abandon a drug shipment he was taking into the U.S.A. just before arriving at the border. Despite the 'shield of sin' (drinking, smoking and so on) in his life at that time, God intervened. He later learned that his partner had already been arrested at customs. Now in his sixties and blind, Antonio believes that he has lost his sight so as to better experience and listen to God. To cite another case from Recalde's study, Amelia left her job in Honduras as a single mother in her mid-twenties and came to Montreal, where she expected to join her child's father. The relationship quickly dissolved, and Amelia found herself without resources 'sleeping on the floor, with nothing to eat'. Without the means to re-establish herself in Honduras, she turned to God (she had had a brief experience in a Pentecostal church before emigrating) and began to go to church. Years later she came to see the times of hardship she went through as 'the work of God', so as to eventually be 'raised up in God'. Today she is married to a member of the same church and has had five more children, all members of the same church.[58]

In sum, religious belief reframes the experiences of migration, resettlement, and difficulties experienced in the host society, such as discrimination and unemployment, and allows immigrants to reinvest them with positive meaning through reference to the presence and intervention of God in their lives. What is more, the religious resources that allow them to do so are often imported from elsewhere – as with Muslim and most Evangelical groups – and to some extent reworked by them in the local context.

Studying Migrants in Religious Contexts

Taking religious groups and activities as a research focus puts migrants, not to mention notions such as 'integration', in something of a different light than when research is explicitly focused on ethnicity or problems connected with the process of migration and resettlement. What we have presented so far shows that, in the religious context, the social agency of immigrants

---

56 Maynard 2009b.
57 Détolle 2009.
58 Recalde 2009.

is paramount. In other words, we see immigrants finding solutions and compensations for the travails associated with migration – separation from family and home, unemployment, deskilling, discrimination, and so on. Moreover, we see immigrants helping each other with longer established individuals assisting newcomers by sharing material resources and information. Finally, relationships between immigrants and the host society are clearly negotiated in a reflexive way in the teachings of many religious groups, and religious leaders often serve as social and cultural intermediaries in the resettlement process.

Often when studying immigrants, the researcher (unless s/he is also a migrant or is of the same ethnic origin) is taken as a representative of the host society, and interaction is framed in majority-minority dynamic of the wider society. Researchers may be confused with social workers or government representatives, and it is sometimes difficult for them to escape their status as members of the social majority. Much of the time, there is an inevitable element of 'studying down' in the research encounter.[59]

By contrast, when the focus is on religion, 'the field' is likely to become an enclave of *étrangèreté*, of foreignness and strangerhood, in otherwise familiar surroundings. The researcher steps into a world that is different from her/his own and is yet surrounded by a society s/he knows well. In the fieldwork context, not only are non-immigrants in the minority, but the cultural norms, language, music and aesthetics of another region of the world are likely to predominate. Often studying immigrant religious groups takes on aspects of 'studying up';[60] in other words, religious hierarchies are at times so pronounced that an ethnographic interview with the leader may be unthinkable, as was the case with several groups in our study. In order to study a religious group, learning about its rituals, beliefs and sacred texts is essential, so that the researcher almost inevitably takes on something of an 'apprentice' role, as for example was the case with Robert Desjarlais in his study of Nepalese shamanism.[61]

Relationships between researchers and those they study are likely to be more complex when immigrant religious groups are the focus of attention than when focusing directly on ethnicity or migration. Much, probably most, research on immigrants (except that done for doctoral and master's theses) is conducted via interviews, when indeed it is not based on more remote methods (questionnaires, analyses of census data, etc.). Studying immigrant religious beliefs and practices, on the other hand, usually requires extended contact with the religious group and its members. Understanding religious behaviour requires not only interviews, formal and informal, but also many hours of observation in ritual and other religious contexts, and often enough, study of the group's sacred texts. Typically, field observations require at least a modicum of participation from the researcher, if only to blend in with the social environment.

59 Hannerz 2006.
60 Hannerz 2006.
61 Desjarlais 1992.

All anthropological fieldwork implicates the subjectivity of the researcher, and without this the intersubjectivity that is necessary for any fieldwork would not be possible.[62] However, supervising over thirty field assistants in the study of religious groups in Quebec, as well as doing such research ourselves, has given us occasion to see that studying religion implicates the researcher's subjectivity in ways that are particularly complex. Unless the researcher is a member of the group studied, s/he is taken to be an outsider to the ethnic group and its migratory history; however empathetic the researcher, direct participation in the experience of the migrants is usually not possible.

Things are different in studying religious groups because the fieldworker can indeed share the religious experience of the migrant if s/he so chooses. Rationalistic dismissals of others' religious beliefs, like Evans-Pritchard's treatment of witchcraft beliefs among the Azande, are no longer typical of anthropologists' attitudes.[63] Some, like Michael Jackson, hold that the truth or falsity and the rationality or irrationality of their subjects' beliefs is irrelevant to their work.[64] Others go much further. King, for example, in his work on vampiric shamans in Siberia, argues that 'analysis proceeds best from the assumption that such entities as spirits and vampires *do* exist'.[65] Peter Geschiere makes a strong case for the actual existence of witchcraft and witches in Africa.[66] Some researchers decide to enter into the spiritual realities of 'others' themselves. Jean-Guy Goulet, for example, found it necessary to engage himself in shamanistic practice among the Dene Tha in Alberta, Canada, in order to learn about it.[67] Elsewhere he argues that opening one's own subjectivity to others' spiritual realities can be a valid and potentially rich dimension of ethnographic research.[68] Meintel has adopted a similar stance in her work on Spiritualists.[69] Without adopting Pentecostal beliefs in any consistent way, Mossière elected to share the ritual emotional experience with the members of the congregation she studied.[70]

The possibility of religious sharing, however virtual it may remain, makes a crucial difference for fieldwork. For one thing, reflexivity, a theme also explored by Fran Meissner and Inês Hasselberg in this volume, becomes a necessary component of the research process. In order to apprehend religious phenomena, researchers are inevitably confronted with their own belief systems and must situate themselves in relation to the beliefs of their subjects, which in turn, is likely to influence their research methods and

---

62 Bloch 1977, 283. Cited by Fabian 1983, 42.
63 'Witches as the Azane conceive them, clearly cannot exist.' Evans-Pritchard 1996, 303.
64 Jackson 1996, 11; Jackson 1989, 101.
65 King 1998, 57.
66 Geschière 1995, 29–35.
67 Goulet 1998.
68 Goulet 1993.
69 Meintel 2006; 2007b; 2011.
70 Mossière 2007c.

strategies. Typically, the student of religion must decide 'how far to go' in participating in the religious activities and beliefs of others, and must explain these decisions to those who participate in the study. In our study, assistants and researchers have not been asked to make their personal beliefs explicit as a condition of doing research, though, in Meintel's experience at least, such questions are frequently encountered from academic colleagues and students. In the vast majority of cases, the religious groups contacted have welcomed researchers and in some cases seem to consider our interest in studying them a form of validation.

The spatial separation between 'home' and a distant 'field' that long characterised the imagined, if not always the real, practice of anthropology has been called into question in recent years.[71] For anyone studying migrants in their own society, the separation between home and field is indeed tenuous,[72] and all the more so when the researcher is from the same group of origin. This has special implications when religion is the focus of study, since the simple fact of frequenting a religious group in one's own city may enmesh the fieldworker in a web of social and material obligations, as several assistants in our study discovered. For example, Senegalese Murids, including women's branches, engage in extensive fund-raising for developing the brotherhood's sacred cities in Senegal; Traore, like any other woman in the group she studied, found herself expected to make substantial contributions to these efforts.[73]

This is not to say that others will accept the researcher's self-definition. For example, Evangelical Christians sometimes take the researcher's assiduous attendance at religious gatherings as a sign of conversion 'in his heart' that is but an augury of the real thing. Moreover, the researcher's position is likely to shift during the course of the fieldwork. As the extensive literature on 'insider' or 'native' research shows, insider/outsider status is never absolute.[74] In studying religious groups, even their own, our field assistants have found that their relationship to the practices and beliefs of the groups that they study changes over time. Insiders adopt critical perspectives on formerly taken-for-granted beliefs and practices; outsiders discover a need to situate themselves in relation to religion and spirituality. In virtually all cases, the informants' religiosity has brought them to question their own (or the lack thereof), and in some cases to develop new spiritual practices of their own (though not necessarily in the same religion as the one they have studied).

71 Clifford 1997; Gupta & Ferguson 1997; Caputo 2000.
72 See Hirvi, this volume.
73 Traore 2010.
74 Narayan 1993.

Conclusion

What we have tried to show here is that studying migrants in their religious groups is likely to reveal new facets of the migrant experience and to highlight the social agency of migrants. Furthermore, studying immigrant religious groups indicates a high degree of adaptation by migrants to their new society, including integration on the religious level, and brings to light the initiatives of such groups and their leaders to orient members' relationships with the wider society. Indeed, we find that religious groups offer considerable assistance to new members in the resettlement process, much as Nancy Foner and Richard Alba have noted.[75] We emphasise that the strength of the sociality of religious groups and the efficacy of the social and material help they give members, particularly new immigrants, cannot be detached from the religious resources they provide. In other words, the strength of these ties and resources derives from the fact that religion provides the group's members with a moral community, one of trust, deriving from a shared vision of the world and relationship with the sacred. Religious social ties are made all the stronger by co-participation in religious rituals, which involves sharing emotionally engaging, sometimes ecstatic, moments of *communitas*.[76]

We have tried to show that when studying ethnicity via religion, the research process takes on added complexity and presents the fieldworker with particular challenges. Studying immigrant religious groups puts the researcher in a situation that in some ways mirrors that of the immigrant: just as the immigrant must situate her-/himself in the normative and cultural context of the host society, so the student of immigrant religion must position her-/himself with respect to the normative and cultural ethos of the religious group. Both engage in considerable reflexivity regarding their adaptation to an alien environment, and in the end, both must accept the risk of being to some degree transformed by the dynamic of intersubjectivity that these encounters involve.

Bibliography

Betbeder, A-L. 2009: Hétérogénéité et force d'intégration dans les temples hindous montréalais. *Document de Travail du Groupe de Recherche Diversité Urbaine.* Montréal.

Bloch, Maurice 1977: The Past and the Present in the Present. *Man* 12: 27, 278–292.

Bouchard, M. 2009: La Mission catholique tamoule: présentation ethnographique et enquête sur la dévotion mariale. *Document de Travail du Groupe de Recherche Diversité Urbaine.* Montréal.

Boucher, Y. 2009: L'Islam en contexte minoritaire: étude de cas d'une mosquée au Saguenay-Lac-Saint-Jean. *Document de Travail du Groupe de Recherche Diversité Urbaine.* Montréal.

75 Foner & Alba 2008.
76 Turner 1975.

Caputo, V. 2000: At Home and Away: Reconfiguring the Field for Late Twentieth Century Anthropology. In: V. Amit (ed.), *Constructing the Field: Ethnographic Fieldwork in the Contemporary World*. New York: Routledge.

Clifford, J. 1997: Spatial Practices: Fieldwork, Travel and the Disciplining of Anthropology. In: A. Gupta, & J. Ferguson (eds.), *Anthropological Locations: Boundaries and Grounds of a Field Science*. Berkeley: University of California Press.

Csordas, T. 2001: *Language, Charisma and Creativity: Ritual Life in the Catholic Charismatic Renewal*. New York: Palgrave.

Csoradas, T. 2002: *Body/Meaning/Healing*. New York: Palgrave.

Desjarlais, R. 1992: *Body and Emotion: the Aesthetics of Illness and Healing in the Nepal Himalayas*. Philadelphia: University of Pennsylvania Press.

Détolle, A. 2010: Alimenter l'identité: Rapport de terrain d'ethnologie culinaire et religieuse au sein d'une pagode bouddhiste vietnamienne au Québec. Working paper published by the Groupe de Recherche Diversité Urbaine. Montréal.

Dubisch J. 2008: Challenging the Boundaries of Experience, Performance, and Consciousness: Edith Turner's Contributions to the Turnerian Project. In: G. St John (ed.), *Victor Turner and Contemporary Cultural Performance*, New York: Berghahn Books.

Dubisch, J. 2005: Body, Self and Cosmos in 'New Age' Energy Healing. In: E. Lorek-Jezinska & K. Wieckowska, (eds.) *Corporeal Inscriptions: Representations of the Body in Cultural and Literary Texts and Practices*, Torun: Nicholas Copernicus University Press.

Ebaugh, H. R. & J. S. Chafetz 2000: *Religion and the New Immigrants*. Walnut Creek: AltaMira Press.

Evans-Pritchard, E. E. 1996: The Notion of Witchcraft Explains Unfortunate Events. In: R. Grinker & C. Steiner (eds.), *Perspectives on Africa: A Reader in Culture, History and Representation*. Oxford: Blackwell Publishing.

Fabian, J. 1983: *Time and the Other: How Anthropology Makes Its Object*. New York: Columbia.

Fall, K. 2007: Pour un Islam du Québec. *Le Devoir*. Montréal: 19 September. www.ledevoir.com/2007/09/19/157463.html. Accessed February 17 2011.

Foner, N. & R. Alba 2008: Immigrant Religion in the U.S. and Western Europe: Bridge or Barrier to Inclusion? *International Migration Review* 42, 360–392.

Fortin, M-N. 2007: *Les jeunes migrants seuls d'origine congolaise: le rôle intermédiaire de la communauté*. Anthropology Master's thesis. Université de Montréal.

Germain, A. & J. E. Gagnon 2003: L'autre, là où on ne l'attendait pas... Les lieux de culte des minorités ethno-religieuses. In: M. Venne (dir.), *L'annuaire du Quebec 2004*. Saint-Laurent Québec: Fides.

Geschière, P. 1995: *Sorcellerie et politique en Afrique : La viande des autres*. Paris: Karthala.

Goulet, J-G. 1998: *Ways of Knowing: Experience, Knowledge, and Power Among the Dene Tha*. Vancouver: UBC Press.

Goulet, J-G. 1993: Dreams and Visions in Indigenous Lifeworlds: An Experiential Approach. *Canadian Journal of Native Studies*, 13: 2, 171–198.

Gupta, A. & J. Ferguson 1997: Discipline and Practice: "The Field" as Site, Method, and Location in Anthropology. In: A. Gupta, & J. Ferguson (eds.), *Anthropological Locations. Boundaries and Grounds of a Field Science*. Berkeley: University of California Press.

Hannerz, U. 2006: Studying Down, Up, Sideways, Through, Backwards, Forwards, Away and at Home: Reflections on the Field Worries of an Expansive Discipline. In: S. Coleman & P. Collins (eds.), *Locating the Field: Space, Place and Context in Anthropology*. Oxford: Berg.

Jackson M. 1989: *Paths to a Clearing: Radical Empiricism and Ethnographic Inquiry*, Bloomington: Indiana University Press.

Jackson, M. 1996: Introduction. In: M. Jackson (ed.), *Things as They Are*, Bloomington: Indiana University Press.

King, A. D. 1998: Soul Suckers: Vampiric Shamans in Northern Kamchatka, Russia. *Anthropology of Consciousness* 10: 4, 57–68.

Levitt, P. 2008: Religion as a path to civic engagement. *Ethnic and Racial Studies* 31: 4, 766–791.

Maynard, S. 2009a: Vivre sa foi sous le regard de "l'autre". Étude de cas de la mosquée Zitouna. *Document de Travail du Groupe de recherche Diversité urbaine*. Montréal.

Maynard, S. 2009b: Vivre au Québec selon l'Islam. Étude de cas d'une association musulmane montréalaise. *Document de Travail du Groupe de recherche Diversité urbaine*. Montréal.

McGuire, M. 2008: *Lived Religions: Faith and Practice in Everyday Life*. New York: Oxford.

Meintel, D. & E. Kahn 2005: De génération en génération: identités et projets identitaires des montréalais de la "deuxième génération". *Ethnologies* 27: 1, 131–165.

Meintel, D. 1984: Migration, Wage Labour and Domestic Relationships: Immigrant Women Workers in Montreal. *Anthropologica* 26: 2, 135–170.

Meintel, D. 1992: Identité ethnique chez de jeunes montréalais d'origine immigrée. *Sociologie et Sociétés* 24: 2, 73–89.

Meintel, D. 2002a: Cape Verdean Transnationality, Old and New. *Anthropologica* 44: 1, 25–42.

Meintel, D. 2002b: Transmitting Pluralism: Mixed Unions in Montreal. *Canadian Ethnic Studies* 34: 3, 99–120.

Meintel, D. 2003: La stabilité dans le flou : parcours religieux et identités de spiritualistes. *Anthropologie et sociétés* 27: 1, 35–64.

Meintel, D. 2006: Événements et non-événements : Une recherche en milieu spiritualiste. In: J-I. Olazabal & J. Lévy (eds), *L'événement en anthropologie : Concepts et terrains*. Ste-Foy: Presses de l'Université Laval, 245–267.

Meintel, D. 2007a: When There Is No Conversion: Spiritualists and Personal Religious Change. *Anthropologica* 49: 1, 149–162.

Meintel, D. 2007b: When the Extraordinary Hits Home: Experiencing Spiritualism. In: J-G. Goulet & B. Granville Miller (eds.), *Extraordinary Anthropology: Transformations in the field*. Lincoln: University of Nebraska, 124–157.

Meintel, D. 2010: Nouvelles formes de convivialité religieuse au Québec. In: S. Fath, S. Mathieu & L. Endelstein (eds.), *Dieu Change en Ville*. Paris.

Meintel, D. 2011: Apprendre et désapprendre : quand la médiumnité croise l'anthropologie . *Anthropologie et sociétés*, 35 : 3, 89–106.

Mossière, G. 2006: "Former un citoyen utile au Québec et qui reçoit de ce pays". Le rôle d'une communauté religieuse montréalaise dans la trajectoire migratoire de ses members. *Les Cahiers du GRES/Diversité Urbaine* 6: 1, 45–61. www.erudit.org/revue/lcg/2006/v6/n1/012682ar.pdf

Mossière, G. 2007a: Sharing in Ritual Effervescence: Emotions and Empathy in Fieldwork. *Anthropology Matters Journal* 9: 1, 1–14. *www.anthropologymatters. com/journal/2007-1/mossiere_2007_sharinGéraldinehtm*.

Mossière, G. 2007b: Emotional Dimensions of Conversion: An African Evangelical Congregation in Montreal. *Anthropologica* 49: 1, 113–124.

Mossière, G. 2008a: Reconnue par l'autre, respectée chez soi: la construction d'un discours politique critique et alternatif par des femmes converties à l'Islam en France et au Québec. *Revue Diversité Urbaine* 8: 2, 37–59.

Mossière, G. 2008b: Une congrégation pentecôtiste congolaise à Montréal: un christianisme du sud bouture québécoise. *Archives des Sciences Sociales des Religions* 143: 195–214.

Mossière, G. 2010a: Mobility and Belonging among Transnational Congolese Pentecostal Congregations: modernity and the emergence of socioeconomic differences. In: A. Adogame & J. V. Spickard (eds.), *Religion Crossing Boundaries: Transnational Dynamics in African and the New African Diasporic Religions.* Leiden: E.J. Brill, Religion and Social Order series.

Mossière, G. 2010b: Passer et retravailler la frontière. Des converties à l'islam en France et au Québec: jeux et enjeux de médiation et de différenciation. *Sociologie et Sociétés* 42: 1, 245–270.

Narayan, K. 1993: How Native is a Native Anthropologist?. *American Anthropologist* 95: 3, 671–686.

Nagata, J. 1988: Religion, Ethnicity and Language: Indonesian Chinese Immigrants in Toronto. *Southeast Asian Journal of Social Science* 16: 1, 116–30.

Recalde, A. 2009: Being a good Christian in Montréal: On how religious principles regulate behavior in the secular world among a group of Latin American evangelicals. *Document de Travail du Groupe de Recherche Diversité Urbaine.* Montréal.

Scott, M. 2010: Mosques Open Doors for Special Welcome. *The Gazette.* Montréal: December 3. www.montrealgazette.com/life/Mosques+open+doors+special+welc ome/3921690/story.html#ixzz1BgTZwsFD. Accessed Febuary 17 2010.

Traore, D. 2010: La communauté mouride et les dimensions de l'expérience religieuse des femmes mourides à Montréal. *Document de Travail du Groupe de Recherche Diversité Urbaine.* Montréal.

Turner, E. 1994: A Visible Spirit Form in Zambia. In: J-G. Goulet & D. Young (eds.), *Being Changed by Cross-cultural Encounters; the Anthropology of Extraordinary Experience.* Peterborough: Broadview press, 71–95.

Turner, E. 1996: *The Hands Feel It: Healing and Spirit Presence Among a Northern Alaskan People.* DeKalb, Illinois: Northern Illinois University Press.

Turner, V. 1975: *Revelation and Divination.* New York: Cornell University Press.

Wikan, U. 1991: Toward an Experience Near Anthropology. *Cultural Anthropology* 6: 3, 285–305.

Yang, F. & H. R. Ebaugh 2001: Transformations in New Immigrant Religions and Their Global Implications. *American Sociological Review* 66, 269–88.

José Mapril

Chawtpohtee in Lisbon

Food and Place among Bangladeshis in Portugal

A Bangladeshi dish called *Chawtpohtee*, to which the title of the present article refers, came to mind when I recalled a specific event that occurred in 2005, right in the middle of my fieldwork among Bangladeshis in Portugal. It was *Id-ul-Ad'ha*, the Feast of Sacrifice, the second most important date in the Islamic calendar, and I had just met Mukitur in a Lisbon mosque for the morning prayers.[1] He was one of the first Bangladeshis to arrive in Portugal and a very important political figure. After the morning prayers, we went, together with other pioneer Bangladeshi migrants, to Zakir's house. As is frequent on such festive occasions, he received us with sweets and tea (*cha*). Everybody sat down around the table and began eating when our host, to the surprise of us all, brought *Chawtpohtee*, a salad of chickpeas, hard-boiled eggs, onions, chillies, spices and tamarind sauce. We were in a hurry because we were supposed to go to a slaughterhouse on the outskirts of Lisbon to perform the *qurban*, the ritual sacrifice of an animal that is customarily carried out on such occasions. In spite of this, everybody was so surprised by the arrival of the dish that we stayed put and began to enjoy the moment. At one point, Mukitur said while eating the salad 'It really feels as if I were in Bangladesh!' This sentiment was shared by everybody, and indeed all seemed to feel a little bit more at home.

Between 2003 and 2008, I carried out a research project about Bangladeshi migration in Lisbon. The project was designed to describe a migration flow that was totally unknown in the literature on Portuguese migration, and thus, for twenty-four months, divided into two periods, I carried out ethnographic fieldwork in Portugal and Bangladesh. I began the fieldwork in the way it always begins: *hanging about* in order to meet and talk to people about their migration experiences, routes and expectations. I wanted to understand and map the role of kin and friends, in Bangladesh as well as in Portugal, in the making and reproduction of migration projects. With this broad objective in mind, I was aware I had to apply a multi-sited-fieldwork[2] approach, and

---

1 Pseudonyms will be used throughout this chapter.
2 Marcus 1986, 1995.

therefore I collected data in several regions of Portugal and in Bangladesh, mainly in Dhaka, from thirteen middle-class households.

After this first period, I decided to take a break of some months and assess my material. One thing was clear by then: there was a dimension to the project that I was missing and which was essential in order to be able to interpret much of what was going on among my interlocutors:[3] Islam and religiosity. Therefore, I prepared for another period of fieldwork, and this time I more focused on Islam and the *ritualisation of the transnational space*[4] between Portugal and Bangladesh. I collected extensive data and participated in the daily life and the organisation of the activities of the mosque. I attended several ceremonies and interviewed nearly seventy Bangladeshis. When I began writing, I had two lines of argument that sometimes seemed to take me in very different directions – transnationalism and Islam. In the end, however, I was able to unite them through the way the ritualisation of this transnational space allowed my interlocutors to continuously produce different places of belonging.

Thus my main theoretical concerns evolved from transnational migration – that is the multiple and permanent political, economic and cultural relations that migrants sustain between the sending and the receiving contexts[5] – to the relationship between transnationalism and the production of localities and the making of places; in other words, the continuous production of spaces of belonging. The world of flow and mobility is dialectically counterbalanced by the production of fixity and place-making, and such processes are visible in the sending of remittances, in the performance of certain rituals and in the (re)production of nationalist discourses, to mention just a few examples.[6]

Later, while going through my field diaries and notes, I came across a topic that was there from the beginning but which I had left totally unexplored in my writings and reflections: food and its daily uses and meanings. Food involves remembering and evoking one's home country, where it is usual to eat certain foods, and the vignette with which I started this article is only one of many examples of this.[7] Mukitur's exclamation while eating *Chawtpohtee* in Lisbon precisely reveals this relation between food and home. *Chawtpohtee* is a very common street food in Bangladesh. In the New Market area in Dhaka (the capital of Bangladesh), it is possible to find sellers, with portable trolleys and plastic benches, who prepare this

---

3 Throughout this text I use 'interlocutor' (instead of 'informant') because it implies a reciprocal relationship in the production of knowledge. 'Informant', on the other hand, frequently assumes an unequal relationship between a person who asks questions and another who simply replies. If the production of ethnographic knowledge is based on intersubjectivity and mutuality, the use of the word 'informant' is misleading.
4 Salih 2003.
5 Schiller, Blanc and Bach 1992.
6 Gupta and Ferguson 1997; Meyer and Geschiere 1999; Olwig 2006; Salih 2002; Veer 1994.
7 Sutton 2001.

dish and *Phuchkaa*, a small pastry one and a half inches in diameter, filled with mashed *Chawtpohtee*. On busy days, one can see people queuing to buy this food. However, the fact that this same dish is now being prepared in Lisbon shows how Portugal has become more and more a place of belonging for Bangladeshi migrants. It is now possible to find in Lisbon the necessary ingredients and cooks who are able to prepare foods that until recently were exclusively prepared and consumed back in the *desh* (the Bengali word for homeland).[8]

Thus re-reading my field-notes in a way called my attention to the fact that in the study of migrations and place the field is not only located in kinship, religion and ritual, or politics but in something much more quotidian: the foodscape. The preparation of certain dishes, the traffic of ingredients and specific culinary practices are essential elements in unearthing the ways by which our interlocutors interpret and embody[9] (see also Vogt, this volume) place in the migration experience.

Food, as Sidney Mintz argues, is intimately linked to the sense of ourselves and to our very social identity. We eat everyday, all our lives, in specific places, surrounded by persons with particular habits and beliefs, and thus all we learn about food is incorporated in a substantive body of cultural materials, historically situated.[10] Food and eating reveals the culture in which one is incorporated and, furthermore, is a way of relating to reality, not only because of its daily centrality but also because it connects the world of things with the world of ideas.[11] This is true whether one is studying the ways ingredients are produced and processed and how meals and food exchanges are perceived (by the consumers) or whether one is researching the global traffic of ingredients, food companies and dietary notions.[12]

This article argues that in migration contexts food reveals – and in certain ways produces – our social and symbolic attachments to certain places. Today, in contexts where migration has assumed great visibility and political importance, who belongs where is frequently defined not only through cultural, religious, linguistic, racial and gendered arguments, and sometimes through a combination of these, but also through food and culinary issues (what food and ingredients belong where).[13] For instance, in the USA, food and multi-ethnicity, related to long-lasting migration flows, have assumed a central importance in the production of hegemonic national narratives and identities around notions of America as a multi-ethnic nation.[14] In certain cases, so called 'immigrant foods' have become part and parcel of the foodscape, while in others they have not been wholeheartedly

8   Gardner 1993; Kotalová 1993.
9   See also Vogt, this volume.
10 Mintz 2001.
11 Mintz 2001: 31, 32.
12 Goody 1982; Mintz 1985; Watson 1997; Bestor 2000; *inter alia.*
13 Geschiere 2009.
14 Gabaccia 1998.

welcomed; indeed, quite the contrary.[15] For instance, a study carried out by Ayse Caglar shows how the *Döner Kebab* in Germany is intimately related to ethnic prejudices and anti-immigration rhetoric.[16] It is perceived not only as an 'immigrant food' but is also as a boundary-marker, demonstrating, through food habits and the senses, the radical 'otherness' of Turkish migrants. Complaints about the smell of garlic, apparently a 'characteristic' of Turkish migrants, were manipulated by conservative sectors to show how this population group does not belong to German society, at the same time as the Kebab has become a symbol of the German *multikulti* model. A comparable process is the introduction of beer and beer-brewing in England by Dutch migrants. This 'foreign' drink was first seen as a potential threat to English society on the basis of rumours that it was poisonous. Later, however, as it became more and more popular, the protests were redirected to focus on questions of profitability and production control. According to some, this profitable business was in the hands of 'foreigners', and it was essential to change this situation.[17]

However, the relation between migration, place and food is also visible in the everyday consumption of migrants themselves. It is also through the consumption of food, and the senses related to it, that migrants continuously produce localities and build a sense of home and belonging in transnational contexts.[18] This article will argue that the foodscape is an idiom through which people evoke memories and produce experiences of familiarity and strangeness, not only symbolically but also socially. Food has an agency in itself because it is frequently a way of producing (or denying) relatedness.

To explore this argument, the article begins with a brief contextualisation of Bangladeshis in Portugal in terms of the relation between the formation of these migration chains and the political economy of migrations in southern European countries. Secondly, it will reveal how the migrants' connection with Bangladesh is continuously re-actualised through the consumption of certain ingredients and dishes, a re-actualisation that has led to the creation of a whole new commercial niche for Bangladeshi products. Thirdly, it will focus on the way food-sharing has been a way of producing, sometimes *ab initio*, relatedness between Bangladeshis in Portugal and thereby of articulating the creation of a new sense of 'community' and home. This will be followed by my concluding remarks.

---

15 In Victorian London, for instance, ice creams were introduced by Italian migrant street-peddlers (Sponza 2002), while the restaurant landscape in Leicester in Britain and San Francisco in the USA, for example, changed considerably with the 'Indian' cuisine and grocery shops that emerged in connection with labour migration during the twentieth-century (Panayi 2002; Mankekar 2005).

16 Caglar 1999.

17 Luu 2002.

18 E.g. Appadurai 1997; Mankekar 2005; Janeja 2010; Hirvi 2010.

Patrons and bachelors

Mukitur was one of the first Bangladeshis to arrive in Portugal in the late eighties of the last century, and he is nowadays a well-known entrepreneur and political figure. He has important ties with the Portuguese media and is frequently called upon to speak in the name of the Bangladeshi 'community' in the public space. In a certain sense, he offers an example on the basis of which it is possible to discuss the history of Bangladeshi migration to Portugal. The number of Bangladeshis in Portugal today is 4500. Like the migrants to Spain and Italy, the majority come from the intermediate social strata, those who in Bangladesh are commonly classified as the 'new' and 'affluent' middle classes, urbanised and with high levels of education.[19] For these segments, coming to Europe is a strategic way to access what they call 'modern' ways of life and adulthood.[20]

This migration chain developed in direct connection with the regularisation processes implemented in southern European countries in recent decades. Several of my interlocutors were already in continental Europe and had arrived in Portugal in search of opportunities for the legalisation of their residence that were lacking elsewhere. The majority followed pre-existing migration chains already established in Europe (in the Federal Republic of Germany, France and Austria, among other states) from the eighties onwards. With the establishment of the dictatorship of General Muhammad Ershad in 1982, several Bangladeshis applied for asylum status in countries such as Germany and France.[21] Later, a substantial economic and social change in southern European countries not only improved standards of living but also changed migrants' position with regard to the international division of labour.[22] These structural changes slowed-down intra-European migrations and, in the short run, led to the arrival of migrants from non-Portuguese colonial territories. Faced with these new migration flows, numerous countries developed legislation and special programmes for the regularisation of immigrants. Many Bangladeshis arrived in Portugal in the context of such regularisation programmes implemented by the Portuguese authorities in 1993, 1996 and 2001–2004 or to join friends and relatives already established in Portugal. After successful regularisation, in which they received either a residence permit (in the case of those who submitted their applications in 1993 or 1996) or a 'permanence visa' (in the case of those who submitted their applications in 2001), many decided to settle in Portugal and invested or worked in commercial activities already set up by a number of Bangladeshis or found employment in the less privileged sectors of the Portuguese economy. Others moved to other European countries either to continue working in their previous occupations or to join family members.

---

19 See also Zeytlin 2006; Knights 1996.
20 Mapril 2008.
21 Knights 1996, 1997.
22 See Malheiros 1996; Baganha *et al.* 1999; King *et al.* 2000.

Initially all were single young male adults, but today most have married in Bangladesh and set up households in Portugal, which means that they have brought their wives and children there. These are the 'patrons' (Portuguese: *patrãos*), or bosses, who are perceived as the most successful migrants and frequently become persons of political and economic importance. At the same time, the so called 'freshies' or 'bachelors' continue working in the lower ranks of the Portuguese economy or in the employ of the pioneer migrants, waiting for an opportunity to start up their own businesses or to save enough money to go back to Bangladesh and get married.

Owing to the specific nature of this migration flow – the search for legalisation opportunities and the globalisation of the migration industry – my interlocutors come from diverse regions of origin in Bangladesh. In total, there are 18 informal regional Bangladeshi associations in Portugal, which in itself indicates that most of my interlocutors did not know each other in their home country. Only now are village and/or regional affiliations becoming more prominent and significant as a result of the formation of migration chains and family reunification processes. In 2006, there were 160 reunited Bangladeshi families in Lisbon, the majority of which were composed of a nuclear family together with another member, either the husband's or the wife's brother – usually the person chosen to come to Europe is the one who displays the greater capacity for coping in a European environment in terms of education and the ability to handle change.

Making home food

As the initial vignette demonstrates, most of my interlocutors maintain a relationship to food that could be called 'nostalgic gastronomy'; that is, food is a way of continuously thinking about the pragmatic, symbolic and emotional ties that many foster with Bangladesh.[23] These transnational links are continuously achieved through activities such as phone calls, internet chatting, e-mails, remittances and travel, but also through a 'gustatory memory'.[24] Eating 'typical' Bangladeshi dishes is not simply a nutritional activity or a habitus that is continuously reproduced abroad but also a way to establish a permanent link with Bangladesh through the consumption of certain substances.[25] It is in the light of such a market that one can interpret the increasing commercialisation of specific ingredients and products. This is a profitable line of business, and some of my interlocutors began selling certain ingredients and dishes in order to offer buyers the experiences of home. Although the majority of those able to set up a business of their own opened small garment shops, a minority invested in grocery shops and restaurants. In the Lisbon metropolitan area one can find four groceries and nine restaurants owned by Bangladeshis, the majority of which are

23 Mankekar 2005.
24 Mankekar 2005.
25 Bourdieu 1977.

concentrated in a central Lisbon area called *Martim Moniz*. In spite of the presence of other immigrant populations, such as Chinese, Cape Verdeans, Indians from Mozambique, Guineans, etc., this is frequently described by many Bangladeshis as a *banglapara* (a Bangladeshi area), where it is possible to find friends, drink *cha* (black tea, with milk, or condensed milk, sugared and sometimes scented with cardamom and other spices), perform prayers or eat a Bangladeshi meal. In total, in this area and adjacent locations, it is possible to find 160 businesses owned or developed by Bangladeshi migrants, most of whom, together with their families, live in the vicinity.

This increasing concentration has created a market for Bangladeshi products ranging from full meals to the ingredients needed to cook Bangladeshi dishes. In Benformoso Street, right in the heart of this Lisbon neighbourhood, it is possible to find four groceries and one restaurant owned by Bangladeshi migrants. The grocery stores are usually small shops equipped with freezers that sell everything from fresh produce to frozen goods. At first sight, these are absolutely indistinguishable from the other South Asian groceries and supermarkets already existing in the area. These were created by Indians who came from Mozambique, both Muslims and Hindus, and established themselves in the area from the late seventies on, after decolonisation. The groceries and supermarkets of both Bangladeshis and Indians from Mozambique sell fresh produce – fruits and vegetables – as well as spices, *ghee* (clarified butter), precooked 'Indian' meals (canned *saag gosh*, *achar* (pickles), Indian- and Iranian-style breads – *rotis*, *chapatis* and *nan* – and also other non-Asian products. When my interlocutors began setting up their businesses, they had to buy many of their products – spices, for instance – directly from the already existing Mozambican Indian supermarkets. Their access to suppliers was very limited, so they had to buy products from their direct competitors, who of course would sell the products at a very high price in order to prevent any sort of competition. Later, however, Bangladeshis were able to buy them directly from the suppliers and became more competitive in this corner of the market. Today, they cater simultaneously to a Bangladeshi and a non-Bangladeshi clientele, and they publically emphasise this flexibility in their announcements, in Portuguese and Urdu, usually on the last pages of a printed version of *The Daily Jugantor*, a Lisbon Bangladeshi daily newspaper, or in flyers distributed around the area, claiming that they provide the essential ingredients for cooking proper 'Bangladeshi' and 'Indian' meals.

A careful look, however, reveals that the publicity of the Bangladeshi groceries appeal directly to the memory of the *desh*. It always also contains a message written in Bengali which specifically emphasises the idea of preparing home food. The phrases used include *deshi kabar*, which literally means food from Bangladesh and *barir kabar*, which implies the idea of home food; that is, food usually cooked in one's own household. In this way, the owners appeal to their commercial spaces as places to buy indispensable and 'genuine' ingredients to prepare regional dishes, not just 'Indian', but also recipes from home, which is equated simultaneously with Bangladesh and the domestic unit, the *bari*.

This constant worry about so-called 'genuine' products from Bangladesh creates very important transnational commercial networks through which certain ingredients travel. A perfect example is fish from the Bay of Bengal. For several of my interlocutors, fish is an important element in their daily diet, while meat is an exceptional food that one eats only on certain specific occasions.[26] It is only with fish from the region that one can cook some of the most emblematic Bangladeshi dishes and celebrate certain festive occasions. A very good example is *Ilsa* fish (in Bengali: *Ilish mash*). This fish is found in the Bay of Bengal and also in the Persian Gulf, the South China Sea and the East China Sea, among other maritime regions, while its riverine habitats include the Indus of Pakistan, the rivers of eastern and western India, and the Padma, the Jamuna, the Meghna and other coastal rivers of Bangladesh. It is a common source of protein in the region and a constant presence in the diet of certain sectors of contemporary Bangladeshi society. Its price has increased considerably in recent years, not only because of over-fishing but also as a result of the politics of water management between India and Bangladesh.[27] Nevertheless, it continues to be considered the national fish of the country and is an integral element in certain festive occasions, such as *Nôbobôrsho* (the Bengali New Year) celebrated on 14 or 15 April and *Pahela Baishakh* (the first day of the first month of the Bengali year). This day begins with a breakfast usually composed of *Pantha Bhat*, with fried *Ilsa (ilish)* fish. *Pantha bhat* is simple cooked rice, soaked and fermented in water and is consumed the following day, mixed with grilled, crushed chilies. It is part of the everyday diet of the poorest segments of Bangladeshi society, but, over the years, it has also entered the menus of middle-class families (from which most of my interlocutors came, as was pointed out earlier in this chapter), especially during the Bengali new year celebrations.[28] Fried *ilish mash* is added to this rice and served together with chilies. In 2005, the *Pohela Boishak* was celebrated in the form of a picnic on the outskirts of Lisbon, where more than forty people partook of *pantha bhat* with fried Ilsa fish bought from a local grocer. The organisers wanted to replicate the Bengali New Year celebrations in Bangladesh, where food and nature assume a symbolically central role. (Here we should recall that the celebrations of the Bengali New Year are linked to the beginning of a new agricultural year.)

Owing to its regional origin, this fish, together with others, has to be imported. The commercial links involved do not connect the fishing industry in Bangladesh directly to the small retailers in Lisbon, but rather are mediated by import and export companies based in the United Kingdom, which is home to the largest Bangladeshi population in Europe.[29] After receiving the goods in England, they are redistributed to several continental European countries, where the presence of Bangladeshis has been increasing over the last decades. Shams, the owner of a grocery store in central Lisbon, has

26 Kotalová 1993.
27 Janeja 2010.
28 Janeja 2010.
29 Gardner 1995, 2002; Gardner and Shukur 1994; *inter alia*.

157

four freezers filled with fish from the Bay of Bengal which he regularly buys from Anglo-Bengali importers in England. This effort to supply ingredients from Bangladesh leads some of the shop-owners to bring with them, in their luggage, some products that are very difficult, not to say impossible, to find in Portugal. One of my interlocutors, for instance, brought in several small packets of a certain appetiser, commonly sold throughout Bangladesh, made of *dal* (fried lentils) and chickpeas, which were quickly sold out in a matter of hours.

Having spotted such a niche, some are planning to create transnational companies through which it would be possible to import Bangladeshi products directly from Bangladesh. For instance, one of my interlocutors registered a company named *Barakatia* in Lisbon, which was linked to another company with the same name, registered in Hamburg, and another one in Dhaka, run by his elder and younger brother respectively. Their main objective is to redistribute foodstuffs from Bangladesh in various parts of Europe where Bangladeshis live.

Occasionally, it is possible in these groceries to find emblematic Bangladeshi sweets that are prepared in private households. In one case, a family from Comilla, a region well known for its tasty *rushmalai* (a sweet made of sugared milk and small pastries) prepared a number of individual portions that were later on sale in several groceries and restaurants.

However, this urge to get ingredients from Bangladesh is not only related to the lack of availability but also partly to the quality and taste of the products themselves, as has been suggested by Katy Gardner.[30] Among my interlocutors, one can frequently hear people saying that ingredients brought from Bangladesh are tastier then the ones on sale in Portugal. For example, I was having lunch with an interlocutor, and for dessert he had bought some mangoes from the local supermarket. We were preparing them and at the same time he began talking about how mangoes were good in Portugal but in Bangladesh they were much better. They were sweeter and tastier. This same argument is applied to the dishes themselves. On several occasions I heard some of my closest acquaintances complaining about the tasteless quality of Portuguese cuisine compared with dishes from Bangladesh.

Together with this offering of products that evoke Bangladesh, all these groceries also specialise in *halal* products, such as chicken, lamb, beef and even sausages (made of turkey meat); a speciality that is also extensively publicised.[31] *Halal* products are usually supplied by other Muslims, Indians from Mozambique or Guineans already living in Portugal, who either import them directly or have small slaughterhouses. In certain cases, the owners resort to networks of informal slaughterhouses, spread throughout the Lisbon metropolitan area, in order to buy *halal* meat, usually lamb and chicken. The *zabah*, the ritual slaughter, which involves the bleeding of the animal and the recitation of a prayer, is performed by the shop owners

---

30 Gardner 1993, 1995.

31 *Halal* means licit or permitted and in the case of meat involves the performance of the *zabah*, the ritual slaughter and bleeding of all animals.

themselves, and the meat is brought to the stores, properly packed, frozen and put on sale. The explanation I was given for such a practice, especially with the pre-existing infrastructure, was that sometimes the suppliers assure buyers that the meat is *halal* when in reality it is not; it is just a trick to sell more products. By slaughtering the animals themselves, however, the shop owners can guarantee their customers that the meat is really 100% *halal*.

Despite the fact that all these Bangladeshi groceries sell similar products, there is a tendency for some specialisation, which, of course, means a substantial reduction in competition between the Bangladeshis themselves. One of the groceries is well-known for supplying frozen fish from the Bay of Bengal, while another is a butcher/grocery store well known for its supply of *halal* meat. Thus all these groceries located in central, Lisbon provide certain products that carry the idea of home food, which means either from Bangladesh or from one's own household. In either case, one interesting element in my interlocutors' discourses is the idea that such food should be limited to private household consumption (see below).

A clear contrast with this situation is offered by the restaurants run by Bangladeshis. Of all the ten restaurants owned by Bangladeshis in the Lisbon metropolitan area only three broadcast their 'Bangladeshiness', and all are located in the same *Banglapara* where it is possible to find the grocery stores. Their main customers are Bangladeshis, and therefore it is possible to find several *deshi* dishes, although these are usually off menu (the main menu essentially offers so-called 'Indian' dishes).[32] The decoration of the restaurants links them directly to Bangladesh: in one of them, there is an emblematic picture of a young girl bent over a pond filed with water lilies, the national flower of Bangladesh. In another, a *carrom* table (*carrom* is a table-top game also known as 'finger billiards' which is very popular in South Asia) and an evocation of *Bangla* pride decorate one of the walls. Finally, the third restaurant refers directly to Bangladesh through its name – *Bangla Restaurante* – and the decorations include quintessential pictures of Bangladesh such as the Bengal tiger, a beach in Cox Bazaar and tea fields in the Sylhet region (famed as the garden of Bangladesh).

The majority, however, consider Bangladeshiness as bad advertisement and publicity for their businesses. On several occasions, I asked my interlocutors why there was not a more significant investment in proper Bangladeshi restaurants where it would be possible to find *Ilsa* fish dishes, Bangladeshi sweets, etc. Every time I was told that Bangladeshi food is a waste of time and bad business. Because they cater to non-South Asian customers, the majority of Bangladeshi-owned restaurants in Lisbon accordingly present themselves only as Indian or South Asian or use references to these regions such as *Star of India, Sitara, Bengal Tandoori*.

An issue common to all these groceries and restaurants is the provision of alcoholic beverages. When asked about this, most of my interlocutors drew my attention to the fact that it is illicit *(haram)* not only to consume

---

32 On several occasions, while sharing meals with my interlocutors, I realised that several Bangladeshi dishes were prepared but not included in the menus.

but also to sell alcoholic beverages. The resulting profits are considered unlawfully earned, and furthermore God might later punish a person who sells alcohol. One of my interlocutors, for instance, argued that in spite of its being good business, he would rather not sell alcohol. Having said this, in the past months several Bangladeshis have been investing in groceries and convenience stores spread through several neighbourhoods in Lisbon. These are open 24 hours, cater to non-Bangladeshis and sell everything from fresh produce to wine and other alcoholic beverages. Unlike these, the groceries in the *Banglapara* still do not sell any alcoholic beverages, and one of the reasons, is of course, fear of social criticism and the potential loss of Bangladeshi customers. The restaurants do, however, offer wine and beer in their menus, and when asked why, they immediately admit that if you run a restaurant you have to be willing to sell alcohol, otherwise your business will fail. That is precisely one of the reasons why important political Bangladeshi figures do not invest in restaurants; otherwise, their charisma and authority would suffer. As Mukitur once said to me: 'I cannot be a leader of the community and have a restaurant selling alcohol, can I?'

Another common line of business is represented by the recent opening of several *Döner Kebab* shops owned by Bangladeshis. The idea was first put into practice by a Bangladeshi, who after seeing the success of a Turkish Kebab house in Lisbon, decided to try his luck in the centre of Lisbon. Today several others have followed his example and opened up *Döner Kebab* shops in the Lisbon metropolitan area.

To sum up, what we have seen so far is how certain kinds of products and dishes are continuously identified with home. Food from Bangladesh, and more specifically from one's household (*bari*), carries connotations of domesticity, comfort, tastiness and authenticity, which appeal to a sense of belonging. This kind of Bangladeshiness is first and foremost something for the home and constituters a very 'bad' commercial product, so my interlocutors argue, for restaurants to sell. It makes for bad advertising when compared to 'Indian' restaurants or *Döner Kebab* shops. However, food does not only represent a semiotic value, the reproduction of a vision of home and the homely, but it also has an actual agency in itself.[33] It is through food exchanges and the sharing of meals that social relations are continuously created and recreated in both Portugal and Bangladesh.

Food exchanges and the 'incorporation' of newcomers

In a previous article, I argued that for Bangladeshis in Portugal, home is the place where it is possible to find one's relatives. The subject was the management of death, and the article described how the most frequent strategy was to send the bodies back to the *desh* because it was the place where people could mourn them. If they were left in Portugal, no one would

33 Appadurai 1981.

pray for their souls; they would be abandoned, it was argued.[34] By 'relative' (Bangali: *atyo*), my interlocutors meant not only a person connected through consanguine ties (linked to wider notions of patrilineage, residential space and its moral co-responsibility), but also one linked by affinity ties and even those with whom one develops friendship ties. In all these, ties are created through the consumption of food and shared meals.[35] Eating together is a way of producing relatedness, to differing degrees, not only with members of the same patrilineage and the household in Bangladesh but also with non-related others, and this kind of process is clearly visible among Bangladeshis in Lisbon.[36]

The sharing of food with relatives who reside in Bangladesh is, obviously, something that Lisbon Bangladeshis can enjoy only occasionally, when they have the opportunity to travel back or when ingredients and foodstuffs are sent from the *desh* through informal channels. In some cases, it takes years before a migrant is ready to pay a visit back to Bangladesh. As one of my interlocutors would say: 'I cannot go back with my pockets empty.' And when the time finally comes, the sojourns are not only spent performing rituals, relaxing and visiting friends and relatives but also eating with them.[37]

During my fieldwork, most of my interlocutors had returned at least once to Bangladesh, usually for a month. These visits frequently occurred in January and February, two months that are commonly perceived as being commercially unfavourable. Coming as they do after the New Year, business in these first two months is very slack in terms of sales, and thus many Bangladeshis who are involved in commercial activities decide to travel back then. In the same years in which I conducted my fieldwork, because of the Islamic lunar calendar, the feast of sacrifice (*qurbani id*) coincided with this visiting season, and thus many seized the opportunity offered by this ritual occasion to renew their membership in a patrilineage and a household by financially sponsoring the ritual and offering raw meat and cooked food. As I witnessed in January and February 2004 while visiting one of my closest interlocutors who was spending his holidays in Dhaka, migrants spend the three days of the celebration visiting relatives and friends and being visited by them, eating sweets and other dishes associated with the sacrificial ritual. Thus, the relationship with Bangladesh and its continuous production as home, in other words, the continuous re-actualisation of relatedness, is partially achieved through food consumption and sharing.

However, it is also through food that new places of belonging are progressively imagined and constructed, especially among certain groups of my interlocutors. When a Bangladeshi family is finally reunited in Portugal, the wife and the children have to be presented to other Bangladeshi families who are already part of the husband's social connections in order that they

34 Mapril 2009.
35 Inden and Nicholas 1977.
36 See Carsten 2000.
37 See also Watkins 2004.

may be included in informal sociability networks. The sharing of meals is a key element in this process and a way to create social relations, sometimes from scratch. Let me give you an example of a specific family.

When I first began the fieldwork for this project in Portugal in 2003, several members of this *poribar* (family), namely the wife, Aisha, and her four sons, Mujib, Raju, Babu and Zubair, had recently arrived in Portugal, to join Fazlur, the head of the household, who had been there since 1996. Fazlur had been involved in a car accident and was in a semi-conscious state in a Lisbon hospital. It had happened when he was still alone in Portugal, and when Aisha heard about the accident in Dhaka, where she was living in her parents' household, she called her brother, Anwar, an architect living in London, and asked him to go to Portugal and see what was going on. When he arrived in Lisbon, the doctors told him that Fazlur's condition was very critical and it was out of the question for him to travel back to Bangladesh, which the family had initially regarded as the best solution. The alternative then was to bring his immediate relatives to Portugal.

With a document from the hospital, Anwar was able to bring his sister and his nephews to Lisbon. In the meantime, and while the process was still under way, Anwar made contact with several other Bangladeshis already living in the country, and during those months he consolidated a social network. When Aisha and her sons arrived, Anwar had already negotiated the shared renting of an apartment with another family, also from the Dhaka district, the head of which was an entrepreneur of a garment shop in central Lisbon. The house was big enough for the two families, and some of the rooms were still used for storage space. As time went by, Anwar and the whole family in Lisbon began to feel excluded and lonely in spite his efforts to incorporate his sister into the existing social networks. This feeling of exclusion was especially difficult because it is usual that when the new wife of a migrant arrives in Portugal (and these were so rare at that time that whenever a new Bangladeshi woman was seen in the *Banglapara*, everybody commented on the fact and wanted to know who she was, when she had arrived, who were her relatives, and so on), she is always incorporated into already existing female networks that meet in regular informal gatherings. In the case of the family under discussion here, they were feeling totally excluded from these existing reciprocity networks, and in order to change this situation Anwar decided to resort to the gift economy.

Together with three of his nephews (Zubair was still very young) and me, he went to an informal slaughterhouse in a northern outskirt of Lisbon and slaughtered two sheep in order to be able to distribute larger portions to their relatives. The meat was evenly distributed in plastic bags, clearly identified with small pieces of paper and stored in the car. When we arrived at the *banglapara* in central Lisbon, Anwar, the maternal uncle, took several of these bags and distributed them through a number of his acquaintances, among whom there was a very successful pioneer and an important political figure and a household made up of male Dhakans. The basic idea was to let people know that his sister and his nephews had just arrived in Portugal. Furthermore, his older nephew argued that through such gift-giving, the receivers would be in debt to them, and, sooner or later, they would reciprocate. Thus, in a certain way, the whole giving of fresh meat was a way to introduce part of the family into the existing social networks and also a strategy for creating reciprocity networks for the future.

Once created, these are constantly nurtured by informal visits, usually performed by women, in which chatter, assistance and hospitality play roles of great importance.[38] With regard to the first, these networks present opportunities for socialising and the sharing of collective news among women, usually in the form of occasional visits or the organisation of afternoon gatherings (together with the children) in several parks around the centre of Lisbon. On the other hand, the network also have an essential caring role, with the participants giving assistance to each other by picking up the children from school, for instance.

The renewal of these networks involves not only various kinds of assistance but also the sharing of food, including sweets and cooked dishes. Visitors are always offered something to eat. Even if one shows up unannounced, every household has always something ready to serve. It can be a simple appetiser, such as *Bombay mix* with egg, *cha* or a coke, or something more robust, such as a whole meal with rice, fish, meat, vegetables, etc. Sweets are also a classic hospitality item, and they are usually offered on certain festive occasions such as the two main feasts of the Islamic calendar. Among the most common sweets are *pitha* (cakes made of rice flour and fried), *shamai* (wheat noodles with sugared milk and spices), *payesh* (rice boiled in sugared milk with cardamom and cinnamon), and *rushmalai* (sweet curd balls in sugared milk). Even if someone comes just to pass on a quick message or to deliver an item, s/he is always invited to stay, sit at the table or in the living room and share something to eat. If this is absolutely impossible, portions of food are given in Tupperware receptacles to be enjoyed later or consumed by other members of the caller's household.

Notions of 'good' hospitality are directly related to the amount and quality of the food presented to guests. On certain festive occasions, it is expected that friends and relatives visit one another throughout the day, to share meals, chat and enjoy the occasion. It is expected that the members of one's social network call at one's house, at least for a while, and on such occasions food is continuously presented to the guests (these rounds are made by men and women alike, but there always has to be someone in the house to receive guests). On the days preceding the festival, people have been busy cooking sweets and other dishes to be enjoyed on these particular occasions, and thus the guests are often overwhelmed by the amount of food offered to them. One can hardly say no, as it is mandatory to eat something. At the end of the day, when everybody is complaining about how full they are and how they will be fasting for the next few days, the discussion invariably ends up being about which houses offered the best food and which the worst. Usually, in the households where, as a result of family reunification processes, there

---

38 For similar examples, see e.g. Werbner 1990; Shaw 2000.

are women to do the cooking, the food is considered much better than in those where men do all the cooking. 'Good' home food is cooked by women, and only occasionally are men considered to be good or competent cooks. Refusal of such hospitality, however, and especially invitations, can be a source of misunderstanding or cause offence, and people may accuse you of regarding yourself as too important to eat at their table. However, the renewal of sociability through the exchange of food and meals does not occur only in domestic units, in relatively private circles, but also on an institutional level, and the place where this happens is the Bangladeshi mosque in Lisbon.[39]

Sponsoring meals, creating 'community'

What is today known as the *Baitul Mukarram* mosque, or informally as the *Bangla* mosque, first started in 2000 in a small flat into which seventy persons could fit. Today, the mosque is located in a warehouse, where five hundred Muslims can perform their daily prayers (*salat* or *namaz*), the Friday congregational prayer (*Jumu'a*), and celebrate most of the events of the Islamic calendar: the two main annual festivities – the *Id-ul-fitr*, the feast marking the end of Ramadan, and the *Id-ul Ad'ha*, the feast of sacrifice – and other occasions such as the Birthday of the Prophet (*Milad-un-Nabi*), the Night of the Prophet's Ascension (*Shab-e-barat*), or the Night of Destiny (*Lailat al-Qadr*) celebrating the revelation of the Qur'an to the Prophet. The mosque is located in the *Banglapara* in central Lisbon and is mainly used and funded by Bangladeshis themselves, in spite of also being frequented by other South Asian and West African Muslims. That is why it was named after the central mosque in Dhaka, the Bangladeshi capital, and has been officially registered as part of the I.C.B., the Islamic Community of Bangladesh.[40]

On several of these ritual occasions, namely, the Birthday of the Prophet (*Milad-un-Nabi*), the Ascension Night (*Shab-e-barat*), the Night of Destiny (the *Lailat al-Qadr*), and, of course, the month of *Ramadan,* food assumes an enormous centrality. In the first three cases, food is served to the congregation after prayers, usually late in the evening. During *Ramadan,* however, meals are served everyday to 350 persons to mark the *iftar,* the breaking of the fast at sunset. The prepared dishes are chicken or lamb *biryanis* (rice, with

---

39 During the fieldwork I carried out in Portugal, the mosque, where I attended several ritual occasions in the course of the year and took part in the preparation of major events, provided an important physical location to engage in participant observation and meet new interlocutors. During this period of research, I interviewed altogether seventy Bangladeshis, many of whom I met in the mosque.

40 I first heard about this place of worship through a Bangladeshi friend, and then we went there together. Since that initial visit, I returned a number of times during the following years and on several occasions interviewed members of the mosque committee (the persons who manage and run the facility). The objective was to follow the changes that that were taking place in this ritual space.

vegetables and meat), *kitchuri* (fried rice with spices, lentils and pieces of meat) or more simply *muri* (puffed rice) with curried chickpeas and fried vegetables in *gram* flour and small pastries such *pecoras* (onion fried with chilies and chickpea flour). Bottled water and *cha* is also distributed.

All these dishes are usually prepared in the mosque kitchen – which in reality is a small room packed with ingredients and an industrial burner – by the members of the management committee who are in charge of the *iftar* committee (which organises these meals throughout the month) and other volunteers. The former group usually consists of 'pioneer' migrants and successful Bangladeshis, entrepreneurs and heads of households already established in Lisbon, while the latter group is composed either of people recruited from among the most recent arrivals, so-called 'freshies', or of the sons of older migrants. As an outsider, I was allowed to be involved with these two groups, and thus one moment I found myself helping out in the kitchen and the next interviewing some of the members of the management committee.

The prayer floor is covered with rectangular plastic strips on which the prepared dishes are laid out, one for each member of the congregation, together with several bottles of water, soft drinks and jars of *cha*. After a short prayer, the congregation breaks the daily fast and follows this with the sunset prayer.

In total, these meals cost up to eight thousand euros, half of which is donated by the members of the mosque committee, while the rest is raised every year from other members of the Bangladeshi community: during the month of *Ramadan,* the members of the *iftar* committee collect donations and other forms of sponsorship from other Bangladeshis. For instance, many of the necessary products, such as rice, vegetables, spices, *muri* (puffed rice), *dhal* (lentils), bottled waters and soft drinks and even the meat are frequently donated by the four groceries mentioned above.

On the days when the fare is not provided by these sources, Bangladeshi households (composed either of families or groups of men) sponsor all or a part of the daily *iftar*. In the latter case, the foodstuff which is usually donated is meat, which is either bought in one of the Bangladeshi groceries or, because of the aforementioned suspicion of the *halal* purity of the produce in these as well as the cost involved, bought directly from the same informal slaughterhouses that we mentioned earlier. In this way, the donors can guarantee that the meat is genuinely *halal*.

All these contributions, both financial and in kind, help with the maintenance of this religious space, and it is generally believed that they constitute acts of merit *(sowab)* that will be rewarded by God in the hereafter. However, this religious facility offers not only a way to communicate with God but also a space where social ties are extensively produced among Bangladeshis. First of all, whenever someone sponsors a meal in the mosque, he always invites not only his relatives but also his close social acquaintances. It is expected that everybody is informed about who is feeding the congregation, and one way of doing this is to have one's relatives and friends in the party that organises the meals. Furthermore, some persons spend heavily, providing various delicacies in the menus in order to make memorable feasts, as if there was a competition to see who can offer the most lavish and opulent *iftar*. In one case, *shingaras* (Somoza-like pasties filled with vegetables and meat) were added to the menu. They were cooked at home and taken to the mosque and laid out on each plate.

These gifts and other forms of sponsorship are felt by everybody to be obligations, and thus even if a household has not previously been able to provide them, the head of the household knows that sooner or later he will have to do so. Those who eat a meal given by someone else know that later on they are expected to reciprocate and themselves sponsor these collective meals. This is enforced by social control. Those who are absolutely unable to do so, like recently arrived migrants, offer their only asset – their manpower – to help in the organisation of the month of Ramadan. In a context marked by huge regional diversities, this gift economy, based on food, seems to be an element of the production of what my interlocutors call *samaj*: the society of those who are Muslims and Bengalis.

Eating together: some concluding remarks

In my concluding remarks, I would like to come back to my initial vignette in order to highlight some important theoretical issues. Mukitur's statement contains an intrinsic ambiguity. On the one hand, food is, as we have seen, a way of remembering Bangladesh, past and present, in which small eating pleasures, such as *chawtpohtee* or *pushcka*, are part and parcel of ones' daily experience. In this sense, the delicacy reveals the participants' attachment to the home country, not only through imagining but also in actual sociability. The links with Bangladesh are not only imagined but also pragmatic. The eating of certain kinds of dishes and the sharing of certain foodstuffs in Lisbon, and in Bangladesh during visits, are constant reminders of these existing ties.

On the other hand, the fact that this same dish is now being prepared in Lisbon constitutes an implicit recognition that the migrant's social ties and symbolic attachments are no longer only with Bangladesh. In Portugal, especially for those with a longer migration history and with more social, economic and emotional investments, Lisbon is no longer simply a port of call but also a place to which people consider more and more that they belong. It is here that they have some of their family members, some of their businesses, some of their friends. If one belongs to the place where one's relatives are, then Portugal is, in a sense, in the process of becoming another place of belonging. For some – the 'patrons' and their families – Portugal is becoming more and more like another home, which they now have to articulate with the *desh*.[41]

41 Rapport and Dawson 1998; Morley 2000.

Bibliography

Appadurai, A. 1981: Gastro-politics in Hindu South Asia. *American Ethnologist*, 8: 3, 494–511.

Appadurai, A. 1997: The production of locality. In A. Appadurai (ed.), *Modernity at Large: The cultural Dimensions of Globalization.* Minneapolis: University of Minnesota Press.

Baganha, M. 2000: Labour market and immigration: economic opportunities for immigrants in Portugal. In: R. King, G. Lazaridis & C. Tsardanidis (eds.), *Eldorado or Fortress? Migration in Southern Europe.* London: Macmillan Press.

Bestor, T. 2000: How Sushi Went Global. *Foreign Policy*, Dec., 54–63.

Caglar, A. 1999: McKebap: Doner kebap and the social positioning struggle of German Turks. In: C. Lentz (ed.), *Changing Food Habits*, Amsterdam, Harwood Academic Publishers.

Carsten, J. (ed.) 2000: *Cultures of Relatedness: New Approaches to the Study of Kinship.* Cambridge: Cambridge University Press.

Gabaccia, D. 1998: *We Are What We Eat: Ethnic Food and the Making of Americans.* Cambridge: Harvard University Press.

Gardner, K. 1993: Desh bidesh: Sylheti images of home and away. *Man*, 28: 1, 1–15.

Gardner, K. 1995: *Global Migrants, Local Lives: Travel and transformation in rural Bangladesh.* Oxford: Oxford University Press.

Geschiere, P. 2009: *The Perils of Belonging: Autocthony: Citizenship and Exclusion in Africa and Europe.* Chicago: Chicago University Press.

Goody, J. 1982: *Cooking, Cuisine and Class: A Study in Comparative Sociology.* Cambridge: Cambridge University Press.

Gupta, A. & J. Ferguson 1997: Culture, Power, Place: Ethnography at the End of an Era. In: A. Gupta & J. Ferguson (eds.): *Culture, Power, Place: Explorations in Critical Anthropology.* Durham, Duke University Press.

Hirvi, L. 2010: The Sikh gurdwara in Finland: negotiating, maintaining and transmitting immigrants' identities. *South Asian Diaspora*, 2: 2, 219–232.

Inden, R. & R. Nicholas 1977: *Kinship in Bengali Culture.* Chicago: Chicago University Press.

Janeja, M. 2010: *Transactions in Taste: The Collaborative Lives of Everyday Bengali Food.* London: Routledge.

King, R., G. Lazaridis. & C. Tsardanidis (eds.) 2000: *Eldorado or Fortress? Migration in Southern Europe.* London: Macmillan Press.

Kershen, A. (ed.) 2002: *Food in the Migrant Experience.* London: Ashgate.

Knights, M. 1996: Bangladeshi immigrants in Italy: from geopolitics to micropolitics. *Trans. Inst. Br. Geogr.* 21, 105–123.

Kotalová, J. 1993: *Belonging to Other: Cultural Construction of Womenhood in a Village in Bangladesh.* Dhaka: University Press Limited.

Luu, L. 2002: Dutch and their beer brewing in England 1400–1700. In: A. Kershen (ed.), *Food in the Migrant Experience.* London: Ashgate.

Mankekar, P. 2005: 'India Shopping': Indian Grocery Stores and Transnational Configurations of Belonging. In: J. Watson & M. Caldwell (eds) *The Cultural Politics of Food and Eating.* Oxford: Blackwell.

Malheiros, J. 1996: *Imigrantes na Região de Lisboa: Os Anos da Mudança.* Lisbon: Edições Colibri.

Mapril, J. 2008: Os Sonhos da Modernidade: migrações globais e consumos entre Lisboa e Dhaka. In: R. Carmo *et al.* (ed.), *A Globalização no Divã.* Lisboa: Tinta da China.

Mapril, J. 2009: O lugar do sacrifício: qurban e circuitos transnacionais entre bangladeshis em Lisboa. *Análise Social*, XLIV, 71–104.

Marcus, G. 1986: Contemporary Problems of Ethnography in the Modern World System. In: J. Clifford & G. Marcus (eds.), *Writing Cultures: The Poetics and Politics of Ethnography.* Berkeley: University of California Press.

Marcus, G. 1995: Ethnography in/of the World System: the Emergence of Multi-Sited Ethnography. *Annual Review of Anthropology*, 24, 95–117.

Meyer, B. & P. Geschiere (eds.) 1999: *Globalization and Identity: Dialectics of Flow and Closure.* Oxford: Blackwell Publishing.

Mintz, S. 1985: *Sweetness and Power: The Place of Sugar in Modern History.* New York: Penguin.

Mintz, S. 2001: *Comida e Antropologia. RBCS*, 16: 47, 31–41.

Morley, D. 2000: *Home Territories: Media, Mobility and Identity.* London, Routledge.

Olwig, K. F. 2007: *Caribbean Journeys: An Ethnography of Migration and Home in Three Family Networks.* Durham: Duke University Press.

Panayi, P. 2002: The Spicing up of English Provincial Life: The History of Curry in Leicester. In: A. Kershen (ed.), *Food in the Migrant Experience.* London: Ashgate.

Rapport, N, & A. Dawson (eds.) 1998: *Migrants of Identity: Perceptions of Home in a World of Movement.* Oxford: Berg.

Salih, R. 2002: Reformulating tradition and modernity: Morrocan migrant women and the transnational division of ritual space. *Global Networks*, 2: 3, 219–231.

Shaw, A. 2000: *Kinship and Continuity: Pakistani Families in Britain.* London: Routledge.

Schiller, N. G., L. Bach & C. Blanc-Szanton 1992: Transnationalism: A New Analytic Framework for Understanding Migration. *Annals of the New York Academy of Sciences*, 645, 1–24.

Sponza, L. 2002: Italian 'penny ice-men' in Victorian London. In: A. Kershen (ed.), *Food in the Migrant Experience.* London: Ashgate.

Sutton, D. 2001: *Remembrance of Repasts: An Anthropology of Food and Memory.* Oxford: Berg.

Veer, P. van. 1994: *Religious Nationalism: Hindus and Muslims in India.* Berkeley: University of California Press.

Watkins, F. 2004: 'Save there, eat here': migrants, households and community identity among Pakhtuns in Northern Pakistan. In: O. Filippo & K. Gardner (eds.), *Migration, Modernity and Social Transformation in South Asia.* London: Sage.

Watson, J. 1997: *Golden Arches East: McDonald's in East Asia.* Stanford: Stanford University Press.

Werbner, P. 1990. *The Migration Process: Capital, Gifts and Offerings among British Pakistanis.* Oxford: Berg.

Zeitlyn, B. 2006: *Migration from Bangladesh to Italy and Spain.* Dhaka: RMMRU working papers.

THE TOLD
AND THE UNTOLD

Clara Sacchetti

'The Typical Southern Italian Woman'

Ruminations on Poststructural Feminist Ethnography[1]

Winter (February) 2000, Thunder Bay[2]

We sit at the kitchen table, sipping our *caffè latte* and eating tasty vanilla-flavored *pizzelle* (waffle-like Italian biscuits). It's winter in the northwestern Ontario city of Thunder Bay, bitingly cold and snowy outside. I asked Giulia if she would be willing to formally speak to me about her gendered experiences of growing up an Italian-Canadian in the supposed 'hinterland' of Ontario.[3] She is, just like me, the daughter of postwar, immigrant, southern Italian parents who, in stories we've both heard over and over again, came to Canada for a better life. Our parents left their native homes to escape *la miseria* (poverty), ensure a brighter future for their children and grandchildren, and secure a social and political life that differed from the chronic chaos of southern Italy. Their dream of a better life in the 'New Country', a term habitually used by Italian immigrants to describe their adopted homeland, has been largely realised: Our parents own their homes; they have had stable well-paying, benefits-rich, working-class jobs; they have well-educated, professional children; and they have many healthy grandchildren, who will, they hope, have middle-class, white collar, professional careers.

1   In keeping with a poststructural sensibility, I have attempted to write this chapter in a recursive and evocative style so that points brought up in one part of the article are taken up differently in other parts. This contrasts with a more typical linear style that tends to correspond, both epistemologically and ontologically, with the assumptions of progressive, 'truthful' data, information or knowledge. These issues are further discussed in the body of the article.

2   The interview, which was not tape-recorded, originally took place in winter (February) 2000 and has been reconstructed from notes I took during the interview. I passed over the reconstructed interview to Giulia in March 2000 for her input and editorial advice. In addition, Giulia reviewed and lightly edited the sections selected for this chapter in autumn 2010 (the full interview is not presented here). I have altered the research participants' names to protect their privacy.

3   Sullivan 2009; Dunk 1994.

Giulia and I are concurrently raising our first children, both girls, both infants. We are liberally educated, working towards postgraduate degrees and undertaking research about our ethnicity in the place we were born and raised. I am busy gathering ethnographic information on the intersections between gender, socio-economic class, immigrant generational position, and the notion of Italian-Canadianness for my social anthropology doctorate; Giulia is investigating the experiences of paid employment among southern Italian immigrant women for her Master of Arts degree. We have met many times in the past to discuss our common research interests and similar ethnocultural background. Unlike other discussants with whom I have been speaking, Giulia is an 'expert' in my research field and is able to connect her everyday experiences to the scholarly literature on Italian-Canadians.

Me: What was it like for you growing up Italian and female in Thunder Bay?

Giulia: Well, I don't think that I really grew up entirely Italian [...] though I was Italian in many respects. My family did all those things your family did – we ate pasta, we were working-class folks with frugal spending habits, we practised the skill of *arrangiarsi,* or making do, [...] and we did our rounds of visiting Italian friends, relatives, and acquaintances when I was little... I remember bringing library books with me everywhere we visited. I'd go to the public library once a week to get a fresh pile of books because buying them was considered a waste of money by Italian immigrants.

Me: What did your hosts think of that?

Giulia: There were always comments [...] about me reading too much. I think everyone felt a bit uncomfortable with it. I came across as uncaring about family, a big no-no with Italians, because I preferred to be alone with my books. I know that my reading bothered some of them, too. Reading means education, and an educated female is considered dangerous in an Italian family. Italian women are not supposed to be overly educated, just enough to get by in Canadian society. Too much education is shunned because it takes away from the traditional duties of being an Italian woman; it makes you *pazza* (crazy), it makes your brains rot and makes you forget about your obligations to your family and to the Italian community. It makes you too independent.

Me: I do understand what you're saying. Many postwar southern Italian immigrants think that university is good but it must be secondary to being an honourable and respectable wife and mother [...]. Education is seen [...] as a potential threat to the unity of the family [...]

Giulia: This is all true. Our parents' ideas of what's right and wrong for women and men come from their own childhood backgrounds [...] It's been hard for me to be in graduate school. My mother keeps asking me when

I will be finished, when I will have a job to show for all of my education, and when I will have more children. I have to keep reminding myself that her questions are part of my Italian side and the work I'm doing on my M.A. is part of my Canadian side. It's hard to keep them apart [...] but it reminds me that I'm not like typical southern Italian immigrant women or their daughters.

Me: So what is a typical southern Italian immigrant woman?

Giulia: If you review the historical and sociological academic literature, which you must know since you're doing research on the topic, there are a number of themes that come up. Southern Italian women are usually subservient to the authority of their husbands. I know this is true from my own experiences since my mother always deferred to my now deceased father. When he was alive, my mother took care of [...] the household, cooking, finances [...] even though she made her own money, had her own job, and had a lot of non-Italian work colleagues. She still had to clear every decision with my father, even though she understood that other Canadian women didn't do the same.

Me: What about the idea, as we've talked about many times before, that Italian women are powerful because they reign over the family and the family is of paramount importance in southern Italian life? Some of the academic literature suggests that women work through their lack of formal power in creative and unusual ways.

Giulia: Yeah, I remember those conversations [...] I am aware of that [...] scholarly writing, and I don't buy it. It's true that Italian women have power... in the domestic sphere. That hardly makes them equal to men. It simply encourages women to be [...] cunning – to be *furbe* (clever). But this is just another indication that women are subservient to men, otherwise they wouldn't have to play so many games to get their way with their husbands. It's really about 'fooling' men into thinking that they've made a decision even though it's really coming from women. Or it's about doing something that your husband doesn't want you to do but doing it in a way that doesn't compromise his authority. I know from my own experiences that my mother always obeyed my father. If my mother disagreed with him, she followed his wishes, not her own. I think this is typical for southern Italian immigrant women [...]; it's true, too, for many of their Canadian-born daughters [...]. That's why being a too educated woman isn't such a good thing [...]. I think [...] that if you go back and take a closer look at the materials you've collected, you'll see that Italian women are taught at a young age to preserve the honour and dignity of their husbands' names. It's that old Mediterranean honour/shame complex; and it's part of the Catholic Church, part of the Catholic school system, even if people aren't aware that it's going on. Men are the public face of the family, and women are not. Italian women are not supposed to work outside of the home – or at least they're not supposed to forget that their earnings are not as important as their domestic chores; the money they make is not supposed to support the family, even if it actually does. A woman's role is to be a wife, mother, and housekeeper.

Me: I'm unsure what to say about that.

As our conversation about southern Italian immigrant womanhood ends, I am baffled by Giulia's comments. Among our many discussions in the past, this is the first time that she has asserted that Italian immigrant women are unequivocally subordinated.[4] What makes Giulia's assertion so powerful is how she ties her own personal experience to some of the existing scholarly literature on Italian immigrant women while discounting any academic work that challenges her assertion. Giulia refuses, despite reminders of our many past conversations, to consider the potential complexities of gender and the ways in which power may be exercised in an unexpected or unpredictable manner. She simply knows better.

This recalls the ethnographic literature on resistance and domination more generally.[5] Lila Abu-Lughod wants feminist ethnographers to think about resistance as integral to the circulation of networks of power; it is a part of, rather than apart from, domination.[6] This is one way for feminist ethnographers to begin coming to terms with the multifaceted ways that peoples' gendered subjectivities are not only produced through the cultural codes of a particular place at a particular time but how they are produced by failing to act in expected, predictable ways. Resistance is about not going along *within* the strictures of going along. Yet this notion of resistance is far richer than it first appears as it opens up questions about the linkages between the unexpected, subjectivities and recent methodological considerations surrounding feminist ethnography. It brings up questions about 'the who' who enacts resistance, how resistance is tracked and who is looking at resistance and why. These sorts of questions move us, I suggest, to consider Patti Lather's, Kamala Visweswaran's, and Gayatri Spivak's insistence that the acts of culling knowledge, particularly knowledge about domination and resistance, must consider the social, economic, political and cultural positions of knowers, of their voices and the contexts through which knowledge emerges at the same time that the unexpected, the unpredictable and the unusual must be grappled with.[7] This is not about casting the latter as expressions of resistance but about coming to terms with the moments of silence, the refusals to answer and the unarticulated – what I refer to in this chapter as 'ethnographic unknowability' – as a regular part of feminist ethnographic practice. Highlighting ethnographic unknowability is grounded, I argue, on a poststructural feminist ethnographic practice informed by Spivak's interrogation of the notion of explanation, Visweswaran's writings about

---

4   See Iacovetta 1992.
5   See Ortner 1995.
6   Abu-Lughod 1990.
7   Lather 2007; Visweswaran 1994, 1997; Spivak 1988.

failure and Lather's evocations of undecidability. I take up these terms in relation to contemporary feminist ethnographic methodology, the attendant issues of field site/place/locale, subjectivity and the importance of how ethnographic unknowability sits side by side with ethnographic knowability. I do this by drawing attention to another ethnographic voice that speaks to the experience of Italian immigrant women, one strikingly different from that of Giulia – a voice that reveals how the collection of ethnographic information (or data or knowledge) may, at times, be a troubling venture.

Spring (April) 2001, Thunder Bay[8]

Twilight encroaches upon us. The sky is a fanciful purple-pink colour, the colour of sky one sees in a classic Group of Seven painting.[9] Maria and I stroll under it at a leisurely pace, breathing in the crisp, cold air that works its way up to the centre of Thunder Bay from the shores of Lake Superior.[10] We walk along a curvy, paved path carved out of a mangled clutter of trees, bush, grass and weeds. We force ourselves to speak louder than usual, hoping our strained voices will carry over the noisy, fast-running brook that hugs the twisting contours of the trail. Maria agreed to an interview after several informal conversations about her experiences as a southern Italian immigrant woman. She is the perfect research participant, a natural storyteller of colourful, lively, suspenseful and gripping tales about southern Italy in the 1940s and 1950s. She regularly speaks about her experiences of growing up as a peasant girl, growing up during WWII, growing up as a farmer and cook, growing up Catholic and, ultimately, growing up with the desire to escape that kind of life by re-making her home in Canada. She

---

8   This conversation has been reconstructed from notes I created immediately after my interview with Maria (the research participant).

9   The Group of Seven, formed in 1920, is Canada's most famous group of painters. Its members challenged traditional European art through the use of bold colours, broad, sweeping brush strokes and a focus on the grandeur of the Canadian landscape. Artists involved with the Group travelled all over central and northern Ontario to such regions as Algonquin Park, Algoma, Georgian Bay, Haliburton and Lake Superior. Works of art depicting trees, sky and water around Lake Superior are popular in northwestern Ontario.

10 Thunder Bay is a small city in northwestern Ontario situated on the western shore of Lake Superior (one of the world's largest freshwater lakes), surrounded by the rugged Canadian Shield, forest, muskeg and swamp. Centrally located in Canada, it was once an important shipping and rail hub for the transport of grain and other products across the country. Academic studies about the city narrowly characterise it as homogeneously rural, Canadian, hyper- masculine and working-class. This portrayal downplays the over 40-year presence of Lakehead University and Confederation College in the city and its more than an century of support for professional symphonies, the promotion of growth in health sciences research and services, an array of professional and amateur theatre troupes, past and ongoing vibrant multicultural expressions and a large white-collar workforce (see Sullivan 2009; Dunk 1994).

repeatedly claims that her decision to leave southern Italy in the postwar era had as much to do with creating a better life for herself as it did with her youthful and naïve desire for adventure. The excitement of immigrating into an unfamiliar English- and French-speaking country, thousands of kilometres away from her native village, inaccessible by land, and across the vast Atlantic Ocean was to some extent tempered by the images of the New Country she had formed from her paternal grandfather's recollections of 'sojourning' in North America in the late 1800s to do dirty, backbreaking, dangerous and low- paying work. His transatlantic employment not only allowed him to purchase decent agricultural land back in Italy but also furnished him with a lifetime of exciting stories about a radically different landscape, the whiteness and frigid cold of a northern Canadian winter, the abundance of food, the different styles of homes in the New Country and the ethnic diversity of the people who lived and worked in Thunder Bay.[11]

Maria seemed genuinely surprised by my request to speak with her more formally. She is, as she tells me time and time again, a functionally illiterate, southern Italian, peasant woman who has nothing to offer a highly educated, Italian-Canadian *ragazza* (girl). She agreed to a formal interview after I pointed out that she had already shared many of her migration stories with me and that I wanted to learn more about the differences between her life in the 'Old Country' (Italy) and Thunder Bay. Before I get a chance to ask my first question, Maria insists that I should not waste my time with her but do some 'real research' by talking to the *biga-shotas* involved with the Italian Cultural Centre. She is referring here to a group of men who run one of the most important Italian organisations in the city.[12] Maria points out that the big-shots possess extensive historical knowledge about Italian immigrants in the city. I explain that I want to speak with immigrant women and that I want to speak with her in particular because she is a gifted storyteller. Maria replies that immigrant women are no different from immigrant men and that their stories are all the same. She then declares that I ought to speak with a local woman known as *il papa* (the Pope), who is active in the city's Italian Catholic church and who is an upstanding citizen. Maria adds that *il papa* was born and educated in Thunder Bay but her parents emigrated in the 1880s. I thank her for the tip but gently emphasise that I am interested

---

11 In the late 1800s, Maria's grandfather laboured in a place known as Port Arthur, which is located today in the northern part of the city of Thunder Bay. Thunder Bay was formed in 1970 by the amalgamation of two bigger centres, Port Arthur and Fort William, with the adjacent townships of Neebing and McIntryre. Although it is not technically correct, Maria, like most inhabitants of the city, talks about Thunder Bay when speaking about her grandfather's 'sojourning'. I also use the name Thunder Bay, rather than Port Arthur, throughout this chapter.

12 In order to qualify as a full voting member of the organisation associated with the Italian Cultural Centre, one must be both male and be able to trace one's paternity to a male of Italian descent. Italian descent is determined by one's last name, and consequently the sons of women of Italian origins who do not have Italian fathers, i.e. Italian surnames, are not eligible for full membership.

in *her* personal immigration experiences. She asserts that she is not a good person to speak to about these matters because she is not a typical, southern Italian immigrant woman, for upon docking at Pier 21 in Nova Scotia (Halifax) in 1957, sea-sick, tired and anxious to stand on land after weeks of living on the Atlantic Ocean, she decided that she would leave all of the trappings of the Old Country behind. With great pride, Maria recounts how she went off to work at an English-speaking laundromat almost immediately upon arriving in Thunder Bay without being able to speak the language of her New Country, without any previous experience in the wage employment sector, without informing her husband and, most importantly, without securing her husband's permission.

A temporary silence ensues. There is an uncomfortable quiet with only the sound of our feet stamping the ground. I finally ask Maria if other Italian immigrant women did the same thing when they arrived in Thunder Bay. She responds that she can't really comment about others, adding that moving to the New Country gave her the chance to 'change things' and become a modern Canadian woman. This was, Maria stresses, not normal. When I ask her to explain a bit more, she tersely announces that she no longer wants to chat about immigration and women. I'm taken aback by Maria's reaction: of the many times in the past that we've talked about her life experiences, she's always been open and receptive to my ethnographic questions, regardless of how many different ways and/or times I've asked them. I decide, for the sake of the friendly relationship I've developed with her, to chat about more mundane matters such as the weather, supper, grandkids' interests and the like. As we come to the end of our walk, I bid Maria goodbye, unsure if I'll ever be able to ask her about the distinctions between a normal, traditional, southern Italian immigrant woman and a not normal, modern Canadian woman.

Ethnographic knowabilities, ethnographic unknowabilities: Understanding Giulia's certainties and Maria's refusals

The two ethnographic vignettes above get me thinking about ethnographic practice by questioning what I think I know about Italian immigrant women. They just as importantly point to the silences around what doesn't get said, broached and grappled with. Giulia's assertion that Italian immigrant women are oppressed is articulated from the position of a presumed competent and reliable knower. Her expertise stems from her educational credentials and scholarly research interests, her life-long pursuit of reading and her talk of Italian cultural traits expressed by the words *pazzo arrangiarsi* and *furbo* and the Mediterranean honour/shame complex. Her expert knowing is bolstered by talk of her own experiences: she is of Italian provenance and has direct quotidian know-how not only of the ways in which Italian immigrant women are expected to act but also of how they do in fact act. Our conversation stalls at the possibility that these women may use the very cultural codes that inform their sense of selfhood in a way that runs counter to that which is expected. There is a steadfast denial of this possibility based on the notion that Giulia is the sort of person who knows what's going on and is the sort of person who is able to give voice to that knowledge.

Maria's talk is radically different, for, unlike Giulia's, it marks a clear moment of ethnographic unknowability.[13] It is possible to simply ignore, downplay or minimise this unknowabiltity by dismissing Maria's comments as unusual or out of the ordinary. Alternatively, it might be looked upon, as emblematic of an immigrant's disjointed and unconscious experiences of place and time, of the culture of the here and there, of one's present-settlement and before-immigration homes. It may well be 'read' as a sign of Maria's discomfort with a public, official interview as opposed to our many previous more casual conversations. In this vein, it could be understood as an expression of Maria's anxiety about the process of transforming informal chitchat into formal ethnographic knowledge and a basic insecurity about the value of one functionally illiterate woman's migration experiences in comparison with the know-how of the big-shots or *il papa*. It may possibly underline Maria's belief that she is an unreliable research participant, someone who will steer an educated *ragazza* down the wrong path. Then again, perhaps it highlights a covert articulation of gender, of the traditional, southern Italian honour/shame complex of private women and public men.[14] Or, conversely, it may represent a research participant's challenge to, or an assertion of power over, a meddlesome educated younger Canadian-born researcher.[15]

I want to suggest that Maria's refusal to fully engage in my ethnographic inquiry, even after securing her consent and even after months of informal banter about her life as an immigrant woman, cannot so simply be understood in these ways. For Maria has regularly laid claim to being a southern Italian immigrant woman during our past conversations at the same time as she is cognizant of how she does not always so neatly fit into its identity mould. She is aware of this contradictory simultaneity and has spoken frequently in the past about the disjuncture between her traditional Italian and modern Canadian womanhood. The reasons for it, however, have eluded our conversations, skirting around the edges of our many talks. The interview, I surmised, would allow me to ask directly about this disjuncture. Despite my best efforts, however, I failed to capture the information that would help me explain how the experiences of Maria's past and present Italian-Canadian selfhoods fit together. Rather than read this failure as a 'bad interview', as an issue that needs to be taken up at another time and/or place, as an effect of the tensions between researcher and research participant or as a covert expression of the honour/shame complex, it might be productive to begin thinking about it as a way to interrogate ethnographic practice generally and the methodology of contemporary feminist ethnography specifically; that is, to critically inspect the assumptions that are made in culling ethnographic

13 See Youdell 2010; Spivak 1988.
14 See Iacovetta 1992.
15 See Bhattacharya 2009; Hedge 2009; McNamera 2009.

knowledge, information, data, etc.[16] Maria's refusal to answer my questions opens up an array of questions about how methodology, i.e. the gathering of knowledge, is intertwined with the problematic of subjectivity, i.e. how people articulate a sense of their selfhood. It raises the question of how a feminist ethnographer goes about getting information while wrestling with what doesn't get said, expressed or broached: Maria's non-answers urge us to reflect upon how we deal with those moments where the ethnographic knowability so clearly, concisely and decidedly voiced by Giulia collides with the ethnographic unknowability voiced by Maria.

The problematic of subjectivity and ethnographic knowing/unknowing (or the explained/the unexplained, success/failure, decidable/undecidable dichotomies, see below) are central matters for poststructural feminist ethnographic practice.[17] I want to begin by asking about how Maria's refusal to deal with my questions in the light of Giulia's expert answers help to illuminate this practice. This gets me thinking about place as well, as my ponderings about the expressions of southern Italian immigrant womanhood in Thunder Bay are located in the very city where I was born, lived away from and, by a strange twist of fate, returned to as the place that is both my ethnographic field site and my current home. It is a place that anchors the telling and re-tellings of my own parents' story of leaving southern Italy, travelling by ship across the Atlantic and settling in Canada in an effort to escape the *la miseria* (poverty) of their isolated, mountainous, agrarian native villages in the Old Country. Talk of the place Thunder Bay is entangled with talk of Italy and with talk about gender, family, farming, Catholicism, pagan festivals, a lack of modern amenities, schooling and hope for a better future. My positioning, however, as a researcher who 'belongs' to the cultural group 'under study', does not automatically furnish me with a deeper, more thorough or more comprehensive understanding of the research participants' migration stories, cultural traits and identities. Nor does it automatically position me as an expert knower because of my supposedly shared culture, history, 'home' and experience with the research participants (unlike Giulia's declared position). The illusions of full identification with a group under study on the part of a 'halfie', native or insider-outsider ethnographer have been thoroughly challenged by feminist work that draws attention to how similarities and differences in class, age, gender, educational levels, disciplinary training, home and generational positions, in a word 'who-ness', come vexatiously into play in the research process.[18]

These critical interrogations of place (i.e. field sites/home) undergird the machinations of feminist ethnography today. Yet there is often something missing in the latter – an omission that points to a poststructural feminist practice committed to looking at ethnographic data and its attendant

16 Harding & Norberg 2009: New Feminist Approaches to Social Science Methodologies: An Introduction. *Signs: A Journal of Women in Culture & Society* 30: 3, 2009–2016.
17 See Britzman 2000.
18 Narayan, 1993; Zavella1993; Abu-Lughod 1990.

uncertainties without automatically reading them as instances of resistance. This draws attention, as well, to the modernist impulse to read unknowabilities as moments of tension that, as Lather emphasises, may operate to 'structure feminist methodology as fertile ground for the production of new practices'.[19] Lather wants us to deal with these moments of tension not by and through the logic of a progressivist 'getting smart' but as a vital element in a poststructural feminist practice that stakes a claim for the importance of continuously grappling with the impossibilities of resolving tension.[20] This follows Gayatri Chakravorty Spivak's claim that a 'certain experience of the possibility of the impossible' needs to be brought into sharp relief.[21] The experience of the possibility of the impossible tells us something about Maria's refusal to speak more fully about her gendered and immigrant sense of selfhood in relation to the spatial southern Italy/Thunder Bay and temporal past/present divides; it tells us something about my expectation that Maria would speak about these issues in a neat, understandable way (the way that Giulia speaks?); and it tells us something about the presumptions about how information, knowledge or data is assembled (i.e. methodology), and its connections to place (i.e. an ethnographic field site). I deal in more detail with some of these knottings below.

Knottings of field sites, subjectivities, and knowabilities

For decades now, older entrenched research practices guiding the division between the ethnographer as Self and the research participant as Other, its unexamined isomorphism with the 'now' of ethnographic writing and the 'back then' of the research participant's quotidian experiences and unreflexive assumptions about the ethnographer's 'home' and the research participant's 'out-of-the-way' field site have been thoroughly challenged.[22] There is no simple way of asserting the dyadic notions of 'the informant Other/the researcher Self', 'us/them' 'tradition/modern', 'our culture/their culture, our home/their field site' and 'Western/non-Western' without inverted commas, extensive explication or rationalisation.[23]

There have, not surprisingly, been many creative responses to these criticisms Some ethnographers have undertaken fieldwork in unprecedented field sites, i.e. the urban village, media, the fashion industry, theatres, cyberspace, science labs, the body and their own backyard.[24] The move to break out of ethnography's normative exotic field site, although needed and much welcomed, is only a starting point. The acceptance of such seemingly pedestrian field sites as legitimate ethnographic locales also begins to open

19 Lather 2009, 224.
20 Lather 2009, 224.
21 Lather 2009, 224; St. Pierre 2000.
22 Wiklund, this volume; Yamaguchi 2010.
23 Meissner & Hasselberg, this volume.
24 Hirvi, this volume; Koikkalainen, this volume.

up concerns over classical ethnography's presumptions about the Self-here-now/Other-there-then binary embedded in past research practices.[25] More importantly, it offers opportunities to contest both the objectivist and experiential techniques of collecting data frequently employed in classical ethnography. While objectivist techniques assume that value-free, impartial, valid, and replicable data is awaiting extraction by an expert ethnographer whose home is elsewhere (i.e. the Self in classical ethnography), experiential ones assume that value-laden, partial, and unique data is embedded in the personal experiences and voices of research participants (i.e. the Other in classical ethnography). One legitimises the amassed data from an outsider perspective, the other from an insider perspective; both rely on the assumption that data is gatherable by and through the stories, tales, narratives, and myths research participants share with researchers in the field. And both have been challenged by concerns about how the ethnographic Self has appropriated, represented, and exploited the ethnographic Other for intellectual, colonial, patriarchal, political and profit-making reasons. These concerns point to the power/knowledge dynamics that continuously underline how one goes about gathering data.[26]

Field sites are nowadays approached as dynamic places that give rise to partial and situated data, information or knowledge constructed through the interactions of the various subject-positions of researchers and research participants (i.e. gender, race, ethnicity, class and so on): questions of place are tied here to the problematic of subjectivity and to the gathering of ethnographic knowledge. These are some of the most salient issues in what is referred to as dialogical ethnography, a research methodology that departs from its objectivist and experiential counterparts by taking seriously how the various contextually-evoked subjectivities of research participants and researchers affect what is thought, what is known, what is known by whom, what is known in particular contexts and locales and how that knowing is collaboratively culled.[27]

These concerns are not, however, new. Feminist scholars have long been at the forefront of articulating similar deep-going critiques, despite the marginalisation of their work.[28] As Sandra Harding and Kathryn Norberg[29] make clear, the feminist movements of the 1970s directly challenged the presumptions surrounding what constitutes good research in the social sciences. Good research was once guaranteed by good objectivist methodology which disentangled the social, political and economic context of the research, as well as the subjectivities of the researchers, from the research results. Value-free, culture-free, politically free, verifiable, replicable and generalizable knowledge was assured by how one went about conducting research, as larger institutional, gendered, immigration, class, racial, ethnic,

---

25 Redwood 2008.
26 Foucault 1998.
27 Britzman 2000; St. Pierre 2000.
28 Visweswaran 1994.
29 Harding & Norberg 2005.

etc., factors were deemed immaterial, pushed aside, made abject. Feminist scholars of methodology revealed how these objectivist presumptions were grounded on androcentric ways of gathering knowledge, which, in turn, produced androcentric knowledge. They claimed that the reliance on an objectivist methodology as the guarantor of 'value-free research' actually produced value-laden androcentric data, information or knowledge. The supposedly value-free, culture-free, politically free, etc., data garnered by the employment of an objective methodology was not only an 'unachievable ideal' but also highly undesirable. In its stead, a biased, partial, and interested research methodology based on women's experiences was valorised as a more responsive and responsible knowledge-gathering practice.[30]

This kind of research was initially tied to a feminist standpoint methodology that endorsed the gathering of knowledge on the basis of listening to women's voices and focusing on what women want to study, ask and know about. The voice of the marginalised, i.e. woman, was deemed to be the path to better, more accurate, research results since the voice of those already in the know, i.e. hegemonic man, was always already distorted by its privilege and power. Current versions of standpoint methodology continue to emphasise the value of women's knowledge but also take account of a multitude of other factors, i.e. gender, race, class, sexualities, etc., and their intersections. They also highlight how quotidian, personal experience articulates with larger institutional forces and how such linkages have the potential to positively transform research participants' everyday life.[31] Feminist standpoint methodologies tend, however, to downplay the power differentials between researchers and research participants[32] – a particularly pressing issue in relation to contemporary feminist ethnographic practice.

Much like other feminist researchers, feminist ethnographers have also focused on the voices, experiences and interests of marginalised, subaltern or subordinated research participants. But they overtly confront the challenges occasioned by the differences in power between researchers and research participants.[33] Indeed, Wanda Pillow and Cris Mayo[34] define contemporary feminist ethnographic methodology by its commitment to producing knowledge in an interactive and collaborative manner (i.e. a dialogical approach). This commitment means that researchers must face up to the social, economic, political and cultural factors that shape ethnographic information by looking at the politics of language, polyvocality and meaning-making; tracking the discourses of culture and community and their attendant vexations; exploring the articulations of power and resistance; and finally, examining the machinations of similarities and difference in relation to femininity, masculinity, race, migration, sexualities, class, age and so on.[35]

---

30 Harding & Norberg 2005.
31 Saul 2003.
32 Cf. Saul 2003.
33 Harding & Norberg 2005; Viswesaran 1994.
34 Lather 2001, 2007.
35 See Pillow & Mayo 2007.

Pillow and Mayo suggest, moreover, that these concerns give rise to the practice of reflexivity, a practice that questions how knowledge is built up in particular contexts and how the different subjectivities of various stakeholders affect research results. Contemporary feminist ethnographic methodology and its attendant practice of reflexivity underscore the partiality of knowledge because of *the partiality of knowledge production*. This does not, as some have misconstrued, promote the production of navel-gazing, fabricated and unreliable knowledge. Such criticisms usually stem from unnamed objectivist methodologies that are tied to colonisation, domination, exploitation, patriarchy and the like.[36] Advocates of current feminist ethnographic methodologies focus on the attempt to give voice to the partialities of subjugated knowledge based on interactions between researchers and research participants' 'authentically personal' or lived experiences instead of abstract theoretical ponderings.[37] Moreover, this way of culling knowledge is said to increase the rapport between researchers and research participants, to allow for the diffusion of power that traditionally traffics within and across the researcher/research participant relationship and to better reveal the experiential differences and commonalities between researcher and research participant.[38] All of this happens in newer feminist ethnographic methodologies through an ethics of care, rather than an ethics of principle, so that feminist researchers are supposedly more concerned with research participants as research participants and less concerned with them as emblematic of categories of knowledge.[39] This is, finally, connected to the increasingly popular use of participatory action research (PAR), which insists that knowledge is practical, belongs to those who generate it and should be used as a tool for research participants to better their lives and to work toward empowerment.[40] These traits constitute, in varying degrees, the basis for a dialogical ethnographic methodology that departs from its objectivist (i.e. the culling of generalizable knowledge from a trained ethnographic researcher) and experiential counterparts (i.e. the culling of knowledge from the experience and interests of the ethnographic research participant). And for some, this is more than enough: all knowledge is partial because it is produced by and through the various, contextually-shifting subjectivities of researchers and research participants.

Contemporary feminist ethnography is informed, in lesser and greater degrees, by these traits.[41] This is laudable and clearly preferable to the value-neutrality and disinterested assertions that surrounded objectivist methodologies (which, recall, are colonialist, exploitative and androcentric). However, an uncritical use of these traits runs the risk of reproducing some of the most obstinate assumptions ingrained in the modernist dream to

36 Visweswaran 1994; Spivak 1988.
37 Hesse-Biber & Piatelli 2007.
38 Hesse-Biber & Piatelli 2007; Pillow & Mayo 2007.
39 Hesse-Biber & Piatelli 2007.
40 Hesse-Biber & Piatelli 2007.
41 Pillow & Mayo 2007.

capture knowledge, however partial, contextual and shifting that knowledge is acknowledged to be. This is perhaps most obvious in topical appeals to culling ethnographic materials through an uncritical notion of participation which claims to give voice to research participants, minimises the power differentials between researchers and research participants, involves research participants in the design, implementation and generation of research results, enhances the research participants' ability to become reflexive about their quotidian life and inspires them to transform their own lives.

However much contemporary feminist ethnographic methodology is positively influenced by the notion of participation, it nonetheless raises concerns in that it may be employed to put rigid boundaries around who, and who does not, count as a research participant. It also tends to be used in a manner that frames communities as discrete and socially homogeneous by downplaying the vexatious differences within a group while minimising the effect of the researcher, who is cast as a facilitator rather than producer, for the generation of partial and contextual data.[42] Critiques of the notion of participation help to open up interrogations about the place of 'who-ness' in ethnographic practice and its knottings with the generation of knowledge more generally. And this, I suggest, leads to questions about what can be known by a particular knower and how that knowability is undergirded by an unknowablity; an unknowability, following Lather, that offers the possibility of 'getting lost in ethnography', of dealing with that which is 'in excess of our codes', of 'dispersing rather than capturing meanings', of 'producing bafflement rather than solutions', and of keeping 'feminist methodology open, alive, loose' such that it operates 'within and against Enlightenment categories of voice, identity, agency and experience'.[43] This recalls a poststructural feminist ethnographic practice that valorises unknowability *qua* unknowability as a critical part of the gathering of data.

On ethnographic unknowabilities: Spivak's explanation, Visweswaran's failure, Lather's undecidability.

The place of unknowability *as* unknowability is, to repeat, too often missing in contemporary feminist ethnography.[44] The dialogical ethnographic call for the partiality of data, its contextuality and its links to the shifting

---

42 Kesby 2005.
43 Lather 2001, 477.
44 Lather 2001, 2007, 2009. Lather, inspired by Spivak, proposes a 'getting lost' kind of ethnography. I am, however, worried by Lather's occasional statements that such moments of 'getting lost' operate as a sort of 'messiness that invites further thinking and doing.' In these instances, Lather implies that the 'provocation of something unknown/unknowable' is an impetus for further exploration, examination and interrogation (cf. Youdell 2010 and St. Pierre 2000 for similar problems). This runs counter to a poststructural feminist methodology that, I contend, recognises unknowability as unknowability.

subjectivities of researchers and research participants may get us away from the assumption that ethnographic data is obtainable by an outside neutral observer; it also may get us away from the assumption that ethnographic data is obtainable by focusing on the personal experiences of certain research participants and/or researchers, as is often the case with standpoint and participatory research methodologies. These methodological approaches are embedded in the modernist dream of capturing knowledge by relying on a modernist belief that data is *a priori* cullable.[45] Spivak long ago warned us of how objectivist, experiential and dialogical methodologies broach the unknown, i.e. unknowabilities, as a motivation to explain what goes on in a particular culture, to unlock the codes and meanings of culture and to chart the machinations, operations and reverberations of a cultural system. Such methodologies are based on the presumption that an explanation, whether partial, experiential or objectivist, about some part of the world is entirely possible. Knowledge gathered by an objectivist outsider, by an experiential insider or through dialogical researcher-research collaboration is grounded on this quest for explanation. Spivak helps put the notion of explanation under critical scrutiny by encouraging us to think about how the 'possibility of explanation carries' with it, in advance, the 'presupposition of an explainable', even if what is explained is recognised as incomplete by an 'imperfect' knower.[46]

In specific relation to contemporary feminist ethnography, Spivak urges us to consider how the 'possibility of explanation' is embedded in debates surrounding the notion of universal womanhood. Spivak argues that the de-stabilisation of a unitary essentialist notion of 'woman' in the 1980s, i.e. the notion that all biologically and culturally defined women equally identify with the category 'woman', led to an acceptance of a heterogeneous notion of 'women', i.e. the notion that women identify, depending on the social, economic, political and cultural context, with many different identity categories (e.g. immigrant, race, ethnicity, age, ability and so on). The move in feminist writing from the singularity of 'woman' to the multiplicities of 'women' parallels the major shifts in feminist ethnography as well, starting with the 'anthropology of woman', moving to the 'anthropology of gender' and settling on an anthropology grounded on concerns over 'difference'.[47] Not surprisingly, then, feminist ethnographers have challenged the prime place of 'woman' by arguing for an understanding of how the intersectionalities of various identity categories give rise to partial knowledge and, in turn, legitimise dialogical ethnography. This is a normative practice in contemporary feminist ethnography that tends to focus on differences both between genders and difference within categories of gender. However, the latter downplays one of the most salient concerns in Spivak's work about 'women': that declarations of the multiplicity of 'women' continue,

45 Spivak 1988.
46 Spivak 1988a, 105.
47 Lewin 2006.

185

nonetheless, to be grounded on the assumption that it is always possible to explain such multiplicity.[48]

Spivak queries how the replacement of an essential 'woman', with an essential multiplicity of, say, southern Italian immigrant women, re-inscribes a modernist logic for explanation by ignoring any attendant unknowabilities. Relying on the multiplicities of 'women', Spivak suggests, does little to get us to pay serious attention to moments 'that are completely inaccessible', moments that constitute a 'blank part of the text', moments that accentuate the unexplained *as* the unexplained.[49] Instead of following modernist methodologies that desire, search for and attempt to master explanation, Spivak implores us to bear in mind how knowledge, data and information are simultaneously intertwined with moments of un-explainability. The two go together. This is a difficult task for feminist ethnographers who expect to produce knowledge in a clear, concise way in order to explain the connections between one's field site and, for example, notions of culture, community, identity, home and migration. Spivak asks us instead to ask about what goes on when we assume the possibility of explanation without considering its impossibility; when, considered in relation to a kind of feminist ethnography grounded on the multiplicity of 'women', explanation is presumed to derive from the right research tactic, technique or information-gathering tool given by the right methodological approach.

Kamala Visweswaran's work is also telling in this regard.[50] Whereas Spivak stresses the notion of the explained and the unexplained, Visweswaran focuses on how feminist ethnographers address failure and success. In relation to failure, she urges us to resist seeing it as a moment that propels knowledge forward, informs us about the mistakes we have made in culling data, encourages us to search more deeply into the lives of our research participants, or serves as a jumping-off point to develop more effective and efficient strategies to get research participants to speak about our research agendas. Ethnographic failure is too often framed as a teachable moment, a temporary check on the road toward eventual success, a stumbling block to overcome. Visweswaran illustrates this treatment of ethnographic failure-as-the-road-to-success by listing examples of standard methodological advice given about interviewing research participants: feminist interviewers ought to begin with open-ended questions so that research participants' guide the interview; feminist interviewers ought to avoid re-directing research participants' answers to suit their own research concerns; and feminist interviewers ought to 'discard their research-oriented time frames in favour of research participants' expectations'.[51] In this vein, failures are cast as ethnographic struggles that are all too often 'recuperated as a success [... so that] future feminist researchers benefiting from this experience will not go on to commit the same errors. They will arrive at an interview, tape

48 Spivak 1993.
49 Spivak 1993, 22.
50 Visweswaran 1994.
51 Visweswaran 1994, 97–98.

recorder in readiness or with a small notebook held discretely in one hand. The assumption is that "better"' methodology will mean better accounts'.[52]

Visweswaran challenges such functionalist views of fieldwork failures by re-casting them as moments that need to be constantly grappled with instead of moments to be overcome. This is a far cry from the familiar ways in which feminist ethnographers usually deal with failure as an emergent question that requires additional effort at another time and/or place; it is a far cry, as well, from how contemporary feminist ethnographers may read failure as an effect of the partiality of data based on the diverse, disjunctive and/or vexed subjectivities of various stakeholders in the research process. In this way, grappling with failure as failure (rather than trying to resolve or ignore or speculate about it) is an important part of a feminist ethnography that helps maintain a critical position in relation to speaking *for* the Other, as is common in objectivist methodology, letting the Other speak in her/his own voice, as is common in experiential methodology and speaking *with* the Other, as is the case with dialogically -based methodologies. Visweswaran centralises the simultaneous double movement of ethnographic failure and success. She asks us to embrace failure as failure by giving space to a kind of feminist ethnography that recognises partiality, indeterminacy and contingency.[53] However she warns us that this kind of ethnography is not simply about making room for the kind of reflexivity championed by contemporary feminist ethnographers. Visweswaran argues that reflexivity may be good at encouraging us to confront how our own biases, assumptions and partialities affect our information-getting practices. But reflexivity, or thinking about the data we've culled and how we've culled it, may not be so good at getting us to confront the plays of power in our information-getting practices; it may, in addition, not be so good at getting us to ask *how* we think we know what we know; and it may not be so good at getting us to deal with the paradox of knowing through not-knowing, of taking seriously the 'practice of deferral [and] a refusal to explain'.[54]

Visweswaran calls attention to the importance of the continuous, never resolved mediations between ethnographic successes and failures. Mediation does not refer here to the resolution of a contradiction, ambivalence or tension; it should not be taken, re-working Lather's words above, to help 'structure feminist methodology as fertile ground for the production of new practices' in order to make 'resolution at least thinkable'. Alternately, mediation does not offer a dialectical solution whereby two opposing terms are brought together in a way that holds on to the specificity of each term while synthesising both into a third term. Patti Lather similarly writes of a kind of ethnography that is based on the 'praxis of stuck places, a praxis of not being so sure, in excess of a binary and dialectical logic that disrupts the horizon of an already prescribed intelligibility'.[55] Lather's

---

52 Visweswaran 1994, 98.
53 Butler 2004.
54 Visweswaran1994, 78.
55 Lather 2001, 482.

call for ethnographically 'stuck places' begins to shore up the saliency, following Spivak, of the aporia in a poststructural feminist ethnographic methodology where gaps of knowing clash with the grounds of knowing, where the certainty of data, information, knowledge is contingent upon its uncertainty and vice versa. Lather promotes a kind of feminist ethnography that is informed by a 'post-critical logic of haunting and undecidables'. Her stress on undecidability leads to a kind of 'philosophical ethnography' that is attentive to 'the certain experience of the possibility of the impossible' and which challenges the quest for the progressive accumulation of data and a faith in the ability to uncover information. She insists on 'a stumbling sort of doing that risks producing what it repeats, a certain respectful mimicking that twists and queers... an undecidability that is never over and done with'.[56] A feminist ethnographic practice based on a never-over-and-done-with undecidability, Visweswaran's notion of failure and Spivak's notion of the unexplained embrace a not-knowing which guards against the desire to assume that knowledge is unproblematically capturable, an assumption, recall, based on modernism's exploitative, domineering, colonialist and androcentric thinking and practice. 'The big question that remains,' writes Lather, 'is the possibilities as well as limits of such an articulation of research practice where we are not so sure of ourselves and where we see this not knowing as our best chance for a different sort of doing in the name of feminist methodology.'[57]

A different sort of 'doing' is a different sort of ethnographic methodology that takes seriously how the question of who knows is connected to how such knowing is structured by and through a knowing/unknowing dyad.[58] Am I therefore to resolve ethnographic unknowabilities by asking Maria, for example, more appropriate questions about her immigration stories? Am I to re-frame my questions so that Giulia is more willing to consider alternative understandings of resistance in relation to the honour/shame complex? Am I perhaps to read Maria's refusal to speak about her refusal to be a traditional Italian woman as a resistance to the honour/shame complex? Is she asserting

---

56 Lather 2009, 224–225.

57 Lather 2009, 225.

58 Less enthusiastic critics suggest that poststructuralism is just an overly reified abstraction that aims to discard the materiality of life and the voices of those to whom ethnographers are indebted. Poststructural feminist ethnographers are sometimes accused here of speaking over the heads of those they are supposedly speaking with by using overblown prose. Yet these remarks often serve to simply reinstate objectivist, experiential and dialogical methodologies. They miss, too, the political and ethical project of poststructural ways of culling knowledge. They put in place a defensive assertion for the value of thick description, of historical data, of the voices of 'informants.' In so doing, these defensive posturings forget about the colonising, exploitative and patriarchal power moves that are embedded in past objectivist methodologies; they forget too, that the move to experiential and dialogical methodologies, although admittedly better, serves to uphold such modernist desires in an effort to continue to capture knowledge, without dealing with how knowing and knowers are simultaneously caught in unknowability.

her power as a research participant over a researcher? Will her refusal to tell me more fully about her migration experiences be overcome at another time, in another ethnographic context and over time as Maria and I develop a stronger friendship? Does Maria's refusal to answer my questions about her position as an Italian immigrant woman stem from my own inability to fully take up a particular role within a given ethnographic moment, i.e. my inability as a Canadian-born researcher of southern Italian provenance to identify myself as an immigrant Italian woman? Is it a question of efficient and effective listening so that my research agenda is better in tune with issues that matter to Maria and Giulia? Am I to read Giulia's expert talk about southern Italian immigrant women as better information? Should I take up Maria's advice that speaking with big-shots and *il papa* will give me more informed migration stories? What violences do I do in trying to get the right explanation from Maria and Giulia about migration, the stories of migration or the experiences of migration on the part of Italian-Canadian women? What gets missed when explanations about migration go awry and when failures are transformed into successes? What kinds of questions should I be asking so that I am in a position to explain away any articulated tensions, contradictions and vexations, so that I can get ethnographically 'unstuck'? Can we, as contemporary feminist ethnographers, deal with unknowabilities in the gathering of data by filling them in with comparative data? Should we frame such stuck moments as opportunities for reflexivity, for thinking about how the 'we' of fieldwork affects how we ask questions and how we generate knowledge in any given context? What is the link between getting the kind of information I am trained to desire and getting the kind of information I don't know what to do with? Are appeals to participation as the panacea to objectivist ways of gathering information another way of overcoming the silences, uncertainties, aporias and refusals of ethnography? Are uncertainties that emerge in the research process always tied to some kind of learning, some morsel of truth, some kind of pragmatic end?[59]

I want to suggest that all of these questions miss the significance of un-knowability *as* unknowability. Unknowability is, I contend, an indispensable part of a poststructural feminist ethnographic practice that takes seriously how one goes about getting and not-getting data for the ethnographic mill. Other methodologies tend to leave intact the modernist assumption that knowledge, data or information is capturable by and through the employment of the right technique, a better research tool or a clever information-gathering tactic. Spivak, Visweswaran and Lather all question this. Working with approaches that valorise the voices of research participants, that place a premium on the co-creation of knowledge, that make declarations about how research ought to be geared at getting research participants to access to their own knowledge, or that make claims about a feminist ethnography grounded on the certainty of community-driven knowledge tends to be grounded on a presumption of explanation, the faith in being able to transform moments of failure into successes and a side-stepping of undecidabil-

59 Dauth 2009.

189

ity. Poststructural feminist ethnographers insist on the simultaneities of success *and* failure, the explained *and* the unexplained, the decidable *and* the undecidable. They acknowledge how the at-the-same-time knowable and unknowable is embedded in the culling of ethnographic data more generally and the culling of migration stories and notions of culture, identity (i.e. gender, class, ethnicity, race, etc.) and 'home' more particularly. Inspired by Spivak, Visweswaran and Lather's work, I want to affirm the central place of knowability/unknowability and how one goes about gathering ethnographic data in the field. This is both the great challenge to, and the great opportunity for, the practice of poststructural feminist ethnography.[60]

Bibliography

Abu-Lughod, L. 1990: Can There Be A Feminist Ethnography? *Women & Performance: A Journal of Feminist Theory* 5(1), 7–27.

Appadurai, A. 1996: *Modernity at Large: Cultural Dimensions of Globalization.* Minneapolis: University of Minnesota Press.

Bhattacharya, H. 2009: Performing Silence: Gender, Violence, and Resistance in Women's Narratives From Lahaul India. *Qualitative Inquiry* 15(2), 359–371.

Britzman, D. 2000: The Question of Belief: Writing Poststructural Ethnography. In: E. St. Pierre & W. Pillow (eds.), *Working the Ruins: Feminist Poststructural Theory and Methods in Education.* New York & London: Routledge.

Butler, J. 2004: *Undoing Gender.* New York: Routledge.

Dauth, H. E. 2009: Thinking with the Heart – Feminist Methodologies and Strategies. schwarzemilch.files.wordpress.com/2009/06/thinking_with_the_heart1.doc. Accessed 10 October 2010.

Dunk, T. 1994: *It's a Working Man's Town: Male Working-Class Culture.* Montreal and Kingston: McGill-Queen's University Press.

Fabian, J. 1983: *Time and the Other: How Anthropology Makes Its Object.* New York: Columbia University Press.

Foucault, M. 1998: *Aesthetics, Method, and Epistemology*, ed. J. D. Faubion. New York: The New York Press.

Gupta, A. & J. Ferguson 1992: Beyond "Culture": Space, Identity, and the Politics of Difference. *Cultural Anthropology* 7(1), 6–23.

Harding, S. & K. Norberg 2009: New Feminist Approaches to Social Science Methodologies: An Introduction. *Signs: A Journal of Women in Culture & Society* 30(3), 2009–2016.

Hedge, R. 2009: Fragments and Interruptions: Sensory Regimes of Violence and the Limits of Feminist Ethnography. *Qualitative Inquiry* 15: 2, 279–296.

Hesse-Biber, S. & D. Piatelli 2007: From Theory to Method and Back Again: The Synergistic Praxis of Theory and Method. In: S. Hesse-Biber (ed.), *Handbook of Feminist Research: Theory and Praxis.* Thousand Oaks, London, & New Delhi: Sage Publications.

Iacovetta, F. 1992: *Such Hardworking People: Italian Immigrants in Postwar Toronto.* Montreal and Kingston: McGill Queen's Press.

Kesby, M. 2005: Retheorising Empowerment-through-Participation as a Performance in Space: Beyond Tyranny to Transformation. *Signs: A Journal of Women in Culture & Society* 30(4), 2037–2065.

60 Youdell 2010; Redwood 2008; Britzman 2000.

Khan, S. 2005: Being Here and Being There: Reconfiguring the Native Informant: Positionality in the Global Age. *Signs: A Journal of Women in Culture & Society* 30(3), 2017–2036.

Lather, P. 2009: Feminist Efforts Toward a Double(d) Science. *Frontiers – A Journal of Women's Studies* 30(1), 222–232.

Lather, P. 2007: *Getting Lost: Feminist Practices Toward a Double(d) Science.* Albany: SUNY.

Lather, P. 2004: Getting Lost: Feminist Efforts Toward a Double(d) Science. AERA Conference, San Diego, April 12–16 2004. www.petajwhite.net/Uni/910/Legit%20and%20Representation/Respreseration%20Precis/lather%20Getting%20lost.pdf. Accessed 22 November, 2010.

Lather, P. 2001: Postmodernism, Post-structuralism, and Post(Critical) Ethnography: of Ruins, Aporias, and Angels. In: P. Atkinson, A. Coffey, S. Delamont, J. Lofland & L. Lofland (eds.), *Handbook of Ethnography.* London: Sage Publications.

Lewin, E. 2006: Introduction. In: E. Lewin (ed.), *Feminist Anthropology: A Reader.* Malden, MA: Blackwell Publishers.

McNamera, P. 2009: Feminist Ethnography: Storytelling that Makes a Difference. *Qualitative Social Work* 8(2), 161–171.

Narayan, K. 1993: How Native Is a "Native" Anthropologist? *American Anthropologist* 95(3), 671–686.

Ortner, S. 1995: Resistance and The Problem of Ethnographic Refusal. In R. Fox (ed.), *Recapturing Anthropology: Working in the Present.* Santa Fe: School of American Research Press.

Pillow, W., S. & C. Mayo 2007: Toward Understandings of Feminist Ethnography. In S. Nagy Hesse-Biber (ed.), *Handbook of Feminist Research: Theory and Praxis.* Thousand Oaks, London, & New Delhi: Sage Publications.

Redwood, S. 2008: Research Less Violent? Or the Ethics of Performative Social Science. *Forum: Qualitative Social Research* 9(2), np (e-journal). http://www.qualitative-research.net/index.php/fqs/article/viewArticle/407/881. Accessed 6 July 2010.

Saul, J. M. 2003: *Feminism: Issues & Arguments.* Oxford: Oxford University Press.

Spivak, C. G. 1993: *Outside in the Teaching Machine.* New York and London: Routledge.

Spivak, C. G. 1990: *The Post-Colonial Critic: Interviews, Strategies, Dialogues.* New York & London: Routledge.

Spivak, C. G., 1988a: *In Other Worlds: Essays in Cultural Politics.* New York and London: Routledge.

Spivak, C. G. 1988: Can the Subaltern Speak? In: C. Nelson and L. Grossberg, (eds.), *Marxism and the Interpretation of Culture.* Basingstock, UK: MacMillian Education.

St. Pierre, E. 2000: Nomadic Inquiry in the Smooth Spaces of the Field: A Preface. In: E. St. Pierre & W. Pillow (eds.), *Working the Ruins: Feminist Poststructural Theory and Methods in Education.* New York & London: Routledge.

Stewart, K. 1996: *A Space on the Side of the Road: Cultural Poetics in an "Other" America.* Princeton: Princeton University Press.

Sullivan, R. 2009: The (Mis)translation of Masculine Femininity in Rural Space: (Re)reading 'Queer' Women in Northern Ontario, Canada. *thirdspace: a journal of feminist theory and culture* 8(2), np (e-journal).

Visweswaran, K. 1997: Histories of Feminist Ethnography. *Annual Review of Anthropology* 26: 591–621.

Visweswaran K. 1994: *Fictions of Feminist Ethnography.* Minnesota, US: University of Minneapolis Press.

Yamaguchi, T. 2010: Impartial Observation and Partial Participation: Feminist Ethnography in Politically Charged Japan. *Critical Asian Studies* 39(4), 583–608.

Yon, D. A. 2007: Race-Making/Race-Mixing: St. Helena and the South Atlantic World. *Social Dynamics: A Journal of African Studies* 33(2), 144–163.

Youdell, D. 2010: Queer Outings: Uncomfortable Stories About the Subjects of Post-Structural School Ethnography. *International Journal of Qualitative Studies in Education* 23(1), 87–100.

Zavella, P. 1993: Feminist Insider Dilemmas: Constructing Ethnic Identity with "Chicana" Informants. *Frontiers: A Journal of Women Studies* 13(3), 53–76.

Sharon R. Roseman

'Hai que entenderse' (We Have to Understand One Another)

Fieldwork, Migration and Storytelling Events[1]

Introduction

Various fieldwork methods can provide invaluable information about people's experiences of migration, including their own conceptualisations of the characteristics and impact of their own or other people's movement between geographical locations. Such movements can be framed by one or more of the following dynamics: refugee status, experiences of economic insecurity or political tension common among emigrants, employment-related geographical mobility wherein workers maintain homes in one location and pursue jobs that require them to commute to work sites and/or be mobile as part of their work,[2] periods of accessing formal education or training, or a desire to take up a new job or rejoin family members who have previously relocated.

This chapter outlines one specific method that can be employed effectively as part of fieldwork conducted to gather data about all of these types of movement: the use of storytelling. As is illustrated in this contribution, it is a key method for studying both current patterns of migration and also movement that took place in the past. The last section of the chapter discusses how this method can be used in several ways. These ways can be divided according to whether the stories are unsolicited or solicited. Unsolicited stories may be assembled when: (a) they constitute an element of participant observation wherein storytelling happens naturalistically as part of social interaction and the fieldworker asks to be allowed to record the stories and possibly also the listeners' reactions to them; or (b) a field researcher can

1   This article is based on research that was funded by the Social Sciences and Humanities Research Council of Canada, the Council for European Studies, McMaster University, Memorial University of Newfoundland, and the Wenner-Gren Foundation for Anthropological Research.
2   See Temple Newhook et al. 2011. Our research group led by Barbara Neis has now further refined the concept of 'employment-related mobility' to 'employment-related geographical mobility'.

supplement on-site data with unsolicited examples of stories about migration that appear in a variety of media from diaries and letters deposited in archives to publically available interactive elements of mass media outlets such as on-line newspapers or personal weblogs. Stories can also be solicited through the use of a number of fieldwork methods, including: (a) as part of individual or group oral history or life story interviews organised by the fieldworker for the research project; (b) using photographic, place-based or other forms of elicitation involving either the researcher or someone else accompanying a storyteller to particular locations; (c) in story circles convened by the fieldworker; these may also involve the production of digital stories that can later be shared in a non-synchronous manner with a wider audience.

In order to illustrate the value of this approach for doing research on employment-related geographical mobility (in this case circular labour migration), a specific case study is introduced; it takes the form of various excerpts from stories told by an elderly man and his wife. They were from Galicia in northwestern Spain and, more than a decade prior to the telling, the man had worked in Switzerland for several years on a seasonal basis while maintaining his home in a Galician village. However, before turning to this case study, it is important to provide a discussion of the broad theoretical framework for this emphasis on the value of collecting people's stories about their lives as part of core fieldwork data. Our research participants' stories can direct our own communications about the social-relational and cultural fields through which we have passed, heard about, or otherwise participated in or studied.

Migrant subjectivity

In *The Human Condition*, Hannah Arendt argues that we should think about human action in connection with 'natality', or being born, because 'the newcomer possesses the capacity of beginning something anew, [...] this sense of initiative'.[3] The anthropologist Michael Jackson draws on Arendt's idea, defining natality as 'the tendency of all human action not only to conserve the past but to initiate new possibilities'.[4] Given that migration involves temporary or permanent settlement in a new geographical location, individuals who migrate are particularly well-positioned to be finely attuned to their initiation of 'new possibilities', as they – like others – continually participate in the remaking of their lifeworlds. If we build on these authors' work in developing an approach to the topic of migrants' subjectivity, we would take into account the existential implications of their experiences and the importance of *praxis* or action.[5]

The approach outlined here allows us to navigate between a number of other common ways of thinking about the study of human mobility,

3   Arendt 1958, 9.
4   Jackson 2005, xxi.
5   Arendt 1958.

and specifically about various forms of migration. One would be an older analytical framework that continues to have a strong ideological force, suggesting that we can evaluate different individuals or migrant populations by assessing the various degrees to which they have 'assimilated' to the mainstream lifeworlds of the host societies in which they have arrived.[6] Another would be the more recent emphasis on migrants' and other individuals' participation in a contemporary world in flux, wherein lives are considered to be more mobile than rooted, and subjectivities are perhaps better conceived of as necessarily suffused with shifting multiplicities and even 'hybridities'.[7]

If we follow Arendt's conceptualisation of human action, we can draw on aspects of both these frameworks. As various researchers have emphasised through specific ethnographic and historical case studies, we do not have to see migrants as *either* primarily assimilating to new ways of acting, speaking, and thinking, *or* simply retaining those that they have brought with them. In Peggy Levitt and Nina Glick-Schiller's terms, migrants very often participate in 'multi-layered, multi-sited transnational social fields, encompassing those who move and those who stay behind'.[8] Nor do we have to consider migrants to be different from other human social actors. Migration does not just entail making choices among behaviours, ideas, material cultures, and so on; it very much involves the basic 'heroism' inherent in all humans, which Arendt noted was not about specific acts of unusual courage but 'a willingness to act and speak at all, to insert one's self into the world and begin a story of one's own'.[9]

Storytelling and memory work

This insertion into the world incorporates storytelling and the ongoing memory work that drives the enunciation and reception of stories. It is often impossible, and indeed analytically problematic, to create an abstract terminological distinction between individuals' specific memories and those that have been variously termed 'social', 'collective', and 'cultural'.[10] 'Cultural memory', as Marita Sturken reminds us, 'does not efface the individual but rather involves the interaction of individuals in the creation of cultural meaning'.[11] Moreover,

> Memory forms the fabric of human life, affecting everything from the ability to perform simple, everyday tasks to the recognition of the self. Memory establishes

---

6   See e.g. Harmann & Gerteis 2005.
7   See e.g. Canclini 1990; Appadurai 1996; Urry 2000; Elliott & Urry 2010.
8   Levitt & Glick Schiller 2004, 1003.
9   Arendt 1958, 186.
10   E.g. Fentress & Wickham 1992; Halbwachs 1992.
11   Sturken 1997, 1.

life's continuity; it gives meaning to the present [...] memory provides the very core of identity.[12]

Whether people are migrants, or are connected with migrants in either sender or host communities, cultural memories establish important continuities between the past and the present, and between the places from which migrants have come and those in which they arrive.

Anthropologists and other ethnographic researchers have long collected people's narrative accounts as part of an explicit focus on different types of narratives ranging from fictional folktales about human encounters with supernatural creatures such as fairies to legends and myths and stories from their own living experiences. Indeed, a series of such stories forms the basis for the development of 'life histories'. The anthropologist Sally Cole, among others, has noted that she employs the term 'life stories' rather than 'life histories' in her ethnography about the lives of women in Vila Chã, Portugal because these women recount stories to her about their lives rather than engage in the work of 'history'.[13] The folklorists Kristin and Eugene Valentine, in writing about the life of 'Maite', their key informant in Santiago de Compostela in Galicia, refer to her as having 'performed culture through narrative', and as a gifted 'Galician Woman Storyteller'.[14] Moreover, as Julie Cruikshank has noted,

> If much of the academic literature seems to universalize or to work against the notion that people lead storied lives in distinctive ways, the primary lesson I learned [...] is that narratives providing the most helpful guidance are inevitably locally grounded, highly particular, and culturally specific. What is important is not just knowing the story but sharing the context for knowing when and why it is told so that conversations can build on that shared knowledge.[15]

These and many other scholars have demonstrated how valuable it is for field researchers to encourage research participants to share their own narrative accounts of their memories, and the connections of these with their current and future situations. Elinor Ochs and Lisa Capps point out that such verbal enactment 'serves as a prosaic social arena for developing frameworks for understanding events [...] a tool for collaboratively reflecting upon specific situations'.[16] As part of this approach to studying migration, we should consider that this memory work helps migrants and those to whom they are connected to move metaphorically between geographical spaces. It also assists those doing research on migration in making the same metaphorical journeys.

12 Sturken 1997.
13 Cole 1991.
14 Valentine & Valentine 1992.
15 Cruikshank 1998, xii–xiii.
16 Ochs & Capps 2001, 2. Also see, for example, Plattner (ed.) 1984 and Jackson 2002.

Emplacement, belonging, and intersubjectivity

Rather than the idea of 'displacement', which implies moving between fixed points in space and time, we can employ the concept of agentive emplacement or 'making place'. When migrants insert themselves in the world, they retell their sense of emplacement and indeed, of belonging, since the experience of belonging is processual, involving emerging meanings as opposed to inert, essential qualities.[17] Hannah Arendt notes that we tell each other stories, but the teller or social agent who tells a story and thus acts 'is not an author or producer' since this story is being inserted into a 'web of human relationships'.[18] Emplacement and belonging are thus intertwined with 'the transformations all experience undergoes as it is replayed, recited, reworked and reconstrued in the play of intersubjective life'.[19] Narrating our experiences through stories does not hold them still for either ourselves or others but 'mediates our relation' with what Jackson terms 'otherness'.[20] Studying migration through storytelling practices allows researchers to examine migrants' intersubjective connections with other people as these emerge from the past and merge into the future.[21]

Storytelling in Galicia

Many Galicians, like people in other parts of the world, describe a shift in the last few decades away from patterns of extensive and regular rounds of inter-household visiting, when it was common to entertain each other by recounting personal narratives. Novels that recreate earlier periods in Galician history also demonstrate how common it was to tell stories in public gathering places such as bars.[22] Despite an undeniably radical shift in sociality and a consequent decline in the previous intensity of visiting and the associated storytelling, it is still common for people to tell stories to each

17 See e.g. Borneman 1992, 18.
18 Arendt 1958, 184; see also Jackson 2002, 22–23; Bakhtin 1981; Merleau-Ponty 1962, 354.
19 Jackson 2002, 23.
20 Jackson 2002, 23.
21 An alternative theoretical perspective, which focuses on immigrants as *individuals* within specific 'new' social and cultural fields rather than on how their experience is similar to the intersubjective experiences of emplacement and belonging of all people, is the framework of acculturation that was part of one branch of anthropology from the 1930s onwards (e.g. Redfield et al. 1936). In the past several decades, this perspective has become more prevalent in the subfield of cross-cultural psychology as opposed to anthropology and has been expanded and refined to include the related concept of intercultural relations. One of the most prominent scholars in this area is John Berry (1997), who has developed an important sub-categorisation of four 'acculturation strategies': integration, assimilation, separation and marginalisation. Also see Berry 1990; Berry 2002.
22 E.g. Méndez Ferrín 1999.

other. This is especially noticeable when they gather for festive occasions such as annual patron saint festivals, when, in addition to going to mass in the local Catholic parish church, families and close friends eat multi-course meals together and attend community dances.[23] However, storytelling is also noticeable in bars and cafés as well as during meals shared by co-workers, students, or the members of social clubs celebrating important dates such as Christmas or the end of the academic year.

The Valentines, whose research is mentioned above, describe the lively storytelling context in which their main informant 'Maite' regularly recounted stories for friends, relatives and people staying in her pension in the early 1980s: 'She would shift from her narrative voice to her characters' voices, with frequent stops for evaluative asides. Her audiences would respond with laughter, assent, and sometimes silence. Maite always became more animated as her audience enlarged.'[24] This description fits well with the many instances I have observed of such storytelling, in both cities and rural communities, in the 1990s and 2000s. However, it is undeniable that there has been a significant decline in its frequency owing to various social and economic changes, including the practice of commuting long distances to jobs, which often means arriving home too late in the evening to have the time or energy to visit others.

As one element in Galician language conservation and revitalisation efforts and also probably in part as a reaction to a decline in vernacular storytelling among friends and neighbours, a tradition of public storytelling by professional or semi-professional performers, known as *conta-contos*, has become popular since the 1990s. The emergence of these performances parallels similar celebrations of the history and continuing currency of Galician popular culture in various genres and media, such as live and televised singing and dancing acts. It is also true that, as in other societies, the Internet has created a new venue for storytelling by and among Galicians, including the creation of diarist documents on social media sites and other forms of weblogs.

In Galician Studies literature, in addition to research on storytelling, there are a number of excellent publications by anthropologists and others who have integrated narrative accounts of specific moments in individuals' lives into autobiographical life history or life story works. These include Marcial Gondar Portasany's book about widows' experiences,[25] Hans Christian Buechler and Judith-Maria Buechler's book recording a woman's orally narrated autobiographical account[26] and Xosé Ramón Mariño Ferro's book on the 'autobiography of a peasant farmer'.[27] Not surprisingly, given the extent of labour out-migration and circular migration in Galicia, the topic of migration comes up in these accounts. For example, in one of

---

23 Roseman 2008, 35–36.
24 Valentine & Valentine 1992, 187.
25 Gondar Portasany 1991.
26 Buechler & Buechler 1981.
27 Mariño Ferro 1986.

various passages in the Buechlers' book *Carmen*, the narrator reports on what she has heard from kin and neighbours who have emigrated for what they see as a long-term but temporary time away from Galicia (in this case in Switzerland, the destination of significant numbers of Galician workers in the period from the 1960s to the 1990s[28]):

> There are some people who've been away for more than twelve years and they're worried that they're going to be sent home, so they want to remain while it's still possible. My sister-in-law worried about that. 'What will happen to us if they send us back to Spain before we have enough money to build our house?' she said. Her husband told her not to worry. 'If they send people home,' he said, 'they'll send home the ones who don't know the language, the newer immigrants. But we speak the language perfectly by now, so you needn't be afraid.'[29]

We now turn to an example of a story about migration to Switzerland recounted by a man who had travelled there in the 1970s to take up temporary work under the 'guest- worker' and 'alien worker' programs that were such an important source of remittances to Galicia prior to the institution of labour mobility between member states of the European Union under the Maastricht Treaty.[30] First, however, it is important to understand the general context and specifically the storytelling thread in which this specific story is set. The term 'storytelling thread' refers to a series of linked stories told about the same or different incidents over a period of time, which can last for days, weeks, months, or, as in this case, for many years.

A case study

María was Pepe's wife and, like Pepe, one of my closest research collaborators in the early 1990s, when I did twelve months of fieldwork in the Galician inland rural municipality of Zas. María died shortly afterwards. Pepe and I often see each other when I return to Galicia for ongoing research. During a visit one year, after our initial exclamations that it was good luck that I happened to find him at home, Pepe told me as if we hadn't both affirmed it many times before: '*A miña difunta era moi boa* (My dead one was a very good person[31])'.[32] Then he went on to tell me once again, as he had on previous visits, what had happened the day that María died: 'She said to me: "*Teño ganas de caldo*[33] (I feel like having some broth),"' And so, '*Fíxenlle o*

---

28 For example, Marina Richter notes that between 1960 and 1980 57% of Galician emigration was to Switzerland. Richter 2004, 267. She cites Alonso Antolín 1984.

29 Buechler & Buechler 1981, 195.

30 Castles & Kosack 1973.

31 All translations from Galician into English are my own.

32 Interview, July 2000. María, Pepe, and other research participants' names are pseudonyms to protect their identity.

33 Some of the original language of these narratives is included in order to better demonstrate the original language and rhythm of such storytelling events.

caldo (I made her some broth); but 'on that day there wasn't *caldo, non había caldo nin nada* (any broth, not broth or anything).'

It is significant that Pepe emphasizes that, on the day of his wife's death, he had carefully prepared a meal of her choice. One of the themes that dominated both María's, and Pepe's, accounts of the last decade of their life together was a situation that, as in many other parts of the world, was one of gender reversal in rural Galicia. Diabetes had taken its toll on María's eyesight, and arthritis troubled her aging bones, and she gradually reduced her household chores to only the most manageable tasks such as letting out their laying hens in the morning and herding them back into their pen at nightfall. Pepe began to do all the cooking, cleaning, and laundry as well as providing some nursing care for María. When María was still alive, he often said to me and to other neighbours when we entered the house while he was giving his wife insulin: '*Eu son moita de cousas. O practicante, o criado, o marido*. (I'm many things: nurse, servant, husband)'.[34] It is also important to note, however, that this gender reversal was also an aspect of men's stories of working in other countries as circular labour migrants.

María and Pepe told me many stories about events in the distant and recent past that involved the same theatrical techniques as the Valentines' informant 'Maite', including character dialogue, gestures indicating actions of themselves and others and sound effects.[35] They inserted these stories into long, layered series of conversations as opposed to telling me isolated, carefully crafted stories. In addition to myself, their audience was often composed of various neighbours of theirs who would stop by. Their stories of the past were thus interspersed with various digressions and observations; they often referred to the contemporary lives of others to illustrate their general points about their own life experiences. After I had known them for some months, I told María and Pepe that I found their stories to be helpful examples of how people recounted their personal experiences and asked if I could study these narratives. They were interested and gave me permission to audio record many of our conversation sessions that took place when I and others[36] visited them, sessions that were filled with storytelling. Like other men whom I know, Pepe often told stories about his years working in Switzerland in the presence of his wife and other listeners. Thus most of these recorded sessions formed part of my use of a participant observation technique, whereby I visited people in their homes in the late afternoons and evenings, when it was common for others also to stop by after many of the day's chores were completed. As was the case with Pepe, it was not infrequent during these visits for people to recount stories about migration as well as many other topics. Migration was always present as a core theme since so many of the neighbours had worked away from the villages in other countries or other parts of Spain. On a few occasions when I came by to visit

---

34 One of many examples that was recorded in my fieldnotes. Interview, May 1991.
35 Valentine & Valentine 1992, 197.
36 Other participants in these events were of course also aware that I was recording the sessions and gave their permission for me to do so.

him, I also elicited stories by asking Pepe to tell us about what it was like to work in Switzerland.

Below is the first of several examples provided here that were excerpted from my recording of his unsolicited accounts of his years in Switzerland. In this case, you can see the interjections of his wife's sister Ana, who is one of those present in Pepe's and María's kitchen on the evening when I tape-recorded this account in 1990, when María was still alive:[37]

Pepe: Aaah, that's right. I cooked [María laughs]. I washed clothes and I did everything. If not, if someone else, ... if I sent out the laundry, one sweater, one shirt, one T-shirt, [...] they would charge for each piece, some handkerchiefs [for example]. For each piece, a franc.

Sharon: Yes?

Pepe: Yes. I would have had to pay.

María: Aaii.

Ana: How much?

Pepe: In our money from here, well our money ... one franc.

Ana: In pesetas?

Pepe: In pesetas, well then when we were there, well ... each franc was worth, was worth close to 20 pesetas.

Ana: Jesus!

Pepe: A franc was only worth around twenty-two.

Ana: Well then it certainly cost you.

Pepe: Hell.

María: Hell. Of course it cost [a lot].

Pepe: It certainly did. Each piece of clothing. For each sock, one franc. It was a slap in the face. For each handkerchief and, and, hell!

Ana: It was a lot.

Pepe: Bloody hell! It was a lot. You had to pay... look how many francs you had to pay. You had to put out half of your hourly salary.

[...]

Pepe: Hell! I washed, I prepared meals, I did the shopping, I brought in meat, I brought, brought in pasta, potatoes, and everything. Don't you see? I went to work for the *contadino* [farmer] and then, afterwards, I didn't pay for the potatoes and also ... the *contadino*[38] was a *labradore*, [farmer]. He worked the land, right?

[...]

Pepe: And the food [to buy]. A chicken would cost you, a little chicken, when I was there, three and a half francs. Four, depending. One that was a little bigger, another a little smaller. Now in the last years [I was there] it cost more and ... that which used to cost three

37 Interview, November 1990.

38 Pepe explained that they spoke a lot of Italian in that part of Switzerland and that many of his co-workers were from Italy. He is indicating here that *contadino* is the Italian word for 'peasant' or 'farmer', using a similar word – *labradore* – which also has these two meanings in the local dialect of Galician.

francs and fifty or four and fifty, had already risen to eight or nine francs. The cost of living had already gone up.

Sharon: Yes. It was very expensive in Switzerland, no?

Pepe: Oooh, oooh. Yes, oooh.

María: Yes.

Sharon: And was the food good?

Pepe: Yes, yes, it was good. Yes, yes. One has to get used to it. The meat was not like what we have here. Like the meat we have in Galicia, that didn't exist. Nor the pork.

María: Well.

Pepe: It was meat, no? But it wasn't.

Sharon: Yes, yes. And the potatoes?

Pepe: Eem. Those grown at home, they were like ours. Let's see if you understand me.

Sharon: Yes.

Pepe: And... the homegrown potatoes weren't like those from here. Oh noooo. Like those in Spain, no. Eh? They didn't have the same consistency as ... they are grown in a different soil, in other soil, that they put down. They don't fertilise them like we do here, no? We use gorse and manure from the stables on the land. That gives crops a different, a different flavour. Let's see if you understand, they had a different flavour there. The potato there was, it was more watery. It was moister. It was to make a more watery meal.

María: Hmmm.

Sharon: Yes.

Pepe: They didn't have any flavour.

Sharon: But you got used to it?

Pepe: You had to get used to it, no?

Sharon: Yes, yes.

Pepe: Then, I made the food just like here ... In order to make a Galician broth, I took a piece of this [indicating the lard hanging in their hearth], no? [...] Or a ham, no? But you had to take everything in separate pieces so that it wouldn't all be taken together at the border. A bottle of cognac ... at the border ... and food. What they allowed to pass was a slab of dried, salt codfish.

This story about both doing unpaid domestic labour and doing a second job of working for food fits into a story thread that coincides with a major cultural theme in rural Galicia: the importance of 'working for the household'[39] to which one belongs even when one is absent. This theme has existential implications since each individual acts on the world through this 'space of belonging',[40] which comprises the physical and social constitution and reconstitution of this household through time. In Pepe's case, his storytelling

39 Roseman 1999.

40 Compare with Jackson 2005, Chapter 2 'Space of Appearances', and Arendt 1958, 72–73.

about his years in Switzerland can also be viewed as a response to his wife María's frequent telling of stories that communicated her warnings and worries about the dangers of men's 'vices' (*vicios*). Here is one example of the many cautionary stories she recounted to me about the situation of other families, often in the presence of Pepe and others. These stories were told in a conversational format, with María requiring my active verbal participation as part of my listening role. Here is an example in which she refers to a family living in another community that had recently lost access to rented land because they could not pay their rent:[41]

Sharon: *¿Lerchán?*
María: *Lerchán. Lerchán...*
Sharon: That means someone who doesn't do anything?
María: Someone who doesn't do anything. Who doesn't work.
Sharon: Is that the worst?
María: It's the worst [*É o peore*]. And 'he' [a man in a nearby village] has this problem. And 'she' [his wife] is not lazy.
Sharon: *Non.*
María: She is hard-working [*É traballadora*].
Sharon: Right.
María: But now the drink has got him inside. Do you understand?
[...]
Sharon: He was hardworking in the past. [*El era traballador antes*].
María: He was hardworking before. But now that he put inside him, now that he drank and drank DRANK AND DRANK AND DRANK [speaking fast and loudly].
Sharon: It's the vice of drinking [a lot]?
María: It's a vice [*É o vicio*]. And now his lungs are gone.
Sharon: He can't [work].
[...]
María: What will she make to eat? Wheat ... They didn't plant maize. They didn't plant wheat ... they were working the fields of [X] ... And, they didn't raise a pig [this year]. But if one wants to make a, a broth. Bah! Nothing. I don't know how they live. It just can't be like that [...] But that's how it is, my dear. Life is like that [*É así, a miña vida. A vida éche así*].

To demonstrate how this theme carried over in Pepe's and María's shared storytelling thread, several years after she died, Pepe employed a narrative account to assure me that he often goes to bars now that his wife has died but spends time there talking with neighbours and playing cards but not drinking any alcohol. As he told me an elaborate story of a recent trip to a bar when these activities took place, this speech event seemed to trigger another memory of a more distant time. He smiled and switched to another

41 Interview, March 1991.

story, about an event that occurred before María died and after she had returned to her home in the village following an operation that she had had in a city hospital – an experience that made her feel extremely anxious. On the day in question, Pepe had come back later than originally planned from running errands in a nearby town and found his wife sitting on the bench outside their house. He told me:[42]

> She was angry, pissed off. She thought that I had gone to the bar [*Estaba enfadada, cabreada. Ela pensou que iba a taberna.*] She really liked calf's liver steaks. I had gone to the doctor's [to get her pills], but then I went and bought her almost one kilo of steak. She was pissed off, but I went in and made her steak and potatoes. And she asked 'What are you doing?' I told her, you think that I was in the bar, but I went to buy these steaks that I'm making for you now.

As I have discussed elsewhere,[43] this concern about 'vices' is a common cultural theme in this part of Spain, where the rural inhabitants have experienced a history of struggling to make ends meet, doing day labour in agriculture, sharecropping, cultivating small plots of land and raising small herds of livestock for subsistence as well as petty commodity production, and doing wage work in areas such as crafts and other skilled trades, manufacturing and service jobs both locally and quite often in migrant destinations in other parts of Spain and abroad. Pepe uses these stories as a general verbal demonstration of his having worked 'for the household' while abroad rather than having fallen into the trap of spending much of his earnings on vices such as alcohol, cigarettes, expensive clothes, going out or even hiring prostitutes. This was a major theme among male emigrants who went to temporary migration destinations without their female partners and a common pattern of behaviour among male Galician workers who took jobs in Switzerland, Germany, France and other European countries even though increasing numbers of women joined them from the 1980s onwards.[44] One can see that, in his story about Switzerland, Pepe is not speaking specifically about vices. However, he is demonstrating that he not only did not spend money on services while working in Switzerland (e.g. paying someone else to do his laundry or cooking), but he also earned some of his food through working extra hours – both examples of frugality and a position of economic inequality familiar to his audiences back home in Galician villages, in which people commonly did day labour for food and a small wage.[45]

He is acting on the world by relaying details about the new environment he encountered when working in Switzerland. Moreover, in so doing, he narrated how, while working there, he remained situated in frameworks that were culturally meaningful to his wife and other neighbours and relatives

42 Interview, July 2000.
43 Roseman 2004.
44 Richter 2004; Buechler 1975.
45 The food made up the larger (or even sole) portion of the wage during difficult economic times such as the 1930s and 1940s.

who had not gone abroad to work. This is not so much an example of either assimilation or the lack of it, or of hybridity, but rather of how stories about migration form part of a place-making experience that is intersubjective. In line with an idea that I quoted earlier from Jackson's work, stories are not fixed but rather 'mediate our relation' with 'otherness',[46] in this case with those who remain behind as much as with those places and people with whom Pepe interacted while working in Switzerland. Part of the intersubjective process is to communicate key concerns and demonstrations of a response to them through stories as María and Pepe did, both with each other and with myself and other listeners. Pepe's story about what he and his relatives regarded to be the outrageous service charges for having one's laundry done in Switzerland was a collectively shared story that created a sense among individuals such as his sister-in-law that the dangers that lay in this migration destination were not only represented by the more obvious 'vices' that were a common concern in rural Galicia but also by less obvious pitfalls such as paying for basic services that were not historically men's responsibilities in Galician rural households.

All the stories cited above illustrate another cultural theme historically common in women's stories but now also in men's in cases where they regularly prepare food. As part of acting in the world, those who prepare food dishes should make every effort to use the highest quality possible food, even when it is food as basic as a simple soup or some cooked potatoes. This idea is part of the assertion of the value of subsistence agriculture that is still common in Galicia despite various challenges to its production and cultural valorisation,[47] and more broadly of the assertion that there are things that make living in Galician villages superior to urban-based lifestyles even though people living in cities can often earn higher and more secure wages. This idea was set against various stories that labour migrants told about people in Switzerland and Germany being 'solitary', 'fino/a' [feeling and acting superior], and needing to be treated 'delicately', about there being less of a connection among people than they were used to experiencing in Galicia. For individuals such as Pepe, this connection was mediated in part through storytelling and commensality.[48] Here is another excerpt from his description of making and sharing food while working as a labour migrant in Switzerland:[49]

> When four of us lived together in one room, we organised everything [...] Today, I'll make the food. Tomorrow, one of the other ones would do it. All together. All together. We would make a pot all together. 'The Galician. It's best that the Galician makes the food, please.' 'The Galician makes the food better than the others'.

---

46 Jackson 2002, 23.
47 Roseman 2004.
48 Note the parallel to the chapter by Mapril in this volume, where he discusses the importance of food among migrants from Bangladesh living in Portugal.
49 Interview, November 1990.

Another storytelling thread in Pepe's and others' accounts of working in Switzerland concerned his relationships with bosses and co-workers. As we can see in the life story of Carmen that the Buechlers published in 1981, this is another common cultural theme in rural Galicia. Carmen told many stories that constituted evaluative accounts of how employers had treated her and others. Here is just one small excerpt from her description of working as a servant when she was a child:

> Then I went to a rich farmer's house [...] his wife was very stingy. She would say to me, 'Do you want to eat this?' I would say 'Yes.' Then she would set it down in front of me, then she'd change her mind and take it away again. Then she'd give me something inferior, telling me that that would do. They would hide the bread on me, for they'd keep it strictly rationed.[50]

In my study of itinerant seamstresses who made their living in Galicia in the past by walking sometimes long distances between villages to spend the day repairing clothing and making new garments for clients who paid them a day wage, the same sort of detailed stories about past bosses were commonly recounted:

> During the difficult period of the 1940s, seamstresses and other day labourers often did not receive a wage or were only paid one peseta. The dependency of this day labouring system, which only covered one's nourishment for a day, was a recurrent theme in the narratives. Sara, who was seventy-four in 1991, worked as a seamstress in the villages for more than forty years. About the wage she commented that 'You were paid by the day, or I mean to say that you collected when you could.'[51]

In comparison, here are three examples of Pepe talking about how he interacted with, and was treated by, his bosses and other workers in Switzerland:[52]

Pepe: I had to learn all of that [he had been explaining a different technique used for construction in Switzerland, as opposed to Spain, when he worked in the former] 'España'. 'Yes'. 'Come here'.

Sharon: España?

Pepe: Yes, yes. They called me ... at first they called me 'España' [Spain] because they didn't know our surnames, nor our names, nor anything. There was a bald guy I dealt with who called me 'Montes' [not anything like his surname] [*Eu tiña un calvo que me chamaba 'Montes'*]. And another one called me by my surname, just as the others came to do. But by the surname. By one's personal name, never.

50   Buecher & Buechler 1981, 2.
51   Roseman 2001, 370–371.
52   Interview, June 1991.

In the second example, he similarly refers to the dehumanising use of general place names for individual workers:[53]

I worked with Castilians, well Spaniards, no? But there were Castilians [there in Switzerland]. And they called me 'Galician!' [as though calling out]. 'The Galician'. And the Galicians and everything goddam else because they [the Swiss employers] had everything. The Castilian, the Italian and every goddam thing.

The third example highlights the common practice of under-employing migrant workers:[54]

Pepe: And it [one's job level] also affected the social security payments. This happened to me, after two years as a *peón* [unskilled labourer] I became a specialist,
Sharon: An *oficial* [a skilled worker]?
Pepe: Yes, a second grade *oficial.*
Sharon: Yes.
Pepe: A second grade *oficial.* And the pay was for an unskilled labourer.
Sharon: Aah.
Pepe: *¿Non ves?* Don't you see [what was going on]?

These last two excerpts are part of a common storytelling thread among labour migrants in which even common benefits such as having one's cost of travelling to migrant destinations paid by the contracting employer, or having a pay raise to reflect experience and increased responsibilities, were interpreted as being awarded to those who had achieved a favoured status with bosses by working extra hard. He even implies that he was rewarded for remaining healthier than other workers. Indeed, the same interpretation underlies Pepe's understanding of being asked to work extra hours beyond those permitted by labour codes. This storytelling thread illustrates how migrant workers, through their marginalised status as temporary residents with impermanent employment contracts, are vulnerable to being exploited by their employers in a variety of ways that other workers are not. The first example went as follows:[55]

Pepe: The first years, I paid, and then the firm, since I was valuable to the firm, they sent for me with everything paid, the trip and everything. The trip, but by train, no? To go by plane, I had to pay the, the...
Sharon (prompting): 'Difference?'
Pepe: The difference. Aaah, see how you're understanding me. I paid the difference, all of it. And without knowing how to read or how to write or anything like that [*sin saber ler nin escribir nin cousa ningunha*]. I had everything really well settled!.

53 Interview, November 1990.
54 Interview, June 1991.
55 Interview, November 1990.

The second example highlights a sense of vulnerability also common among those on migrant worker contracts:[56]

Pepe: And then after two years that I had spent there, working, they sent the contract here [to his home in rural Galicia] again. And now it was with more money [...] Well, before they had me at seven an hour and for me, they moved me up to ten. Then they moved me up to ten. Because I was worth it as a worker, I was worth it. I worked like a horse [...] There you could not miss work, on Mondays, on Tuesdays, you could not miss work. If you were sick, you had to go to the doctor or the doctor would have to come see you in your bed ... visit you at your bedside [...] I didn't fall ill or anything. I was always strong like a horse. That's luck, no? And then I made my food, washed my clothes and I worked for the *contadino* [farmer] with the permission of my boss. I went to work when ... on Saturdays, on Saturdays. On Saturdays they didn't work. And if the firm had a day, had to work some hours you went on the sly.

Sharon: Uum.

Pepe: The boss went on the sly: 'You come and we'll watch out for you.' *Alá*. That [is] how it was. So that they wouldn't give a fine, no?

Sharon: Aah, yes.

Pepe: For us, nothing. The one that would be fined would be him [the boss] [...] The week ... the work week was five [days] nothing more [...] He trusted me for the Saturdays, for the two or three or four hours before lunchtime. He'd say to me: 'Pepe, you'll come and do this thing for me.' Because the other ones weren't up to it ... What one guy could do in a week, I could do in half a day.

Sharon: But how did he pay you for this day?

Pepe: What? *Aii*, for these days. That day that I would go to work?

Sharon: Yes.

Pepe: For the boss?

Sharon: Yes.

Pepe: I didn't have any deductions. The deductions were for the other hours of work ...

Sharon: Deductions for your housing?

Pepe: It would have been for social security. I don't know what it was for...

These examples of stories told by María and Pepe indicate that, although they clearly faced many economic constraints, they were active in the making of their lives, and their passage was not static. Labour migration, which ended up affording them the ability to purchase their small house and some land, as well as contributing toward Pepe's old age pension, was something that

---

56 Interview, November 1990.

was a 'storied' and mediating experience as much as were other aspects of their lives. This couple's affection for each other was evident, from the way that they continued to flirt with each other and smile even in their last years after decades of marriage, and the strength of this bond probably led to them telling me to record their struggles as well as their good times. Both privately emphasised to me how 'good' the other person was. Ruth Behar and David Frye, in writing about peasant marriages in the León province in Spain, from the eighteenth century to the 1970s, emphasise that the verb used to refer to a good relationship versus a weak one was not 'the bourgeois sentimentalising language of love'[57] but rather the notion of 'understanding one another' expressed in the reflexive verb form *entenderse*. The same notion is still used in Galicia, and applies not just to married couples but also to relationships between parents and children, siblings, in-laws, other relatives and neighbours.

As in other locations with a history of extensive out-migration and circular migration, there is ample potential for social conflicts between those who have been labour migrants and those who have not. For example, some households have large migrant remittances that they can spend on new cars, new homes and other goods that their neighbours cannot afford. At the same time, the neighbours who remain behind often take on extra burdens in caring for people in the community as well as undertaking key volunteer work that is necessary for the maintenance of community-wide initiatives and events. In some cases, one or both parents have left their children to be raised by relatives (most often grandparents); this was common in Zas and other Galician municipalities at the time when Pepe and many of his neighbours travelled to other European countries to pursue employment opportunities.

This situation can also produce misunderstandings and tensions; for example, between caregivers and parents and between absent parents and their children. To judge from my findings in conducting extensive participant observation in Galicia since 1989, storytelling is one of the most effective interactional activities for reducing the tensions produced by the sort of spatial, economic, and social disjunctures that attend migration processes. When migrants are able to tell vivid stories about their time away from their home area, and their relatives and neighbours are able to respond to these stories and tell ones of their own that may even belong to the same storytelling thread, this constitutes a 'willingness to act',[58] and involves important processes of transformation that attend ongoing experiences of emplacement and belonging. It allows for people to work on *entenderse*.

Therefore, studying storytelling events as well as the stories that form different storytelling threads is an important aspect of research on migration. The recognition of the existence of storytelling threads helps us to see that stories should not be viewed as isolated events but rather that, through

57 Behar & Frye 1988, 29.
58 Arendt 1958, 186.

storytelling, people are 'collaboratively reflecting upon specific situations'[59] over the long term. In locations with an extensive history of either out-migration or in-migration, in order to better understand the nuanced way in which memory work is integrated into shared understandings of the present and projections of the future, it is crucial that we study people's stories about past as well as present periods of migration, and see how these interact with the other stories that people tell.

Storytelling in studies of migration

There are several ways to collect storytelling data as part of a fieldwork project. These are now outlined in sequence, with the first major distinction being between those using unsolicited and solicited stories. One basic point that should never be overlooked is the need to pay attention to how and when storytelling forms a natural aspect of people's interaction, to participate in such storytelling if it is appropriate (as both a listener and perhaps also a storyteller), and to ask research participants if they will agree to your collecting material from these storytelling moments after an appropriate degree of rapport or the establishment of a collaborative research relationship has been established.[60] Unsolicited stories can be collected from conducting participant observation in the same physical location as the research participants, by the use of telephonic or computer-mediated communication, as is discussed by Hirvi and Koikkalainen in their chapters in this volume, or from individuals whom the fieldworker has not met but whose stories form part of archival collections or public media publications.

The use of the participant observation method to study migration can yield very valuable information about the migration experience as well as about how migration fits into the ongoing, active, intersubjective and collaborative creation of cultural meanings through time. This is shown in the examples from my fieldwork provided above. In developing an in-depth understanding of these emergent meanings, it is important to study the interconnections between stories, how stories fit into specific storytelling threads, and the frequent use of stories to communicate back and forth between individuals. As with the rest of these methods, such storytelling may take place in locations to which migrants have moved (even if only temporarily), locations from which they have travelled, or in spaces in between since many migrants tell stories on their way to or from migration destinations. This methodological approach is discussed by Vogt, whose work in this volume focuses on her interviews with Central American migrants in transit in Mexico. In these cases, research participants recount stories about their lives to the fieldworker and perhaps also to a wider group

---

59 Ochs & Capps 2001, 14.
60 Pink 2006.

audience most often composed of members of existing social networks such as their relatives, friends, neighbours, and co-workers.

Stories about migration can also be found recorded in a variety of media, and they may constitute an important set of data in a fieldwork project, whether one is dealing with past historical periods or the present. Locations where stories may be narrated include private documents such as personal letters or diaries later deposited in publically accessible archives. The documents might also be directed at broad public audiences in the first instance, as is the case with contributions to newspapers and magazines, pre-programmed material or unsolicited calls or letters broadcast by radio or television stations, or individuals' weblogs. The last-mentioned case includes social networking sites which can be regarded as a form of shared diary, although, as Hirvi and Koikkalainen point out in their chapters in this volume, there are important ethical questions to consider with respect to accessing and, when appropriate, gaining permission to use such data. All of the foregoing may be particularly valuable in studying migration since the field researcher (or project team) can look for media produced or deposited in both sending and destination points.

It is also possible to explicitly solicit stories, through a directed conversation as part of participant observation or through other methods including unstructured or semi-structured oral history or life story interviews. Stories about migration may also be elicited through the use of photographs and other mnemonic cues, including physical places.[61] Given that a variety of oral genres, including personal narratives about people's experiences, thoughts and feelings as well as culturally shared knowledge, are sometimes transmitted as part of recognizable expressive culture traditions,[62] people will often find it easy to comprehend why a researcher is asking them to recount stories. The elicitation of stories within group activities is often less threatening for the participants than other forms of data elicitation such as structured interviews or surveys may initially be. More recently, newer media methods have been developed that allow field researchers to work in new collaborative ways with those from whom they solicit stories, and not only to make voice or video recordings of people's storytelling and later transcribe these into written texts but also to produce digital stories that incorporate their voices and photographic or videographed images.

Stories can be solicited explicitly from individuals whom a field researcher is interviewing in private, and some stories may be of a private nature. In such circumstances, the person telling them may not mind if they are part of a set of research data but would prefer that they be relayed to others than the fieldworker through the use of a pseudonym and the suppression of any key identifying details. In other cases, as is indicated above, people may prefer

---

61 In a related manner, Lisa Wiklund in this volume describes how her understanding of the perspectives of the Japanese migrants working in creative professions in Williamsburg, New Jersey was enriched by her having visited the physical locations in Tokyo that her informants told her were significant for them.

62 E.g. Valentine & Valentine 1992; Cruikshank 1998.

to tell their stories to a group since this is a common context for storytelling in many societies. Convening storytelling events as part of projects on migration can be a more familiar and resonant experience for many of those collaborating in the field research than other group research methods such as structured focus groups. Like the other methods mentioned here, it can be used in both sender and host communities and may be particularly welcome as part of leisure time in migration destinations, especially in cases in which field research is being conducted on a group of migrants who come from the same localities, regions or countries.

One method for soliciting stories is through looking at photographs, which may have been taken by the ethnographer(s), the research participant(s) or others. Ethnographers have used photographs to interview people formally at least since the mid-twentieth century.[63] This method is described, for example, by John Collier Jr. and Malcolm Collier with reference to research that they conducted with other research team members among Acadian farmers in a Canadian Maritime province[64] and among Navajo research participants in New Mexico.[65] In a 1957 article, John Collier employs the term 'photo-interviewing' and noted that they had more than one goal in showing people photographs and asking them to reflect on the visual images. One goal was to 'find a way to read from photographs evidence that was not understandable'[66] to the researchers, who may, in some cases, have taken the pictures. Another was that 'photographs can trigger responses that might lie submerged in verbal interviewing.'[67] In recent years, there has been an increased use of this and other forms of mnemonic elicitation. This increase is due to the growth of visual anthropology and sociology, and the exploration of various ways of working collaboratively with research participants. An emphasis on collaborative methods of both data collection and the dissemination of research results recognises explicitly that knowledge is produced intersubjectively. Indeed, in her book *Doing Visual Ethnography*, Sarah Pink notes that she prefers not to use the word elicitation when referring to the method of 'interviewing with images'[68] because processes of intersubjectivity entail something other than one person 'eliciting' information from another. Rather, she states: 'Photographic interviews can allow ethnographers and informants to discuss images in ways that create a 'bridge' between their different experiences of reality'.[69] In some cases, individuals are asked to recount stories about specific places or photographs (which they may have taken themselves as part of participatory

63 Pink 2006; Collier & Collier 1980.
64 They note that they purposefully use a pseudonym for the location in Collier 1957. The Canadian Maritime provinces are New Brunswick, Prince Edward Island, and Nova Scotia.
65 Collier 1957; Collier & Collier 1980.
66 Collier 1957, 846.
67 Collier 1957, 854.
68 Pink 2006, 82.
69 Pink 2006, 84.

photography). The *[murmur]* project has designed one form of place-based elicitation that does not rely on face-to-face contact between research participants and researchers.[70] The participatory *Photo Voice* initiative also has a number of examples of people recounting stories specifically about migration, such as the 2009 *Moving Lives* project.[71] An excellent example of the use of place-based elicitation in a field study of migration is in Lawrence Taylor and Maeve Hickey's book *Tunnel Kids*[72] about children and young persons who make their living on, and literally under, the border between Nogales, Mexico and Nogales, Arizona in the United States. In one chapter of this book entitled '*Lugares importantes*/Important places', a young woman takes the anthropologist (Taylor) and the photographer (Hickey) to see a variety of places to interview and videotape her friends' stories including those about where they had slept when they first arrived in this part of Mexico.

Closely connected to projects such as *[murmur]* and *Photo Voice* is the use of digital storytelling, which can be used to great effect to study stories about migration. Digital storytelling is a term that arose in the United States and the United Kingdom to describe the development of the use of digital technology to create illustrated, narrative accounts of individuals' lives that could be shared with others.[73] The Center for Digital Storytelling in California defines a digital story as 'a short, first person video-narrative created by combining recorded voice, still and moving images, and music or other sounds'.[74] These narratives are often compiled as part of storytelling workshops. In such workshops, stories are told first in face-to-face storytelling circles prior to the creation of the digital story product. Such methods and their impacts are now well documented and can be used by ethnographers to study a variety of migration situations. Digital storytelling initiatives have been used as part of the goal of mainstream media outlets to encourage members of the public to engage in an interactive relationship with web site content. Some of these initiatives are very relevant to the topic of migration. One would be some of the stories collected as part of a BBC-sponsored project called *Capture Wales*.[75] Moreover, this method can lead to people sharing (and perhaps communicating reactions to) each other's stories on the World Wide Web. As the digital storytelling activist and theorist Joe Lambert reminds us, telling stories can be transformative in the sense that they can provoke in listeners emotional reactions and new ways of thinking about their own lives.[76] With new technologies, the process of leading 'storied lives'[77] and acting on the world has new possibilities.

70 http://murmurtoronto.ca/about.php. Accessed May 2 2010.
71 http://www.photovoice.org/projects/uk/moving-lives-2009. Accessed October 2 2010
72 Taylor & Hickey 2001.
73 See, for example, Lambert 2010.
74 http://www.storycenter.org/index1.html. Accessed October 2 2010.
75 Helff & Woletz 2009.
76 Lambert 2010.
77 Cruikshank 1998.

Summary

This chapter demonstrates the importance of including the collection of stories, and the study of storytelling events and venues, in field research on migration. The theoretical framework for the employment of this methodology draws on Hannah Arendt's and Michael Jackson's ideas about human action and intersubjectivity as well as Marita Sturken's and John Borneman's discussions about emerging processes of producing 'cultural memory' and 'belonging'. A core assumption is Peggy Levitt and Nina Glick-Schiller's point that migrants often participate in 'transnational social fields' rather than moving from one to another circumscribed social space. In connection with these ideas, the argument is also rooted in demonstrations of the significance of recognising that 'people lead storied lives'[78] as part of their collaboration with each other in writings by Julie Cruikshank, Kristin Valentine and Eugene Valentine, and Elinor Ochs and Lisa Capps. To illustrate the value of this approach, case material is used from a study of labour migration among individuals from Galicia in Spain who live in a sender location for extensive circular migration to Switzerland, Germany, France and other countries that began in the 1960s. Finally, several different specific methods for assembling data from people's stories and storytelling contexts are outlined, with special attention being paid to the importance of appreciating the value of collecting both unsolicited and solicited stories.

Bibliography

Alonso Antolín, M. C. 1984: *La emigración gallega assistida a la República Federal de Alemania, Francia y Suiza*. Madrid: Instituto Español de Emigración.

Appadurai, A. 1996: *Modernity at Large: Cultural Dimensions of Globalization*. Minneapolis: University of Minnesota Press.

Arendt, H. 1958: *The Human Condition*. Chicago: The University of Chicago Press.

Bakhtin, M. 1981: *The Dialogic Imagination: Four Essays*. C. Emerson & M. Holquist (trans.), Austin: University of Texas Press.

Behar, R. & D. Frye 1988: Property, Progeny, and Emotion: Family History in a Leonese Village, *Journal of Family History* 13: 1, 13–32.

Berry, J. W. 1990: Psychology of Acculturation: Understanding Individuals Moving Between Cultures. In: R. W. Brislin (ed.), *Applied Cross-Cultural Psychology*. Newbury Park: Sage Publications, 232–253.

Berry, J. W. 1997: Acculturation and Adaptation. In: J. W. Berry, M. H. Segall, and C. Kagitçibasi (eds.), *Handbook of Cross-Cultural Psychology*. Boston: Allyn and Bacon.

Berry, J. W. 2002: Acculturation and Intercultural Relations. In: J. W. Berry, Y. H. Poortinga, M. H. Segall, & P. R. Dasen (eds.), *Cross-Cultural Psychology: Research and Applications*. Cambridge: Cambridge University Press.

Borneman, J. 1992: *Belonging in the Two Berlins: Kin, State, Nation*. Cambridge: Cambridge University Press.

---

78 Cruikshank 1998.

Buechler, J-M. 1975: The Eurogallegas: Female Spanish Migration. In: D. Raphael (ed.), *Being Female*. The Hague: Mouton, 207–214.

Buechler, H. C. & J.-M. Buechler. 1981: *Carmen: the Autobiography of a Spanish Galician Woman*. Rochester, Vermont: Schenkman Books.

Cole, S. 1991: *Women of the Praia: Work and Lives in a Portuguese Coastal Community*. Princeton: Princeton University Press.

Collier, J. Jr. 1957: Photography in Anthropology: A Report on Two Experiments. *American Anthropologist* 59: 5, 843–859.

Collier, J. Jr. & M. Collier 1980: *Visual Anthropology: Photography as a Research Method*. Revised edition. Albuquerque: University of New Mexico Press.

Cruikshank, J. 1998: *The Social Life of Stories: Narrative and Knowledge in the Yukon Territory*. Lincoln: University of Nebraska Press.

Elliott, A, & J. Urry 2010: *Mobile Lives*. London and New York: Routledge.

Fentress, J. & C. Wickham 1992: *Social Memory*. Oxford: Blackwell.

García Canclini, N. 1990: *Culturas híbridas. Estrategias para entrar y salir de la modernidad*. México: Grijalbo.

Gondar Portasany, M. 1991: *Mulleres de mortos. Cara a unha antropoloxía da muller Galega*. Vigo: Edicións Xerais de Galicia.

Halbwachs, M. 1992: *On Collective Memory*. L. A. Coser (ed. and trans.). Chicago: The University of Chicago Press.

Harmann, D. & J. Gerteis 2005: Dealing with Diversity: Mapping Multiculturalism in Sociological Terms. *Sociological Theory* 23: 2, 218–240.

Hartley, J. & K. McWilliam (eds.), *Story Circle: Digital Storytelling around the World*. Malden and Oxford: Wiley-Blackwell.

Helff, S. & J. Woletz 2009: Narrating Euro-African Life in Digital Space. In: J. Hartley & K. McWilliam (eds.), *Story Circle: Digital Storytelling around the World*. Malden and Oxford: Wiley-Blackwell.

Jackson, M. 2002: *The Politics of Storytelling: Violence, Transgression and Intersubjectivity*. Copenhagen: Museum Tusculanum Press.

Jackson, M. 2005: *Existential Anthropology*. Oxford: Berghahn Books.

Lambert, J. 2010: *Digital Storytelling: Capturing Lives, Creating Community*. Third edition. Berkeley: Digital Diner Press

Levitt, P. & N. Glick Schiller 2004: Conceptualizing Simultaneity: A Transnational Social Field Perspective on Society, *International Migration Review* 38: 3, 1002–1039.

Mariño Ferro, X. R. 1986: *Autobiografía dun labrego. Estudio novelado de antropoloxía*. Vigo: Edicións Xerais de Galicia.

Méndez Ferrín, X. L. 1999: *No ventre do silencio*. Vigo: Edicións Xerais de Galicia.

Merleau-Ponty, M. 1962: *Phenomenology of Perception*, C. Smith (trans.), London: Routledge & Kegan Paul.

Newhook J. T., B. Neis, L. Jackson, S. R. Roseman, P. Romanow, & C. Vincent. 2011: Employment-Related Mobility and the Health of Workers, Families, and Communities: The Canadian Context. *Labour/Le Travail* 67, 121–156.

Ochs, E. & L. Capps 2001: *Living Narrative: Creating Lives in Everyday Storytelling*. Cambridge: Harvard University Press.

Pink, S. 2006: *Doing Visual Ethnography*. Second edition. London: Sage.

Plattner, S. (ed.) 1984: *Text, Play and Story: The Construction and Reconstruction of Self and Society*. Washington: The American Ethnological Society.

Richter, M. 2004: Contextualizing Gender and Migration: Galician Immigration to Switzerland. *International Migration Review* 38: 1, 263–286.

Roseman, S. R. 1999: ¿*Quen manda*? (Who's in Charge?): Household Authority Politics in Rural Galicia. *Anthropologica* XLI, 117–132.

Roseman, S. R. 2001: Vendiendo la labor, vendiendo los conocimientos: un estudio antropólogico de las modistas de taller y de las costureras ambulantes gallegas. *Semata: Ciencias Sociais e Humanidades* 12, 370–371.

Roseman, S. R. 2004: Bioregulation and *Comida Caseira* in Rural Galicia, Spain. *Identities* 11, 9–37.

Roseman, S. R. 2008: *O Santiaguiño de Carreira. O rexurdimento dunha base rural no Concello de Zas.* A Coruña: Baía Edicións,

Sturken, M. 1997: *Tangled Memories: The Vietnam War, the AIDS Epidemic, and the Politics of Remembering.* Berkeley: University of California Press.

Taylor, L. J. & M. Hickey 2001: *Tunnel Kids.* Albuquerque: University of New Mexico Press.

Urry, J. 2000: *Sociology beyond Societies: Mobilities for the Twenty-First Century.* London: Routledge.

Valentine, K. B., & E. Valentine. 1992: Performing Culture through Narrative: a Galician Woman Storyteller. In: E. C. Fine & J. Haskell Speer (eds.), *Performance, Culture, and Identity.* Westport, Conn.: Praeger Publishers.

Contributors

Inês Hasselberg is a DPhil candidate in anthropology at the Global Studies School, Sussex University (UK). Her doctoral dissertation aims to understand processes of deportability in Britain. Her research is funded by Fundação para a Ciência e Tecnologia.

Laura Hirvi is a doctoral student at the Department of History and Ethnology at the University of Jyväskylä (Finland), who is about to submit her dissertation in which she explores how Sikhs with a migration background living in Helsinki (Finland) and in Yuba City (California) negotiate their identities. Hirvi spent the academic year 2009–2010 as a Fulbright visiting student at the Center for Sikh and Punjab Studies at UC Santa Barbara. Her latest publications include 'The Sikh Gurdwara in Finland: Negotiating, Maintaining and Transmitting Immigrants' Identities' published in 2010 in the journal *South Asian Diaspora* and a chapter on the work and migration histories of Sikhs in Finland in an edited volume on *Sikhs in Europe*, which was published by Ashgate in 2011.

Saara Koikkalainen is a doctoral candidate at the University of Lapland (Finland). Her doctoral research in sociology focuses on the mobility of skilled labour in the European Union, and in particular on the transfer of cultural capital. In 2010 she spent six months at the University of California, Davis as a Fulbright visiting student researcher and in 2012 another six months as a visiting student at the European University Institute in Florence (Italy). Her recent publications include 'Europe is my Oyster', a refereed article on the labour market experiences of Finns abroad in the Finnish Journal of Ethnicity and Migration (2009), 'Welfare or work: migrants' selective integration in Finland', a co-authored chapter in a volume edited by Emma Carmel, Alfio Cerami and Theodoros Papdopoulos (2011): *Migration and welfare in the 'new' Europe* (Bristol: Policy Press), and a volume co-edited with Elli Heikkilä (2011): *Finns Abroad: New Forms of Mobility and Migration* (Turku: Finnish Institute of Migration).

José Mapril holds a PhD in anthropology from the Institute of Social Sciences, University of Lisbon (Portugal). His dissertation was on transnationalism and Islam among Bangladeshis in Lisbon. Currently he is a lecturer in Anthropology at the New University of Lisbon and a post-doctoral research fellow at CRIA-IUL (Centre for Anthropological Research, Lisbon University Institute). In recent years, he has worked on religious education and liberal citizenship and currently is developing a project on expectations and transnational politics among Bangladeshis in southern Europe. He is member of the CRIA executive committee and a review editor of the journal *Etnográfica*. He has published in both national and international journals.

Deirdre Meintel is a professor of anthropology at the Université de Montréal (Canada) and has worked on ethnicity and migration in Canada, the United States and Cape Verde. Her more recent research and publications focus on religion and modernity. She is currently directing a broad study of religious diversity in Quebec, Canada.

Fran Meissner is a doctoral research fellow at the Max Planck Institute for the Study of Religious and Ethnic Diversity (Germany) and a DPhil candidate at Sussex University (UK). Her research is on super-diversity in urban areas and how this can be studied through the social networks of numerically small migrant groups.

Géraldine Mossière is an assistant professor at the Faculté de théologie et de sciences des religions de l'Université de Montréal (Canada). Her research projects focus on contemporary religion in the contexts of migration and globalization, and she works with African Pentecostal congregations in Quebec. She is also interested in issues of religious subjectivities and mobility, and she has published on religious conversion, in particular the conversion of women to Islam.

Sharon R. Roseman is a professor in the Department of Anthropology at Memorial University of Newfoundland (Canada). She is a specialist on human mobility, memory, paid and unpaid labour, class, gender, cultural and language politics, and media studies. Her research projects deal with Galicia, one of Spain's Autonomous Communities, and with the Canadian province of Newfoundland and Labrador. Among her recent publications are the books *O Santiaguiño de Carreira. O rexurdimento dunha base rural no Concello de Zas* (Baía Edicións, 2008), *Recasting Culture and Space in Iberian Contexts* (co-edited with Shawn Parkhurst, SUNY Press, 2008), and *Antropoloxía das mulleres galegas. As outras olladas* (co-edited with Enrique Alonso Población, Sotelo Blanco Edicións, 2012).

CLARA SACCHETTI is a postdoctoral fellow at the Frank Iacobucci Centre for Italian Canadian Studies at the University of Toronto (Canada). She received her doctorate in Social Anthropology, in which she investigated the discursive and ambivalent nature of the Italian-Canadian identity, from York University, Toronto. Sacchetti's work has appeared in *Renegade Bodies: Canadian Dance in the 1970s* (eds Allana C. Lindgren and Kaija Pepper), *Italian Canadiana, Migration Letters*, the *Semiotic Review of Books*, the *Boston Book Review*, and *TOPIA*. She is also co-editor of *Superior Art: Local Art, Global Context* (DefSup, Thunder Bay) and *The Economy as Cultural System* (Continuum, UK, forthcoming).

HANNA SNELLMAN is Professor of European Ethnology at the University of Helsinki (Finland). She has carried out studies on migrant workers in Finland, Sweden and North America and on fieldwork methodology.

WENDY A. VOGT received her PhD from the School of Anthropology at the University of Arizona (USA). She is now an assistant professor in anthropology at Indiana University-Purdue University, Indianapolis (IUPUI). Her dissertation is based on fifteen months of ethnographic research with Central American migrants and local residents in transit spaces in southern Mexico. Her work focuses on the historical political economy of violence and inequality, migration, gender, feminism and human rights.

LISA WIKLUND is a PhD candidate and teacher in ethnology at the Department of Cultural Sciences, University of Gothenburg (Sweden). Her forthcoming dissertation examines how work is organized in creative cosmopolitan environments. Her research focuses on the neighbourhood of Williamsburg in Brooklyn, New York City and the young Japanese people who have moved there to work in creative professions. Her research interests include urbanity, cosmopolitanism, work and national identity/ethnicity, and also issues related to the new challenges and possibilities for fieldwork in a globalized world. Her latest publication was a chapter for the book *Etnografiska hållplatser. Om metodprocesser och reflexibilitet* (Studentlitteratur 2011, ed. K. Gunnemark).

Studia Fennica Ethnologica

**Making and Breaking
of Borders**
*Ethnological Interpretations,
Presentations, Representations*
Edited by Teppo Korhonen,
Helena Ruotsala &
Eeva Uusitalo
Studia Fennica Ethnologica 7
2003

Memories of My Town
*The Identities of Town Dwellers
and Their Places in Three
Finnish Towns*
Edited by Anna-Maria Åström,
Pirjo Korkiakangas &
Pia Olsson
Studia Fennica Ethnologica 8
2004

Passages Westward
Edited by Maria Lähteenmäki
& Hanna Snellman
Studia Fennica Ethnologica 9
2006

Defining Self
*Essays on emergent identities
in Russia Seventeenth to
Nineteenth Centuries*
Edited by Michael Branch
Studia Fennica Ethnologica 10
2009

Touching Things
*Ethnological Aspects of Modern
Material Culture*
Edited by Pirjo Korkiakangas,
Tiina-Riitta Lappi & Heli
Niskanen
Studia Fennica Ethnologica 11
2009

Gendered Rural Spaces
Edited by Pia Olsson &
Helena Ruotsala
Studia Fennica Ethnologica 12
2009

LAURA STARK
The Limits of Patriarchy
*How Female Networks of
Pilfering and Gossip Sparked the
First Debates on Rural Gender
Rights in the 19th-century
Finnish-Language Press*
Studia Fennica Ethnologica 13
2011

Studia Fennica Folkloristica

Creating Diversities
*Folklore, Religion and the
Politics of Heritage*
Edited by Anna-Leena Siikala,
Barbro Klein &
Stein R. Mathisen
Studia Fennica Folkloristica 14
2004

PERTTI J. ANTTONEN
Tradition through Modernity
*Postmodernism and the Nation-
State in Folklore Scholarship*
Studia Fennica Folkloristica 15
2005

Narrating, Doing, Experiencing
Nordic Folkloristic Perspectives
Edited by Annikki Kaivola-
Bregenhøj, Barbro Klein &
Ulf Palmenfelt
Studia Fennica Folkloristica 16
2006

MÍCHÉAL BRIODY
**The Irish Folklore Commission
1935–1970**
History, ideology, methodology
Studia Fennica Folkloristica 17
2007

VENLA SYKÄRI
Words as Events
*Cretan Mantinádes
in Performance and
Composition*
Studia Fennica Folkloristica 18
2011

**Hidden Rituals and Public
Performances**
*Traditions and Belonging among
the Post-Soviet Khanty,
Komi and Udmurts*
Edited by Anna-Leena Siikala &
Oleg Ulyashev
Studia Fennica Folkloristica 19
2011

Studia Fennica Historica

**Medieval History Writing and
Crusading Ideology**
Edited by Tuomas M. S.
Lehtonen & Kurt Villads Jensen
with Janne Malkki and
Katja Ritari
Studia Fennica Historica 9
2005

Moving in the USSR
*Western anomalies and
Northern wilderness*
Edited by Pekka Hakamies
Studia Fennica Historica 10
2005

DEREK FEWSTER
Visions of Past Glory
*Nationalism and the
Construction of Early Finnish
History*
Studia Fennica Historica 11
2006

**Modernisation in Russia since
1900**
Edited by Markku Kangaspuro
& Jeremy Smith
Studia Fennica Historica 12
2006

SEIJA-RIITTA LAAKSO
Across the Oceans
*Development of Overseas
Business Information
Transmission 1815–1875*
Studia Fennica Historica 13
2007

Industry and Modernism
*Companies, Architecture and
Identity in the Nordic and
Baltic Countries during
the High-Industrial Period*
Edited by Anja Kervanto
Nevanlinna
Studia Fennica Historica 14
2007

CHARLOTTA WOLFF
**Noble conceptions of politics
in eighteenth-century Sweden
(ca 1740–1790)**
Studia Fennica Historica 15
2008

**Sport, Recreation and Green
Space in the European City**
Edited by Peter Clark,
Marjaana Niemi & Jari Niemelä
Studia Fennica Historica 16
2009

**Rhetorics of Nordic
Democracy**
Edited by Jussi Kurunmäki &
Johan Strang
Studia Fennica Historica 17
2010

**Studia Fennica
Anthropologica**

On Foreign Ground
*Moving between Countries and
Categories*
Edited by Minna Ruckenstein
& Marie-Louise Karttunen
Studia Fennica Anthropologica 1
2007

Beyond the Horizon
*Essays on Myth, History, Travel
and Society*
Edited by Clifford Sather &
Timo Kaartinen
Studia Fennica Anthropologica 2
2008

Studia Fennica Linguistica

MINNA SAARELMA-
MAUNUMAA
**Edhina Ekogidho – Names as
Links**
*The Encounter between African
and European Anthroponymic
Systems among the Ambo
People in Namibia*
Studia Fennica Linguistica 11
2003

Minimal reference
*The use of pronouns in Finnish
and Estonian discourse*
Edited by Ritva Laury
Studia Fennica Linguistica 12
2005

ANTTI LEINO
**On Toponymic Constructions
as an Alternative to Naming
Patterns in Describing
Finnish Lake Names**
Studia Fennica Linguistica 13
2007

Talk in interaction
Comparative dimensions
Edited by Markku Haakana,
Minna Laakso & Jan Lindström
Studia Fennica Linguistica 14
2009

**Planning a new standard
language**
*Finnic minority languages
meet the new millennium*
Edited by Helena Sulkala &
Harri Mantila
Studia Fennica Linguistica 15
2010

LOTTA WECKSTRÖM
**Representations of
Finnishness in Sweden**
Studia Fennica Linguistica 16
2011

Studia Fennica Litteraria

Changing Scenes
*Encounters between European
and Finnish Fin de Siècle*
Edited by Pirjo Lyytikäinen
Studia Fennica Litteraria 1
2003

Women's Voices
*Female Authors and Feminist
Criticism in the Finnish Literary
Tradition*
Edited by Lea Rojola &
Päivi Lappalainen
Studia Fennica Litteraria 2
2007

**Metaliterary Layers in Finnish
Literature**
Edited by Samuli Hägg,
Erkki Sevänen & Risto Turunen
Studia Fennica Litteraria 3
2009

AINO KALLAS
Negotiations with Modernity
Edited by Leena Kurvet-
Käosaar & Lea Rojola
Studia Fennica Litteraria 4
2011

**The Emergence of Finnish
Book and Reading Culture
in the 1700s**
Edited by Cecilia af Forselles &
Tuija Laine
Studia Fennica Litteraria 5
2011

**Nodes of Contemporary
Finnish Literature**
Edited by Leena Kirstinä
Studia Fennica Litteraria 6
2012

www.ingramcontent.com/pod-product-compliance
Lightning Source LLC
Chambersburg PA
CBHW081738270326
41932CB00020B/3320